continued . . .

"Sielski chronicles the lives of these two athletes and illustrates how their personalities and values were formed from interactions with family, friends, coaches, and community. In the process, he writes of much broader topics in contemporary American life: dreams, competition, resolve, war, honor, sacrifice, and true heartbreak." —*Library Journal*

"Both young men come alive as unique individuals as special as they are ordinary." —*Booklist*

FADING ECHOES

A TRUE STORY OF RIVALRY AND
BROTHERHOOD FROM THE FOOTBALL FIELD
TO THE FIELDS OF HONOR

Mike Sielski

BERKLEY BOOKS, NEW YORK

THE BERKLEY PUBLISHING GROUP
Published by the Penguin Group
Penguin Group (USA) Inc.
375 Hudson Street, New York, New York 10014, USA
Penguin Group (Canada), 90 Eglinton Avenue East, Suite 700, Toronto, Ontario M4P 2Y3, Canada
(a division of Pearson Penguin Canada Inc.)
Penguin Books Ltd., 80 Strand, London WC2R 0RL, England
Penguin Group Ireland, 25 St. Stephen's Green, Dublin 2, Ireland (a division of Penguin Books Ltd.)
Penguin Group (Australia), 250 Camberwell Road, Camberwell, Victoria 3124, Australia
(a division of Pearson Australia Group Pty. Ltd.)
Penguin Books India Pvt. Ltd., 11 Community Centre, Panchsheel Park, New Delhi—110 017, India
Penguin Group (NZ), 67 Apollo Drive, Rosedale, North Shore 0632, New Zealand
(a division of Pearson New Zealand Ltd.)
Penguin Books (South Africa) (Pty.) Ltd., 24 Sturdee Avenue, Rosebank, Johannesburg 2196,
South Africa

Penguin Books Ltd., Registered Offices: 80 Strand, London WC2R 0RL, England

The publisher does not have any control over and does not assume any responsibility for author or third-party websites or their content.

PRINTING HISTORY
Berkley hardcover edition / September 2009
Berkley trade paperback edition / August 2010

Berkley trade paperback ISBN: 978-0-425-23453-2

The Library of Congress has cataloged the Berkley hardcover edition as follows:

Sielski, Mike, 1975–
    Fading echoes : a true story of rivalry and brotherhood from the football field to the fields of honor /
Mike Sielski. — 1st ed.
        p.   cm.
    ISBN 978-0-425-22974-3 (trade pbk.)
    1. Buckley, Bryan.   2. Umbrell, Colby, 1981–2007.   3. Soldiers—Pennsylvania—Doylestown—
Biography.   4. Iraq War, 2003—Biography.   5. Doylestown (Pa.)—Biography.   I. Title.
    F159.D7S54   2009
    956.7044'34092274821—dc22
    [B]
                                                                                    2009017001

PRINTED IN THE UNITED STATES OF AMERICA

10   9   8   7   6   5   4   3   2   1

Most Berkley Books are available at special quantity discounts for bulk purchases for sales promotions, premiums, fund-raising, or educational use. Special books, or book excerpts, can also be created to fit specific needs.

For details, write: Special Markets, The Berkley Publishing Group, 375 Hudson Street, New York, New York 10014.

When I think of an officer in the Army, I think of someone who has a variety of talents and skills. An officer is smart, physically strong, mentally tough, and is highly motivated and capable. These admirable qualities create a leader.

—Colby Umbrell

If you're an able-bodied male in Doylestown, you're probably going to play football.

—Bryan Buckley

PREFACE

Connections

Until the dawn of the twentieth century, the notion that there was an organic link between athletics and military life was not part of the conventional wisdom of American culture. That fact may be difficult to understand now, if only because the language of the armed forces so permeates the language of sports, particularly of football. A quarterback is a "field general." An athlete who plays in spite of physical or emotional trauma is a "warrior." An important contest is often described as a "battle." And on and on. These clichés are so embedded in the vernacular of athletics that nowadays we give barely a thought to the connection that they imply or to how that connection came to be made.

The idea that participation in sports may help prepare a young man for the rigors of war was never expressed more succinctly or eloquently than it was in a famous remark attributed to the Duke of Wellington: "The battle of Waterloo was won on the playing fields of Eton." Fifty-four years after the Seventh Coalition vanquished Napoleon and his army, four years after Robert E. Lee's surrender at Appomattox, Rutgers and Princeton played the first game of American intercollegiate football, in 1869, and the concept that athletic competition could cultivate the best attributes of a soldier now took tentative root in the country's system of higher education. "At the schools that were starting football games in the northeast, the virtues of the Civil War were supposed to be brought to bear," said Andy Kozar, the author of the book *Football as a War Game*. "Self-sacrifice, courage, discipline, public spirit—football was a place where schools could develop those kinds of things."

In 1890, military officers made the first inroads toward implementing athletics into the training of their men. Lt. C. D. Parkhurst, in a series of essays called "The Practical Education of the Soldier," argued that physical training was the most vital aspect of a soldier's preparation for battle and that sports and exercise encouraged "quick and unthinking obedience to orders." That same year, Army and Navy played their first football game against each other, and soon enough, the U.S. government began to use the spirit of Wellington's words as a guiding principle for military and public policy. Two powerful forces contributed to this development: the prospect of war, and the desire for sex.

Under the presumption that the 1916 Mexican Revolution might lead to all-out war, President Woodrow Wilson invaded Mexico twice and marshaled the National Guard along the Mexican-American border. The 100,000 troops filled their downtime at Mexico's saloons and brothels, frequenting them so often that, in early 1917, Washington was receiving reports that America's fighting forces were rife with venereal disease. In response, the military called on service organizations, such as the YMCA and the Red Cross, to create camps and events that emphasized participation and competition in sports and physical activity, including relay races, cross-country runs, and baseball and basketball leagues. U.S. military leaders considered the programs so successful that President Wilson, in 1918, wrote a formal proposal to make athletic participation compulsory in the Army. The military complied, and as historian Steven W. Pope wrote in 1995, "Official integration of sport into military training sparked a wave of competitive team sports" among civilians. By 1921, seventeen states had passed legislation mandating some form of physical education in their schools. The value of athletics had been revealed to the entire nation.

Meanwhile, a little town in southeastern Pennsylvania—a town whose only public school did not, as yet, have an athletic program of any kind—was growing. And year by year, the town would continue growing, continue changing, keeping time with the rhythms of a new America, where the games a child could play had become part of the rite of passage into adulthood. Come the close of the century, the town would find itself tethered to one sport in particular, and it would produce two young men who regarded their transitions from the playing field to the battlefield as seamless, as natural chapters in the stories of their lives.

ONE

Departure

Wednesday, July 26, 2006

Already he had written his own eulogy, typing it on his laptop in the sure and steady strokes of a Marine who knew, but did not fear, that he might soon die. The speech was a reckoning, an explanation of why he had decided to stop playing football and pursue a cause for which he was willing to sacrifice himself, and after he had finished it, Bryan Buckley kept writing. Five letters followed, each addressed to one of his five closest friends: Corey, Spratty, Ed, Matt, Dave. He wrote more. He provided instructions for his funeral. He did not want to be buried at Arlington National Cemetery. He did not want sadness or despair to mar the day. *Go have some beers,* he wrote. *Laugh about the dumb stuff I've done.* He had printed out the letters and the eulogy, stuffed them into an envelope, sealed it, and given it to his brother-in-law Chris DiSciullo during his last visit to Doylestown, Pennsylvania, to the place where he had grown up. Bryan then had asked Chris and his wife, Kim— Bryan's eldest sister—to honor a single request: No one was to open the envelope unless something happened to him during his deployment in Fallujah, during the seven months he was scheduled to spend in the deadliest city in Iraq. These were his most private and personal thoughts and memories. These were his words to the people he loved . . . should he never see them again. He even told Kim that he had marked the envelope with a pen, creating, in effect, a bar code on it. If someone opened the envelope, read its contents, and resealed it before Bryan returned home, he would know.

His father, Bill, did not know that he had done all this, or whom Bryan wanted to deliver the eulogy. His mother, Connie, did. She knew what he had written and whom he had selected as his eulogist. Some things are just easier to tell mothers, and some things are easier to ask of fathers—things such as assembling weaponry, which is what Bill Buckley had been doing during the days before his son's deployment with the 2nd Battalion, 8th Marine Regiment. With much of Bryan's gear strewn about his living room floor, Bill had sat on the couch amid the mess, looping survival cord through the magazines of 5.56-mm ammunition that Bryan would load into his M4 rifle. Having the magazines knotted to his weapon would allow Bryan to keep the bullets closer to his fingertips, reload more quickly, and lessen the chances that he'd be left defenseless in the chaos of a desert firefight.

Bryan's decision to become a Marine had surprised Bill. Sure, as a boy, Bryan was at his dad's knee often, asking questions about Bill's three years with the U.S. Army Security Agency, the electronic intelligence branch that was the antecedent to the National Security Agency. Bill told Bryan what stories he could—so much of his work was still classified—and he taught Bryan to shoot a rifle when the kid was thirteen, taking him up to the hunting and fishing club that Bill belonged to in Pike County, Pennsylvania, near the Pocono Mountains. The kid bagged a deer his first time out. But football had been so integral to Bryan's daily life, particularly when he was playing in high school for Central Bucks West, that until Bryan announced to his parents that he was giving up football and joining the military, Bill had never stopped to consider his son's future without the sport. Through Bryan's middle

school, high school, and college years, there always had been another
game to play. Now, here was Bryan, the youngest of Bill and Connie's
four children, at twenty-six years old. Soft pink freckles still dotted his
face. Splayed along the inside of his left forearm was a striking tattoo:
a blue-black trident. At six feet one and 190 pounds, he was leaner and
lighter than he had been as a high school or collegiate football player.
Most of his light brown hair had been shorn away, and his physical
training for the military had shaved away even the slightest bit of excess
body fat, like stone from a sculpture, as if the Marines had stripped
away all that had been unnecessary about him. Here was Bill Buckley's
son, shoving clothes and gear into a duffel bag and a backpack, a lieutenant in the U.S. Marine Corps, 4th Platoon Commander in 2–8's Fox
Company. Bill was proud of him. He didn't say so just then. He just
kept looping that cord through those magazines.

These last few days—the whole month, actually—had been a swirl
for Bill and Connie. On Saturday, the two of them had flown down on
one-way tickets from Philadelphia International Airport to Jacksonville, a small city of tattoo parlors, dry-cleaning shops, and Southern
fast-food restaurants hard on the southeastern coast of North Carolina.
Bryan had bought a house near Jacksonville in December, a tidy two-
story single on an isolated cul-de-sac a mile east of Camp Lejeune, the
Marine Corps base that had become his office and was the practice field
on which he was preparing himself and the forty-five Marines in his
platoon for what they would face in Fallujah. *Fallujah.* Connie still
couldn't say for certain how she'd react once it sank in that the youngest of her four children was leaving and might never come home. She
and Bill had thrown a going-away party for him on July 1 at their
home, with two hundred family members and friends filling the house
and spilling over into the backyard to say good-bye to Bryan, no one
dwelling on the dark unknown of Bryan's departure. Still, at different
times during the day, a few partygoers asked Connie the same question:
"How are you going to deal with this?" How the hell did she know?
"You have faith in him," she'd tell them, and she'd force a smile and

plop a spoonful of potato salad on a guest's plate and return to the party and try not to think about the question then and there. She still had three and a half weeks before he left. She still had time to figure it out.

Now, that time had all but expired. Fox Company's 230 Marines were scheduled to depart Camp Lejeune at midnight, a series of buses shuttling the men forty-five miles to Cherry Point, North Carolina, the largest air station in the corps, and this is how Bill and Connie Buckley were spending their final hours with their son before he boarded one of those buses: They were running an annoying, time-consuming errand on a stinking hot summer day. The temperature was climbing to 90 degrees, the air heavy, and the three of them were driving to a Staples so that Bryan could photocopy a batch of articles and memoranda, a scouting report of the Iraqi insurgency, that he planned to pass out to his platoon. Typical Bryan—he had waited until the last minute to take care of this task. But more than the inefficiency, more than the uncomfortable humidity, what exasperated Bill and Connie was that Bryan paid for the copies—$144 worth—out of his own pocket. "For God's sake, Bryan," Connie said, "can't you do this at the base?" He said no. He wasn't allowed. Worse, he already had dropped close to $700 on various accessories that the government didn't issue to Marines—batteries and cold-weather clothing, for instance. His father, unlike Connie, did not say a word. This was how they had always been, throughout their thirty-three years of marriage. Connie was the firecracker: a redheaded, outgoing woman who spoke in bursts of italics. Bill's dark gray hair was a bit longer than a buzz cut; he wore glasses, loved Elvis Presley's music, and had a more measured temperament. His words and gestures were precise, purposeful. He stood in the store, watching Bryan shell out more of his own money, and though he did not say so at the time, Bill Buckley thought it appalling that the richest country in the world—a country fighting, and laboring to win, a war it had chosen to initiate three years earlier—couldn't afford to make its own photocopies.

*   *   *

Back at Bryan's house, the swirl now swept him up, too. He changed into his sand-colored camouflage uniform and baseball cap. The rest of his personal gear was packed, or at least he thought it was. Was it? He sifted through his short-term memory, running down the list of things he had to bring with him (his uniforms, his body armor, his rifle, his 9-mm pistol) and the list of things that the corps already had shipped over to Iraq in anticipation of the company's arrival (machine guns, optics). The minutes sped by. Was everything packed? He wasn't thinking about where he was going, just what it would take for him to get there.

This was his frame of mind now, a mentality that more and more was singularly focused on *the mission* and the next moment therein. He would joke with friends that someday he would move back to Doylestown to settle down, raise a family, coach his kids' football teams . . . but that would be years into the future, not here, not now. Part of the reason he'd bought this particular house was that it was on such a sequestered, quiet street. It was close to the base and therefore convenient, yes. But it was also far enough away from the relative bustle of downtown Jacksonville that Bryan could surround himself in silence if he so chose, could have time in that cocoon he sometimes created for himself. Even the inside of his house featured minimal distraction—save the bar that Bryan and Bill had built on the second floor (complete with a shiny gold keg tap) and the television, couch, and assorted DVDs in the living room. The carpeting was slate gray. The walls were mostly bare—a few photographs. The back patio faced thick, green woods. A man could lose himself in thought in a place like this if he wanted to, and Bryan often did. He always had. In high school, hours before a Friday night CB West football game, he would return home from school, scarf down a plate of pasta that Connie had prepared, go up to his room, and close the door—never emerging, never talking to his family members until he saw them on the field after the game had ended. When

Bill and Connie first picked up on Bryan's pregame routine, the way he would retreat within himself, they wondered about it and worried. They didn't understand it. As Bill said later, "Parents hear things about kids and drugs" and how teenagers behave. But there was nothing sinister about what was going on behind that door. Usually Bryan was watching television or reading his playbook or, in the phrase he often used, "going to that place [he] needed to get to" before a big game, and Bill and Connie learned something about dealing with their son: There were times when you could talk to him, and there were times, like now, when you couldn't . . . and didn't dare try. Connie could see that her son was on edge; his answers to her innocent questions were short, impatient. He hadn't eaten all day. He was a Marine in a Marine town, and his country had called him to duty, and the time had come for him to answer. His was an all-consuming role.

At 7 P.M., he decided it was time for him and his roommate, Scott Helminski, another platoon commander in Fox, to leave for the base. Connie wanted to accompany them, but logistically, that didn't make sense. There was no reason for her and Bill to be at the base so early; they'd be standing around with nothing to do for at least five hours. So they agreed to carpool: Bryan and Scott would drive to Camp Lejeune at seven in Bryan's blue 2000 Chevrolet Blazer, and Scott's girlfriend would drive Bill and Connie over in Scott's car at eleven. That way, Bill and Connie could go back to his house and tidy up the place before driving the 475 miles back to Doylestown in Bryan's Blazer.

They lasted until ten before piling into Scott's car and pulling out of Bryan's cul-de-sac. They couldn't wait any longer. Heading west on Route 24, an expansive four-lane highway along which drivers adhered strictly to the 55-mph speed limit, Bill and Connie could look to the left and see the long, high metal fence along the northeast border of Camp Lejeune's eighty-five-mile perimeter, a fence now festooned with homemade banners and signs asking husbands, fathers, and brothers to come home soon, to stay safe, to remember how much they would be loved while they were away. Once they reached Lejeune, they parked near a half dozen contracting trailers, each some sixty feet long, that were serving as offices as the base underwent renovations. One was functioning as Fox Company's headquarters, and inside was Bryan, with the rest of Fox's leadership: the three other platoon commanders, the four platoon sergeants, and the company commander, Capt. James Mingus. There were plenty of parking spaces around the trailers, and Bill noticed how quiet the base seemed to be.

When his cell phone hummed to signal his parents' arrival, Bryan went outside and found Bill and Connie. The buses' departure time to Cherry Point had been pushed back to 2 A.M., so rather than have his parents sit in his car for three more hours, Bryan invited them into Fox's trailer. There, the officers had piled their bags on the floor—their rucksacks on one side, their long, green C bags on the other. Bill and Connie sat at Bryan's desk and listened. The officers were in the middle of a meeting, reviewing the mundane details of the company's travel itinerary: ride the buses from Lejeune to Cherry Point; fly in a Boeing 777 jet from Cherry Point to Nova Scotia, from Nova Scotia to Ireland, from Ireland to Budapest, and from Budapest to Kuwait City. Between flight durations and layovers, the trip would take more than twenty-four hours. The company would spend one or two days in Kuwait for processing and paperwork. That was where the mundane would stop and the dangerous would start. For Fox then would fly to Al Taqaddum Airbase in central Iraq, and a C-130 would need to make at least two trips to transport the entire company to the base. The travel time from Kuwait to Al Taqaddum was only an hour, but to avoid any anti-aircraft threat, each flight would end with a combat landing. Instead of coasting in on an incline, the C-130 would drop to the ground like a hawk in pursuit of prey, its nose jutting downward at a sharp angle during its descent, the Marines on board jarred out of their seats as the landing gear made contact with the tarmac.

Connie kept her eyes on Bryan, who fiddled with a switchblade as the meeting continued. He would never admit that he was nervous, she said later, no, not her son, but there he was, opening the blade, closing it, flipping the knife into the air and catching it, open, close, flip, catch, open, close, flip, catch, until there was a small line of red penciling across one of his fingers. He had cut himself and didn't know it. He didn't stop playing with the knife. Some things, a mother just notices.

After the meeting ended, Bryan, Bill, and Connie left the trailer and walked across the street to Lejeune's musty basketball gymnasium, where Fox's enlisted men were killing time. Some of them were clustered into groups, huddled together, sitting in silence. Some of them were praying. Some of them were curled up in the fetal position, sleeping. Some of them were talking to each other or to family members. Some of them were shooting baskets. Each was waiting in his own way. The sight shocked Connie. It saddened her, too. She estimated that three-quarters of the men had no family members there, no one to see them off, and in her mind, it was a stretch even to refer to the people before her as men. What she saw were eighteen-, nineteen-, twenty-year-olds, most of whom were dressed just like Bryan. What she saw were kids. She was expecting older, harder warriors, with facial hair as rough as sharkskin and chins on which someone could strike a match. She was expecting *Marines*. There was one who stood out to her—a big guy sitting in the corner of the gym, his arms covered in tattoos that blended into the tones of his camouflage—and she leaned over to Bryan and said, "Nobody's going to be able to see him."

"He's one of the snipers, Mom," Bryan said. "That's the idea."

The buses arrived on time, and the Marines filed out of the gym. Those who had family and friends on hand hugged them before climbing into the buses, and Bryan did, too, though on his terms. All of Bryan's life, Connie had called him her "one-armed hugger" because of the way he showed affection—or, more accurately, because of his reluctance to show too much affection. It was just something he always did, that lean-in half hug, as if he were the host of a Hollywood cocktail party, and he did it once more in the Camp Lejeune parking lot by the buses, wrapping one of his arms around Connie, then Bill: just one.

As Bryan fell back in line with the men of Fox Company, his back to his parents, Bill stood nearby, holding a camera.

"Yo, B.," he said, and he pressed the flash button.

The photo caught Bryan as he was still turning around to acknowledge his father. In the photo, he is glancing over his right shoulder, his military cap square on his head, a sly smile on his face. He looks confident, ready. It was the last glimpse Bill and Connie got of him before he boarded his bus.

From inside the Blazer, they watched the buses pull away, and Connie pressed her hand to the glass as Bryan's bus passed across the passenger's-side window. It was 2:02 A.M. on Thursday, July 27. She noticed that, too. They started back to Bryan's house, winding their way out of the more than 153,000 acres of sand and swamp that composed the base, out to Route 24 again, saying nothing to each other. Talking about an emotional night would only make it more emotional. Words would only lead to tears. When they got back to Bryan's house, they went to bed. They didn't sleep much.

Bryan had planned to rent out his house while he was in Iraq. Early that morning, Bill and Connie woke and began packing up whatever personal valuables Bryan had left behind—his computer, clothes, DVDs, CDs, and the like—fitting what they could into his car, padlocking the rest in his most spacious bedroom closet. At 8 P.M., they closed the house's front door, locked it, and left. Driving through the dead of night from Jacksonville to Doylestown, Bill and Connie Buckley didn't stop at a motel, and they didn't speak to each other. For eight and a half hours, the only sound in the Chevy was low music coming from the stereo, 475 miles of Elvis.

On his bus, Bryan passed out the "scouting report" he had compiled for the forty-five men of 4th Platoon, ordering them to have the entire packet read by the time they touched down in Kuwait City. "Get your head in the game," he told them. "This is it." It was all he said, and once he sat down, most of the Marines slept, and when they weren't sleeping, they hooked headphones to their ears and let their iPods take them away. The scene was part of the delicate balance Bryan and Fox Company's other officers sought to strike among the men during the trip. With Fox Company facing a six-hour layover in Ireland, for instance, the men saw a bar at the airport terminal but only stared at it with trepidation, most of them under the U.S.'s legal drinking age of twenty-one. They stared, that is, until Mingus, the company commander, declared, "I don't care how old you guys are. We're getting drunk in Ireland. Let's get a fucking beer." The officers wanted their men to be loose and relaxed, but not so much so that the men lost their edge and sharpness. They wanted them to be prepared, but not so tight and anxious that they would freeze up at the worst time.

To that end, the dossier that Bryan distributed to 4th Platoon included a six-thousand-word essay by David Kilcullen—a lieutenant colonel in the Australian Army, a Ph.D., and an expert in counterinsurgency tactics—that recently had been published in *Military Review*. The essay was titled "Twenty-Eight Articles: Fundamentals of Company-Level Counterinsurgency," and it was the last of Kilcullen's articles that Bryan wanted the men of his platoon to remember most.

28. Whatever else you do, keep the initiative. In counterinsurgency, the initiative is everything. If the enemy is reacting to you, you control the environment. Provided you mobilize the population, you will win. If you are reacting to the enemy, even if you are killing or capturing him in large numbers, then he is controlling the environment and you will eventually lose. In counterinsurgency, the enemy initiates most attacks, targets you unexpectedly, and withdraws too fast for you to react. Do not be drawn into purely reactive operations: Focus on the population, build your own solution, further your game plan, and fight the enemy only when he gets in the way.

Kilcullen's recommendations were particularly timely, given the state of Iraq. In May, the Directorate of Intelligence, a division of the Joint Chiefs of Staff, had disseminated to the intelligence community a classified report that detailed just how dire the situation in Iraq was for American troops and that contradicted President George W. Bush's public insistence that all really was well. The number of attacks by insurgents and al-Qaeda in Iraq had risen steadily since the start of the year to an average of six hundred to seven hundred per week in May, and Al Anbar Province—where Fallujah and Ramadi, another thicket of insurgents, were located and where Bryan and Fox Company were headed—was the nexus of the violence. It had been for a long time. Insurgents had ambushed and killed four American contractors with the Blackwater security firm in Fallujah on March 31, 2004—shooting, slashing, and stabbing the bodies, then burning them until they were charred. After Iraqi boys beat the bodies with flip-flops to show, according to author Bing West in his book *No True Glory*, "that Americans were scum under the soles of their shoes," a mob of *mujahedeen* hung two of the corpses from a girder, two black sacks swaying for all to see. The incident precipitated the Bush administration's decision to have the Marines mount a full assault on Fallujah, to level a city of two thousand blocks and more than 250,000 people. But the Iraqi Army refused to fight, and after less than a week of intense fighting, the Marines withdrew under orders from U.S. Central Command, creating a vacuum that the insurgents were happy to fill; the city became their safe haven. As a recognition that Fallujah was at a minimum symbolic of the insurgency's defiance of the United States' power and presence in Iraq, ten thousand Marines went back into the city seven months later, in November, destroying its infrastructure and attempting to survive what is now regarded as the most brutal combat that American troops had experienced since the Vietnam War. By the end of the battle, the Marines had taken the city, but Fallujah was damn near dust.

Since then, the situation in Al Anbar had hardly improved. Insurgents streamed back into the area, surreptitious as always. In fact, on

July 27, 2006, the same day that Fox Company began its journey to Kuwait, four Marines were killed in Al Anbar. Lance Cpl. James Higgins, 22, an old soul from Frederick, Maryland, whose favorite singer was Frank Sinatra and whose favorite comedians were Abbott and Costello, had been shot in the chest. His unit had been stationed at Camp Fallujah. The three other Marines—Lance Cpl. Adam Murray, 21, of Cordova, Tennessee; Cpl. Timothy Roos, 21, of Cincinnati, Ohio; and Pfc. Enrique Sanchez, 21, of Garner, North Carolina—had died at the same time, their Humvee destroyed by a large roadside bomb in Ramadi, thirty miles west of Fallujah. Murray, Roos, and Sanchez were the twelfth, thirteenth, and fourteenth men of 3rd Battalion, 8th Marine Regiment—a Camp Lejeune battalion—to die over the previous four months. At the time of the classified report's release, roughly 130,000 U.S. troops and another 263,000 Iraqi military and police were in the country, most of them on the defensive because they were fighting enemies who could vanish among the local population, who might fire randomly at American troops and, by doing so, compel the unit to waste a day in pursuit of phantoms. After all, the insurgents still regarded Fallujah as *their* city. They had owned it, and they wanted it back, and to carry out a counterinsurgency in such an environment—an urban area of five square miles, a confining grid of mosques and alleys and three- and four-story buildings where the full 360 degrees around you presented a threat—the Marines couldn't simply outmuscle the guerrillas. That was the lesson from Fallujah in 2004. *We have to get smarter*, Bryan knew, and in playing his part in that process, he had to trust his men to think freely, to make the right call for the right reason at the right time, even when he or another officer wasn't available to give them an order. In war, there were always such occasions.

In that way, Bryan reasoned, what he expected out of his men wasn't so different from what his football coach at Central Bucks West, Mike Pettine, had expected out of him. Though Bryan understood that football and war really weren't comparable, the basic principle guiding his actions and decisions in each arena was the same, and he had learned that principle long before he became a Marine. Countless times over the three years he played at West, Bryan had heard Pettine—in pregame speeches and team meetings, in that gravelly, bass-drum-deep voice of his—drive home a core coaching value: that a coach cannot play the game for his players, that he can only give them the tools for success, that it was up to each player to apply those tools. Moreover, as a team captain in his senior season, 1998, Bryan had a unique position, apart from any of his teammates, as the player whom Pettine trusted most to make sure his message reached every single CB West player. Truth be told—and Pettine admitted as much himself—the coach ceded some control of the locker room, of a hundred teenage boys, to one of their peers. If the quarterback threw to the wrong receiver, if a linebacker didn't blitz through the right gap, Pettine wouldn't give the quarterback or the linebacker an earful. He'd give *Bryan* an earful. It had been a sacrifice sometimes to be the whipping boy and the team leader at the very same time, but what happened that season had made the measure of abuse he took worthwhile.

Eight years later, that season remained a touchstone for him. Now that they were friends, Bryan could kid Pettine about those tongue-lashings, but he still gripped those memories and their meaning tightly. His parents had taught him to be responsible for himself and his actions, but to Bryan, Pettine had expanded that notion. Pettine had taught him accountability—to be responsible not just for his actions but for the actions of those around him—and never had their relationship felt more valuable to Bryan, more relevant, than it did right now. Bryan had played football in prep school, and he had played football in college, but no coach he encountered at those higher levels had affected him in the same way. No one else came close. Bryan loved his parents and his siblings and his circle of friends. He considered Chris DiSciullo not merely his brother-in-law but another older brother, which was why he had entrusted Chris with the contents of that envelope. But he believed that no one understood him better, as a person or as a Marine, than Mike Pettine did, and that meant Bryan had a task to complete in Iraq. He had to find time to write and send a letter back to Doylestown, and in it, he had to ask Pettine an awful question. He had to ask him if, God forbid it was necessary, Pettine would deliver the eulogy that Bryan had written for his own funeral. . . . *Once you accept that you might die, you have two choices. You either die on your knees, or you die standing up and fighting. If I go, so be it. The need of the many outweighs the need of the few, and if my death helps to save the lives of other Americans, I accept it because I'm serving a cause greater than myself.* . . . Yes, he wanted his old coach to say those words.

At Cherry Point, he had paused before taking his first step onto the plane, reminding himself that he might never walk on American ground again. Now, Fox Company would soon land in Kuwait City, and Bryan glanced down the aisles at the faces of his men, harking back to a long-time ritual of his, one he carried out before every football game. He'd survey the locker room, and he knew his teammates were ready to play, to *win*, when each of his teammates had a look on his face that made it clear he planned, in Bryan's words, to "fuck someone up." He wanted to see that look from his Marines now. Their weapons were clean, their expressions narrowing stares. He saw it.

The plane landed, and the exit door opened. In another two days, at most, Bryan would arrive at Camp Fallujah. When would he find time to write that letter to Pettine, to the man whom he credited so much for molding his character? Kuwait City's mean temperature in July and August reaches 111 degrees Fahrenheit, but that day, the thermometer rose to an incomprehensible 133 degrees. Hot wind gusted into his face, as if the exit doorway were the mouth of a giant blow dryer. To that moment, there had been 2,573 U.S. military deaths in Iraq since the war started. Those four Marines had died just a day after Bryan had one-armed his mother and father and smiled that confident smile and left Bill and Connie to watch him, through the window of a car, disappear. Grains of sand pricked his skin. What would he say in the letter? Sweat beaded on his forehead. He felt like he might get sick. Maybe he should start the letter this way: *I could never thank you enough for what you did for me, Coach. . . .*

He squinted against the sunlight and stepped out of the plane into the hellish heat.

TWO

History

Tuesday, September 1, 1998

The football field wasn't so much a football field as it was an expansive lawn with goalposts, fit for the front of one of the elegant, colonial-style homes that rose, alp-like, from the emerald earth of central Bucks County, Pennsylvania. A slight hill sloped up from the student parking lot behind Central Bucks High School East to one sideline, and beyond the opposite sideline were trees, nothing but trees, a wall of them tall and green and brown. There were no bleachers or stands surrounding the field, just a low, gray chain-link fence and an oval track of charcoal gravel; it was a practice field, nothing more. But on days like this, when the sky was clear and the sun was warm and practice felt like one of the touch football games he had played with his father in the yard, Colby Umbrell was happier nowhere else.

The previous spring and summer had been memorable for him— life-changing, in a way. He had attended a football camp at the U.S. Military Academy, an experience that reconfirmed a lifelong desire: to become a cadet and then an officer in the U.S. Army. The thought had been a daydream for him when he was a young boy; his family's annual vacations to Washington, D.C., and to Arlington National Cemetery stirred a sense of patriotism within him, and after he experienced first-hand, if only for a few days, the history and honor at West Point, his mind and heart were fixed on the goal of getting there. Since participating in the camp, he had received a nomination to the academy from his congressman, Republican Jim Greenwood, and playing football for Army now had become an option for him, too, because he had bulked up so much over the previous months. Charlie Packman, the new strength coach for CB East's football team, the Patriots, had had players pair up as workout partners during the off-season, and Colby and one of his best friends, quarterback Steve Kreider, had attacked Packman's weight-training program with vigor. Kreider had put on fifteen pounds, but Colby had put on thirty-five, adding mass and muscle in anticipation that he would change positions on East's offensive line from his junior year to this, his senior season. He had played center the year before; he would play offensive and defensive tackle this season. The extra weight took him up to 240 pounds. Standing six feet one, he had a puffy blond crew cut, a slight gap between his two upper front teeth, and a large lower jaw that jutted forward as if it were in search of a left hook. During practices and games, he usually did not say much.

Colby's reticence had been the reason that Larry Greene, East's head coach, at first hadn't selected him to be one of the Patriots' team captains. At the team's season-ending banquet in 1997, Colby had sat stunned at his table when Greene announced the names of East's senior captains for '98—Kreider, Phil Laing, and Bryan Scott—and he wasn't among them. Greene, like everyone else on East's team, didn't question Colby's work ethic, but he just wasn't sure that Colby had the right personality to be a captain. Kreider? He was gregarious, the quarterback, a natural choice. Laing? He was the sort of kid, Greene thought, who looked like he'd started growing facial hair at age six. Laing was going to start at fullback and middle linebacker. Scott? He sang in the school choir, started for the varsity basketball team, was an all-district-caliber sprinter, was respected and well liked by most of East's student body—and was perhaps the best high school football player in Pennsylvania. A tailback and safety, Scott seemed to have an NFL-ready body at age eighteen, a chiseled six feet two, 205 pounds. Penn State was the front-runner in the race to recruit him.

Eventually, Greene reconsidered his decision and named Colby a captain, too. But that initial disappointment was a lasting memory for Colby for years afterward, perhaps because he had looked forward to his senior season as his last, best chance to change the dynamic of a football rivalry that for nearly thirty years had defined his hometown of Doylestown. For most of those years, CB East had been the redheaded stepchild to its neighbor in the school district: Central Bucks West. It wasn't that East didn't have a respectable program. The Patriots had won a league championship in 1979; had reached the district playoffs in 1996, Colby's sophomore year; and were perennially a better-than-average team in the Suburban One League National Conference, which comprised ten schools in the suburbs north of Philadelphia. It was that West was the premier high school football program not just in the National Conference, but arguably in all of Pennsylvania.

Once, the schools had been one. Because of increasing enrollment, Central Bucks High School had split in 1969 into two schools—one on Central Bucks High's campus on the southern end of Doylestown Borough, the newer building five miles to the northeast in bucolic Buckingham Township. By 1998, the two schools, which still house students in grades ten through twelve, had more than 3,100 students between them, roughly 1,700 of whom went to West. It was not the only advantage that West had over East. Over the subsequent twenty-nine years after the split, all of them under Mike Pettine, CB West's Bucks won 281 games, 22 league or conference titles, and 2 state championships in Class AAAA, the highest enrollment classification in Pennsylvania. As a matter of routine, they were ranked in USA Today's weekly poll of the top twenty-five high school football teams in the country. They accomplished all of this, in large part, because of Pettine—his decision to stay at West after the split, his football acumen, the force of his will. Just the year before, in 1997, as East was limping to a 4–6 record, West won its second state title, going 15–0 and beating Upper St. Clair 44–20 in the championship game on a snow-sprinkled Mansion Park Stadium in Altoona. One program had a history of supremacy and excellence. The other had always been trying to catch up.

Since 1969, East had beaten West only twice. Colby's father, Mark, had played running back and linebacker for the Patriots, graduating from East in 1973, and he had lost three times to West—by a combined score of 111–12. Colby had lost twice. The one-sidedness, though, didn't temper the rivalry's intensity. The annual Thanksgiving matchup between the two teams, held from 1971 to 1992, drew as many as fifteen thousand people to the football stadium at Doylestown's Delaware Valley College. After the game was moved from Thanksgiving to accommodate West's annual appearances in the district playoffs, the Bucks and Patriots would play on the final weekend of the regular season, and students, alumni, parents, and community members filled instead a smaller venue: War Memorial Field, the stadium on West's campus where both teams played their home games.

There were older high school football rivalries in Pennsylvania. Germantown Academy and Penn Charter, members of Philadelphia's Inter-Academic League, began playing each other in 1887; theirs is believed to be the longest continuous series in the country. There were rivalries that clung faster to custom. Easton and Phillipsburg (New Jersey), two schools separated by the Delaware River, have met every Thanksgiving since 1914, refusing to reschedule their game even if one or both teams had playoff games on the following Saturday, playing two games in three days if it meant maintaining tradition. But in terms of the two teams' quality, proximity to, and familiarity with each other, by the fall of 1998 East-West had become perhaps Pennsylvania's best. Two of the Central Bucks School District's four middle schools—

Tamanend and Lenape—matriculated students to East and West for tenth grade, so boys who one year had sat next to each other in math class and had lined up next to each other on the offensive line were often on opposite sides of the rivalry the following year. "You wanted to beat them more than anything," Kreider would say later. "You didn't hate the guys, though. They were your friends. It was the only game where, when you were playing against them, guys on the other team were picking you up."

From that same pool of players, West had emerged as a nationally recognized program, and though the Bucks' success cast a shadow over East, the Patriots, with the start of the '98 season just three days away, regarded themselves as a viable threat to West's dominance. The four captains promised to provide a level of leadership that East had not possessed in '97—too many cliques on that team, too many guys out for themselves. Apart from that intangible aspect, Colby considered this a much deeper, more talented team. The Patriots' prospective start-ers were all seniors and juniors, and sophomore Brandon Scott, Bryan's younger brother, had shown potential at tailback in training camp. Colby told a reporter from the *Intelligencer*, one of Bucks County's two daily newspapers, "We can do a lot more of what we want to do." "More" included beating West, an ambition that had been on Colby's mind since he was at Lenape Middle School. Come November 7, the date of the East-West game, it would be no small satisfaction to him to walk off War Memorial Field as a winner, wearing the Patriots' red, white, and blue, to shake the hands of those West players, to have them know that, just once, the Central Bucks East Patriots got the better of them. That he had grown up with so many of the West players would only sweeten such a victory. They were, after all, the same kinds of kids from the same kinds of families and backgrounds.

One of Colby's teammates at Lenape, in fact, was now a West captain.

Bryan Buckley.

* * *

There are two Doylestowns. There is the borough, twenty-five miles north of Philadelphia, two and a half square miles in size, with a population of just more than eight thousand, the political epicenter of Bucks County as the county seat and the home of the county courthouse. And there is Doylestown Township, a penumbra of more than fifteen square miles encircling the borough. Another seventeen thousand people reside there. Generally, when you ask people born in the suburbs and towns surrounding Philadelphia where they are from, they will say, "Suburban Philadelphia." But when you ask people who live in Doylestown, be it the borough or the township, where they are from, they will say, "Doylestown." It is a telling if subtle modification. The place is part of their identities.

William Penn originally owned the land on which Doylestown was founded, selling some twenty thousand acres in 1682 to the Free Society of Traders, a company of wealthy Quakers who wished to encourage settlement throughout Pennsylvania. Among the men who settled the land was Edward Doyle, the son of an Irish immigrant, who in turn bequeathed a particularly choice portion of the property to his son William. William's tract of land included an intersection of two narrow roads of dirt and dust. The north-south road ran from Easton, one of America's first industrial cities, to Philadelphia; the east-west road connected the Delaware River to the Schuylkill River. A man who clearly understood the value of leisure, William Doyle decided that what those passing through his settlement needed first was a place to have a drink. In 1745, he opened Doyle's Tavern on the northwest corner of the intersection, which became the northwest corner of Main and State streets, the eye of activity in Doylestown.

"With the opening of Doyle's Tavern," according to a history of the town, published in 1988, "these crossroads were destined to become a commercial haven, a place where the business of law, agriculture and merchandising could thrive."

Indeed, Doylestown was never tethered to one industry, as the northern part of Pennsylvania was to anthracite or the western part of the state to steel. Amid verdant, fertile land, Doylestown, for one sixteen-year period in the 1800s, was the only municipality in the world that owned and operated its own gristmill, but there was always more to the residents' livelihoods than just their rural surroundings. The 1856 opening of a railroad line into the town led to a population surge, and from the mid-nineteenth century to the mid-twentieth, Doylestown maintained an economic and cultural balance of professionals, artisans, farmers, small-business owners, and artists. There were two primary ethnic communities: an English section that made up most of the town, and a German section in the hills of the northeast end. Catholics, Jews, and Democrats were sparse. Just after the turn of the century, when a paperboy named James A. Michener began his rounds delivering newspapers at four each morning, he could recite the name of every homeowner in Doylestown. Soon, Michener's hometown became a haven for other men and women of letters. Pearl S. Buck, Oscar Hammerstein, Moss Hart, Budd Schulberg—all of them either rented or purchased property in Doylestown. They joined the influx of New Yorkers and Philadelphians, drawn there by the fieldstone houses and pastoral setting, who now regarded the town as an ideal place to either vacation or begin a new life away from the choking bustle of the city. Above these new residents towered two stone castles built in the early 1900s by archaeologist Henry Mercer—the first his renowned museum of more than fifty thousand everyday items; the second called Fonthill, which he made his home.

The growth continued into the latter half of the century, part of a remarkable period of countywide expansion. From 1960 to 2000, Bucks County's population doubled from 300,000 to 600,000, and many of those new residents put down roots in Doylestown and its adjacent communities: New Britain, Chalfont, Warrington, Buckingham, Lahaska, Pipersville, Bedminster, Jamison. For downtown Doylestown, though, there was a cost. Shopping centers sprang up at the borough's membrane, draining customers from the merchants and small businesses. By 1962—the year that the house in which Mark Umbrell and, eventually, Colby Umbrell grew up was built—eight storefronts and two hotels loitered on Main Street, unoccupied, and those stores that had survived were dilapidated, their awnings frayed and tattered, their signs corroded and stained. The downtown's situation was so dire that, in 1964, the county's redevelopment authority proposed using more than $700,000 in urban renewal funds to tear down twenty-eight buildings, including the historic Fountain House, the four-story hotel that stood at the intersection of State and Main, the very spot where William Doyle had opened his tavern. But two local businessmen, Joe Kenny and Frank Shelley, created "Operation '64," a campaign to persuade local banks to underwrite improvement loans at lower interest rates, property owners to refurbish their buildings, and the borough council to hold down taxes. With Kenny and Shelley convincing enough residents and merchants that the people of the town had a stake in each other's success and survival, the campaign worked.

"It gave them the motivation to renovate," Betty Strecker, a former member of the borough council and a local historian, recalled. "Everybody knew everybody."

This was the Doylestown that Mark Umbrell knew as the youngest of Joe and Dorothy's four children—a town where you didn't have to lock your front door at night, a town where Mark, as a sophomore football player at CB East, could meet Nancy Macy, a sophomore member of the color guard at CB West, on a canoe trip and know he would spend the rest of his life with her. They went to college together at Lock Haven University, then returned to the central Bucks area when Mark opened Middle Bucks Mechanical, his heating and air-conditioning company. And this was the Doylestown that Bill and Connie Buckley discovered when, as a young married couple, they visited Connie's sister in New Britain and decided that central Bucks County was where they wanted to live, too. Bill had been a city kid, a native of northeast Philadelphia, and Connie had grown up in the blue-collar suburb of

Upper Darby, west of Philadelphia. But they bought a house just outside Doylestown Borough in the spring of 1973, only three-quarters of a mile from CB West and War Memorial Field, and when they finally arrived at the new home after an interminable drive up Easton Road, one of Bill's buddies who had agreed to help them move in cracked, "Hey, are we still in Pennsylvania?"

Bill and Connie laughed, but they never left. They—like Mark and Nancy, who bought and moved into Mark's boyhood house, on the east side of the borough, in the early 1990s—bore witness to Doylestown's continued evolution. It retained its small-town charm and remained culturally diverse, if not racially so. (Ninety-six percent of the borough's and township's residents were white.) The art deco of its County Theater, a tiny movie house that showed independent and foreign films, contrasted with the Victorian-era Fountain House and the Federal style of "Lawyers' Row," the string of law offices on Court Street, next to the county courthouse. Yet as more people relocated to the central Bucks region, modernity crept in to coexist with the traditional. Doylestown mutated into a sphere of affluence, of professionals, its median household income more than $46,000—not necessarily the sort of hardscrabble hamlet that usually aligns itself closely with high school football. Opening in the heart of town were boutiques, organic-food stores, organic-clothing stores, trendy bars that offered pastel-colored drinks, restaurants that would serve you ostrich if you knew to ask for it. The Woolworth's on the east side of Main Street, where bike-riding boys and girls could stop for an ice cream soda, closed in 1993, and The Gap replaced it. A few years later, the first floor of the Fountain House became a Starbucks.

Still, everybody knew everybody. That was how Doylestown could sustain so strong a sense of community despite the assimilation of outsiders and the town's disparate social foundations. A heavy Quaker influence remained in and around the town (Michener himself had been raised a Quaker) and with it the social justice and pacifism that was inherent to the Society of Friends. But the people of Doylestown were also supportive of those among them who volunteered for battle, a spirit that first manifested itself in the aftermath of April 12, 1861—the day that the first shots of the Civil War were fired at Fort Sumter. Three days later, Gen. William W. H. Davis notified the governor of Pennsylvania that his company, the Doylestown Guards, was prepared to join the fight to save the Union. On April 26, when "the last good-bys [*sic*] were said, the company was ordered to 'fall in,' and, at the word, marched off, the drum and fife playing a lively tune," Davis wrote in his book *History of the Doylestown Guards*. "The march through the streets to the railroad station was an ovation: The whole population had apparently turned out, and cheer upon cheer was given. A large crowd had collected at the station, and, as the train moved off, with the Guards aboard, the cheers were repeated."

Not long after the Guards completed their three-month tour of duty, Davis organized the 104th Pennsylvania Volunteers, a 501-man regiment that trained on the ground that became Central Bucks West's campus and served with the Army of the Potomac in Virginia. Over three years, the 104th lost 239 men, sustaining severe casualties at the battle of Fair Oaks on May 31, 1862, before returning to Doylestown in September 1864.

"A martial spirit always prevailed in spite of the sentiment of the Friends against it," Davis wrote in a footnote to *History of the Doylestown Guards*. Doylestown's "citizens never failed to respond to the call of the authorities when their services were required."

It was true then, at the nation's lowest hour. And it would be true, as two families would learn, a century and a half later.

Colby Umbrell and Bryan Buckley were not close friends. They played football together at Lenape Middle School, but they knew *of* each other more than they knew each other. Each had his own group of friends, his own formative experiences as a boy. The Umbrells were an East family, and the Buckleys were a West family. In Doylestown, that distinction made a difference.

The oldest of Mark and Nancy's four children, Colby had a natural intelligence and inquisitiveness for topics or activities that interested him. In school, if a subject bored him, he did just enough work to get by. "His grades weren't what they should have been, and he wasn't as conscientious as he knew he needed to be," Ann Kuntzmann, Colby's guidance counselor at Lenape, recalled. "Those were the kinds of things that we talked about. Basically, my job was to kick him in the butt now and then and try to get him to put out a little more." But the pursuits that he enjoyed received his full attention and passion, and football was foremost among them. Sundays were set aside for watching his and his family's favorite pro football team, the Philadelphia Eagles, but Friday nights were special. Friday nights were for East games, and during the games of tackle or two-hand touch that he and his friends from the neighborhood played together, Colby imagined himself not as Randall Cunningham or Reggie White or Ricky Watters, not as an Eagle, but as a Central Bucks East Patriot. When the Central Bucks School District realigned its enrollment boundaries the year before Colby began high school, giving him the choice to attend either East or West, it was really no choice at all.

"Anybody can go to West and win," he told his parents. "I want to go to East and win."

Away from football and school, Colby didn't mind palling around with his three siblings: his sister, Casey, and his brothers, Bruce and Adam. He drew his own comic books, creating a character called "Liver Man" who resembled the human organ, and he learned early in life how to laugh at himself, even as his parents or other authority figures were teaching him a lesson. One day in 1994, when Colby was thirteen and the average computer user was beginning to discover the power and reach of the Internet, Mark and Nancy found in their son's room a notebook filled with photos that he had printed out on their home computer—photos of naked women. Rather than castigate Colby for committing a common sin of male pubescence, Mark and Nancy carried out what they considered a more effective method of punishment: They pinned all the photos on the walls of Colby's room. When Colby arrived home from football practice at Lenape, his parents said hello to him, and he ran upstairs to get cleaned up and changed. They waited and listened. Silence. Then, Colby came back down the stairs at a much slower pace, walked into the kitchen, and said sheepishly, "Well, I guess I've lost my Internet privileges."

Mark and Nancy smiled to themselves, and nothing more about the matter needed to be said. The family, after all, had dealt with worse news than the revelation that a thirteen-year-old boy liked to look at naughty pictures. At age thirty-one, Nancy was diagnosed with breast cancer. She had a lumpectomy. Colby was in second grade at the time, and whenever he asked what was wrong with her, Nancy, in a soft voice that made it seem as if she were apologetic for speaking, would tell him that she had a "bad germ" inside her, hoping that the euphemism would be less alarming to him. Thanks to the surgery, Nancy survived the cancer, but her son never took her good health for granted. For years afterward, Colby couldn't shake the memory of what he thought and felt when he was seven and he found out his mother might die.

Connie Buckley called the youngest of her four children "Baby Bryan," and she was, in all likelihood, the one person who could get away with it. Bryan Buckley was the youngest kid in his family and the youngest kid on his block, and if he was to hang out with those older boys, he had to prove he could—prove it to himself, if not to them. It was an inner drive that he himself could never explain. He had to be the best at whatever he did. He just had to.

In Bryan's pursuit of excellence, football, as it did for Colby, came first. Bill and Connie had been going to West games ever since they had moved into town. All of their neighbors went to the games; it was the thing to do on a Friday night. Bryan went to his first East-West game on Thanksgiving 1987 when he was six, and he was instantly hooked. In December 1991, Bill drove the two of them 250 miles to Altoona to watch West beat Erie Cathedral Prep, 26–14, for the Bucks' first state championship, and during that game, Bryan turned to his father and, as if he were a character in a Matt Christopher story, said, "I'm going to play for them someday." He did not go back to Altoona two years later, when West, after losing its second game of the season, made something of a Cinderella run (as much of a Cinderella run as West could make, that is) to the state final. Instead, Bryan pedaled his bike over to the house of his friend Brian Spratt, and the two of them lay on the floor in the Spratts' basement, listening on the radio as West took a two-touchdown lead against North Hills, a team that featured future NFL linebacker LaVar Arrington, then a freshman. The notion that West could win a state title against such odds—*The Bucks weren't supposed to make it this far! Arrington's the greatest player in Pennsylvania history, and he's only a ninth-grader, and West's still gonna beat 'em!*—intensified Bryan's yearning to be part of the program, even after North Hills scored two touchdowns and a two-point conversion in the game's final four minutes to win, 15–14.

The Buckleys were an upper-middle-class family. Bill worked as an engineer for C. B. Ives, an industrial equipment company in the suburbs west of Philadelphia, and Connie was a field manager for Weight Watchers, overseeing franchises in four counties. It would have been easy for them to spoil their children: Steve, Kim, Maureen (who went by the nickname Moey), and Bryan. They didn't. On Saturday mornings, Bryan usually woke to the sound of clanging coming from the garage, of Bill digging through his toolbox, and Bryan would bury his head under his pillow because the noise meant he'd be spending the weekend helping Bill repair the fence or pave the driveway or finish some landscaping project in the backyard. If Baby Bryan wanted something—free time on a Saturday, a starting spot on his middle-school football team, a shot at playing for CB West—he would have to *earn* it.

Thursday, September 3, 1998

Jim Benstead was quite possibly the only Oxford-educated middle-school football coach in America. After playing wingback and running back under Mike Pettine and graduating from CB West in 1980, he headed to the University of Arizona to begin his studies in international law. There, he got his first experience as a head football coach . . . with one of the university's powder-puff intramural teams. Oxford then granted him admission—based on his grades at Arizona, not on his powder-puff win-loss record—opening the door for him to travel to Warsaw, Moscow, and Leningrad to research his doctoral dissertation on the U.S. response to *perestroika*.

Late in the summer of 1988, he had returned to Doylestown after those eight years away. It was supposed to be a short visit—see his family, say hello to friends—while he decided whether to work in New York, Washington, or London. He stopped by West, shuffling down the concrete staircase at the west side of the building that led down to Pettine's office, shaking his old coach's hand, hearing Pettine say eight words that made Benstead rethink his future.

"Your alma mater, Lenape, doesn't have a coach."

Benstead couldn't believe it. The feeder system to one of the finest high school football programs in the country was missing a coach? He headed over to Lenape, located across the street from War Memorial Field, and told the administrators there that he was willing to volunteer as the head coach for two weeks. What Benstead ultimately understood, from that casual meeting with Pettine, was that he had left Doylestown without really leaving it. What he discovered, after those first two weeks at Lenape, was that he wanted to coach, and he wanted to do it in his hometown. He opened up a private practice in an office on Court Street, along Lawyers' Row, so that he could focus on what he called "the three Fs": his family, his firm, and football.

"Coaching is in your blood," Benstead, a squat man with a cherubic grin, said later. "As soon as you got with the kids, you realized, particularly at junior high, that a kid can make a right or left turn. They're at an extremely moldable age. I liked the fact that you could form or help some of these kids one way or the other. I'm not talking about your Buckleys or your Colbys; they're like bedrock. Those guys were formed when the world was flat. People say, 'What did you do to make a kid like that?' You don't make kids like that. Their parents make kids like that. Those guys are gems."

Never did Benstead hide his agenda when it came to coaching his eighth- and ninth-graders. He wanted the kids to have fun, particularly those who might never play football in high school or college. He wanted the team to win games, and win it did. The smallest of the four Central Bucks middle schools, Lenape went undefeated in 1993 and 1994, then went 7–1 in 1995, Bryan and Colby's ninth-grade season. (Each of those teams autographed a football for Benstead, and he mounted the three mementos on a shelf in his law office.) But because many of the players would play for West, he also wanted to introduce them to a streamlined, simplified version of Pettine's playbook. If Pettine had thirty pass plays in his repertoire, Benstead ran ten of them. If Pettine used six short-yardage formations, Benstead used two of them. Though Benstead's approach may have helped Pettine maintain continuity and excellence in the West program, it engendered some resentment in the community, for it was difficult to argue that Benstead wasn't, to some degree, favoring players who would go to West and shortchanging those who would go to East. That one of Benstead's assistant coaches, Leo Carey, was the father of Mike Carey—the assistant head coach at CB West and Mike Pettine's right-hand man—didn't do much to assuage that resentment. For their part, Mark and Nancy Umbrell liked and respected Benstead, but they also prepared Colby for the reality of his situation. They told him not to tell too many people that he was planning to attend East. They didn't want any bias, overt or subconscious, to hinder him. Colby, of course, didn't listen. He told anyone who asked that he was going to East, like his dad.

Three years had passed since Benstead coached Colby and Bryan, but neither was ever far from his thoughts. He regarded football as a metaphor for life, as a revealer of character—trite concepts, he knew, but true nonetheless. In that context of competition, though Colby and Bryan may have shared only a word or two between swigs of water during a slow moment at practice, Benstead considered them soul mates. All he ever needed to know about Bryan, he learned the first day he met him. Before a preseason practice, this seventh-grader—five feet six, 120 pounds, chest out, shoulders back—had stuck out his hand, looked Benstead in the eye, and introduced himself.

Benstead was impressed. He wanted to test the kid.

"You realize," he said, "that you have to be at least a hundred twenty-five pounds to play, right? Have you considered playing elsewhere?"

"No," Bryan said.

Colby was quieter, more businesslike off the field, Benstead found. On the field . . . well, there was one play that stood out to Benstead whenever he remembered coaching Colby. An opposing offense had tried to run a sweep against Lenape's defense. Playing defensive end, Colby took on one blocker with his inside shoulder, just as Lenape's coaches had taught him, and he shuffled off and took on a second blocker with his hands, just as Lenape's coaches had taught him. The coaches never taught him anything about a third blocker, but Colby put his head down and collapsed the pile, thereby knocking down the running back behind the pile who was carrying the ball. "That was grit," Benstead recalled. "That kid just dug his cleats in and said, 'Not on my watch.' It was beautiful."

And it was three years ago. Three years. The time had rushed by. They were on the cusp of their senior seasons now. Colby's began the next night, Friday, against Spring-Ford; Bryan's, the night after that against Upper Darby. Both games were at War Memorial Field. Jim Benstead would be there, as most everyone around Doylestown would. Three years. Damn, he missed coaching those two guys, and he always would.

THREE

The Opening Weekend

Friday, September 4, 1998

The most that the sixty-three-year-old man could do was use his left hand to thump the left side of his chest like a bass drum, say the words "Hey" and "Right here," and smile, and Neil Zanetti was doing all of these things at once. He sat in his wheelchair near the south end zone of War Memorial Field, his feet strapped into the chair's stirrups and hovering above the fresh grass. At the two refreshment shacks on each end of the stadium, hot dogs cooked on rotating broilers and buttered popcorn warmed under hot neon-yellow lamps, the late-summer night mixing the musks of timeless customs and new beginnings. One by one, players from the Central Bucks East football team, players whom Zanetti had coached the season before, jogged over to him before their game against Spring-Ford to pat his shoulders and rub his head, as if he were a Buddha statue, and he smiled and thumped his chest and tried to speak to them, but the words came out in a loud, confusing garble. The stroke that Zanetti had suffered in April had taken away so much from him—including, for a long time, his memory. For months afterward, he could not remember that he had been an assistant football coach at East for two years, that he had been the school's varsity baseball coach for close to ten years, that these faces had names. All of those experiences and relationships were just whispers in his head that he strained to hear once he curled up on the ground behind home plate and started to convulse and quiver during a ball game in the spring.

Zanetti still could not stand up by himself. The right side of his body was paralyzed, and his aphasia—the condition in which the mouth and voice struggle to form the words that the brain tells them to form—made it difficult for him to communicate with anyone, even his wife, Bonnie. He had lived in a rehabilitation center since the stroke. But things, slowly, were becoming familiar to him again. His widening eyes made it clear that he recognized a few of the young men on the team, including Colby Umbrell, as each of them bent down to say hello to him. In his pregame speech to the Patriots, Larry Greene had been careful not to tell his players to win the game for Zanetti, an avuncular figure to many of them; Greene did not want to put that sort of pressure on them. All he asked was that they play forty-eight minutes of good, hard football, so that afterward they could look their former coach in the eye with clear consciences. "We're *playing* this game for Z," he had made sure to say.

And the Patriots did play hard, though for extended stretches of the game they did not play particularly well, save for two players: Colby and Bryan Scott. Spring-Ford was a AAA team; its enrollment classification was one level below East's, which meant that the Patriots, based on the size of the pool from which they could draw talent, would be favored to win. Nevertheless, East trailed 7–0 at halftime before Jamie Rotonda, Spring-Ford's quarterback, fumbled twice inside his 20-yard line in the third quarter, and Scott ran for a touchdown after each turnover, allowing East to hold a 14–7 lead late into the fourth quarter. Scott gashed Spring-Ford's defense all game long, rushing for 142 yards on twenty-two carries, the Rams for some reason sticking with an unusual alignment. They put only six men on the line of scrimmage and played man-to-man coverage on almost every play, ostensibly daring the Patriots to hand the ball to Scott. Perhaps Greene and his offensive coordinator, Bart Szarko, should have done so more often. Kreider completed only one of his ten pass attempts, which made Greene's preseason goal of diversifying the offense to prevent teams from focusing too much attention on Scott appear unattainable.

Worse, with three minutes and fifteen seconds left in regulation, Kreider threw his second interception of the game, setting up Spring-Ford at East's 27-yard line. Forty-one seconds remained when, on fourth down from the East 10, Rotonda pitched to fullback Brant Gadzicki, who sprinted to the right before chucking the ball back across the field to Rotonda for a touchdown, cutting East's lead to 14–13. The call stunned the Patriots; they had seen nothing during their game film reviews during the week that suggested Spring-Ford would try such a play.

When the Rams decided to attempt a two-point conversion, Greene sent out his goal-line defense, banking that Colby would continue what had been, to that point in his high school career, the game of his life. Even with the weight and muscle he had added during the off-season, he had retained the quick first step of a lighter defensive tackle, and Spring-Ford hadn't been able to block him all night. He twice sacked Rotonda and collected thirteen tackles. (Later, Greene said that no player he had coached had ever made thirteen tackles in one game until Colby did.) He and his teammates had to make a play now, because a loss to any AAA team, even in the first game of the season, would damage East's chances of making the district playoffs. More, it would suggest that no other team in the Suburban One League National Conference, especially CB West, should take the Patriots seriously.

At the snap, Colby bulled forward, and Spring-Ford's offensive linemen hesitated, as if they weren't ready for the snap. Rotonda fumbled the ball. With Colby pushing, the pile of bodies caved in on top of Rotonda and the football. Everyone on the East sideline and in the home half of the bleachers exhaled.

After time expired and they began celebrating their victory, the East players paused to gather as a group near the south end zone, where Neil Zanetti had watched the entire game. All of them, except for the four captains, knelt down on one knee. Scott, Kreider, Phil Laing, and Colby walked toward Zanetti, bearing a gift: a red-and-white football signed by every East player. Only after the captains tucked the ball under Zanetti's left arm did the rest of the team stand, each of them raising his helmet like a torch and cheering for a man who now couldn't walk, couldn't speak in full sentences, and couldn't contain his joy. Those whispers were a little louder.

"What you did for that man," Greene told his players, "was exciting."

Until he saw the horse in the hallway during his first year as a special-education teacher at CB East, Larry Greene considered his most acute moment of culture shock to be his first day as a student at Cheltenham High School. It was the beginning of his sophomore year. His father had taken the job as the Cheltenham School District's superintendent and moved the family to the Philadelphia area from the town of Marshfield in Massachusetts's Irish-heavy South Shore. From a small-town school, Greene felt overwhelmed at first by Cheltenham High's size—the school had more than 1,800 students at the time—and its diversity when compared to Marshfield. (As an example of that diversity, Cheltenham's alumni include Reggie Jackson, the Hall of Fame baseball player, and Benjamin Netanyahu, the former prime minister of Israel.) But Greene found his niche on the football team. By the end of that sophomore season, he was starting in the secondary. By the beginning of his senior year, he had grown to five feet ten and 185 pounds, a big defensive back for those days, and had become skilled enough to play Division III ball in college. But above all else, high school football had given him an identity, a way to adjust to his new school and to form and sustain friendships. He never forgot that.

Though he was skilled enough, according to his own evaluation of his ability, to play only Division III football, Greene tried to play Division II football at American International University in Boston. He lasted two years, long enough to get his grades to a respectable level, then transferred to La Salle University in Philadelphia, mostly because it was the only school he could find that would accept the credits he had accrued at AIU. A criminal justice major, he encountered Doylestown for the first time in 1975 when, as part of his senior project, he worked from January to May at the Bucks County Juvenile Detention Center, just outside Doylestown Township. One day, during a tackle football game in the center's yard, a twelve-year-old boy who had ball-peen-hammered a man to death was slammed headfirst into an outdoor radiator, opening a gash in his forehead. Greene locked handcuffs onto the kid's wrists and drove him to Doylestown Hospital. *Man, this is podunky,* he thought as he stood in the hospital's waiting area. It was only fair that he would judge the town so harshly, because based on the way they were looking at him, the people of Doylestown thought he had cracked the kid's head open.

Upon completing his criminal justice degree, Greene decided he couldn't reconcile his aims and aspirations with his experiences at the juvenile center. Time after time, he saw kids from broken homes, kids who had run away from alcoholic fathers, kids who struggled in school and made stupid mistakes—good kids thrown into the system alongside the worst seeds, with murderers and violent felons. He realized he wanted to help the good ones. He took a job at a home for neglected children, coaching them in basketball and football, and went to night school at one of Penn State's satellite campuses to get a degree in special education. It took him five years to finish, five years of working with abandoned and cast-off kids for meager pay each day and going to school each night, but at least now he knew exactly what career path he ought to take. He applied for as many special-ed teaching jobs as he could. Central Bucks East scheduled an interview with him on July 24, 1980. It was his twenty-seventh birthday. The interview's outcome served as a perfect gift: East principal Jim Gallagher needed a special-ed teacher and an assistant football coach, and he hired Greene for both positions.

For Greene, East took some getting used to. During his daily forty-minute ride from his apartment near Philadelphia, he wondered how he, a guy who had lived in and around two of the major metropolitan areas in the Northeast, had landed a job at a countryside school. Early in his teaching tenure, he happened to be sitting in his office one afternoon when he heard a clip-clopping sound in the hallway. He stepped out of his office, peered down the hall, and saw a female student bending over a water fountain to get a drink, her hand holding the reins of what was presumably her pet horse.

"Excuse me," Greene said to her. "You can't bring a horse into a public building."

"Why not?" the girl asked.

He couldn't think of a satisfactory answer.

Over time, he adjusted. He coached the Patriots' offensive line and their defense before becoming East's head coach in 1987, only to resign in January 1992 in protest of the Central Bucks School District's institution of an open-enrollment policy. The policy allowed students who lived in West's attendance area to go to East, and vice versa, and to Greene, it sent the wrong message to student-athletes about the importance of high school sports—that it was acceptable to attend a school solely for its sports programs. Greene also reasoned that if a prospective football player—or, more likely, the player's parents—had the choice between a dominant program and a merely respectable one, the gap between West and East would only grow wider. On Thanksgiving 1988, Greene's second East-West game as a head coach, the Patriots had tied the Bucks 14–14, snapping West's fifty-three-game winning streak, but if the most talented players in the district all went to West, when would such a result happen again? And what was to stop a West booster from trying to lure a player to Pettine's program? Larry Greene knew that he was staring at a stacked deck.

"I didn't think," he said later, "that's what high school football was all about."

So he stepped down, on principle. He never accused West of recruiting players, never suggested that there was anything nefarious going on—just took another head coaching job, commuting forty-five minutes each afternoon from East to Pennsbury High, in lower Bucks County. There were days, though, when he was so tired that he wouldn't remember having driven from one school to the other, and having settled in the central Bucks area by then, he hoped a time would come when he could coach again at East. It did. After the Central Bucks School District rescinded the open-enrollment policy, East rehired him in 1996.

At first meeting, Greene seemed to possess the requisite qualities of a full-fledged disciplinarian, but he counterbalanced the instructive authoritarianism that most football coaches employ with that semi-social-worker streak that he'd developed while working at the juvenile center. His voice was raspy, his speaking style clipped and direct, almost a bark, and he talked in an accent that was neither Bostonian nor Philadelphian but a combination of the two; it could best be described simply as urban. He had a paunch and a wide, flat mouth and a full head of short gray hair, and he used earnest, empathetic clichés that coaches often recite. Somehow, though, they sounded more sincere coming from him. At the end of every East game, he gathered his players together and told them to hug their parents, enjoy themselves over the weekend, make sure they were diligent about their schoolwork, and, above all, be safe. Larry Greene wanted to win football games, and he wanted his players to enjoy themselves, and he didn't regard those notions as being mutually exclusive.

"First, I talked about being a winner in everything you did—commitment to winning not just in sports, but in life," Greene explained years later. "The second thing was, I wanted kids to leave knowing I gave them the best program that I was capable of giving them and that our assistants were capable of—that we didn't cut corners, that we worked harder than they did in terms of preparation, that we gave every kid a fair shot. I never went home thinking I screwed a kid. I would say there were a few kids who I wished I handled differently and some I think I might have been too tough on. But I think every kid left there thinking they got a fair opportunity, and I hope they also left there thinking, 'Hey, not only was this a successful experience, but I had fun.' I often said to kids, 'If it's not fun, it's the worst place in the world to be.'

"Once in a while, you'd have a father who wanted it more than the kid, and it's sad to see. Every year, you'd see one or two kids out there who were out there for the wrong reasons. And I often said to my coaches, 'This isn't Boys Town. We're not Father Flanagan. We're here to play football and develop skill.' Sometimes, you get frustrated because I think adults look at it like, 'This is the last chance for my son to get a little discipline.' Or, 'Hey, this is like camp. He needs to do something.' And the kid had no more of a right to be there than the man in the moon."

That philosophy was part of the reason that Greene appreciated Mark Umbrell's involvement in the East program. While Colby was still a ninth-grader at Lenape and before Greene decided to coach again at East, Mark had lobbied Robert Laws, the superintendent of the Central Bucks School District, to allow ninth-graders to use their respective high schools' weight rooms. At the time, East had two linemen, Josh Mitchell and Mike Moosbrugger, who were about to enter their senior seasons, were Division I prospects, and were more than 275 pounds apiece, and Mark thought that if Mitchell and Moosbrugger were going to drive-block his son at practice each day, Colby, then a 185-pound sophomore, deserved at least a chance to prepare his body for the pounding. Greene supported Mark's push to change the policy, and after the district relented, Mark became the president of East's football parents' booster club and spearheaded a campaign to renovate the school's weight room. By the early part of Colby's senior season, Greene could pick out one voice from the bleachers on the Patriots' game films, one proud parent screaming his support above everyone else's. He could pick out Mark's voice, could visualize Mark's round, ruddy face reddening, and he liked that he could do that. "Some parents are just over the top with their kids, but Mark wasn't over the top with Colby," Greene said later. "You could see he relished the development of his son. He loved that Colby played at his dad's alma mater, and he loved that he was winning games. The kid was becoming a man."

At heart, though, the kid was still a kid. In eighth grade, Colby and his friend Brandon Heath had armed themselves with screwdrivers one day and competed with each other to see who could collect more screws. (By the end of day, the Lenape Middle School janitors were more than a little perturbed, since several doors were hanging by a single hinge and light-switch plates kept popping out all over the building.) As a senior, Colby still possessed the same fondness for pranks and general goofiness. It became a common pregame occurrence for him—a seventeen-year-old, husky from chin to feet, not a speck of Motown soul in him except in his own mind—to dance in a crowded locker room to the Jackson 5. That was Colby. He told corny jokes. At home, he sang stupid songs until Casey, Bruce, and Adam couldn't stand hearing him. He and Steve Gonzalez—one of East's starting guards, one of Colby's best friends—spent much of each practice trying to make each other crack up. Once, Colby won their personal laugh contest by attempting to kick an extra point—and accidentally hitting Greene in the head with the ball.

"Being like everyone else," Gonzalez said later, "was his idea of having nothing to do."

That was the contradiction at Colby's core: He made time for silliness, but he also had a quieter side that gave off the misleading air of a dumb jock. The East coaches sometimes couldn't tell if he was being serious or if he had the driest sense of humor on the team, if he was trying to be respectful or possessed exquisite comedic timing. During one film session, the coaches and players watched a sequence in which an opposing offensive lineman drove Colby backward twenty yards, a poor play by Colby, uncharacteristic. Bill Heller, East's defensive line coach, cracked, "Hey, Umbrell, what are you doing, playing defensive back?"

"Coach," Colby said, "I believe I'm at right defensive tackle."

He snapped his answer back at Heller so quickly, with such officiousness, that Heller, Greene, and the rest of the team erupted into guffaws. Football film sessions can be lousy. They're long. The room is dark. Everyone is tired. The coaches are picking the players apart. The players want to go home and relax. So do some of the coaches. And Colby's answer ripped through all of that gauze. Yet Greene, for one, could never say for certain why Colby had said what he said in the way he said it. Was he trying to be funny? Was he just being serious and sincere? Long after Colby had graduated, Larry Greene would smile as he retold that anecdote, but he never did get an explanation for Colby Umbrell's answer.

Castles. Quakers. An accent on the arts. James Michener and his eight-hundred-page tomes on worlds exotic and eternal. Compared to those aspects of Doylestown's culture and history, the success of the Central Bucks West football team seemed out of place. Indeed, before Mike Pettine assumed control of the program at Central Bucks High, life in Doylestown had never been so strongly linked to football. The sport was just part of the town's scenery.

At the beginning of the twentieth century, a "Young Men's League" competed against teams from other Bucks County towns. (The *Intelligencer* reported on October 26, 1903, that the league defeated a team from New Hope 18–0, even though New Hope had recruited talent from Lambertville, New Jersey, including "a center weighing 210 pounds." Doylestown, meanwhile, "at most did not average more than 130.") The Blue Sox, an independent men's team sponsored by an organization called the Doylestown Football Association, did play in the mid-1920s, and in 1925, the association's members voted to fund the establishment of a football program at Doylestown High School. Yet neither Doylestown High nor its reincarnation, Central Bucks High, forged a reputation as a football power. From 1925 to 1966, Doylestown/Central Bucks had more losing seasons (nineteen) than winning ones (eighteen) and went a combined 180–163–34. The record was nothing embarrassing, but nothing that would unite a community, either, not until early 1967, when John Kracsun resigned as Central Bucks High School's head football coach to take a high school coaching job near Pittsburgh. On May 15 of that year, Doylestown became a football town—not because Kracsun had resigned, but because one of his assistants was promoted to replace him.

Mike Pettine had grown up in Conshohocken, a town west of Philadelphia, in a neighborhood of row houses, cracked-concrete basketball courts, and industrial warehouses—a clannish existence in the early 1950s. The Pettines lived in the Italian-Catholic section of the town, not far from the Irish-Catholic section, which wasn't far from the Polish-Catholic section, which wasn't far from the WASP section. As a boy, Pettine knew that the one way he could get out of doing chores around the house was to tell his father, "I'm going to play ball." The trade-off was that young Mike couldn't run back home to ask his father, a mechanic, to fight his battles for him. When several older boys commandeered the Pettines' basketball court, the one Mike and his buddies had built themselves, Mike complained to his father that he couldn't play on his own court. His father gave him two choices: sit and wait to play, or find a way to get into the game.

"The competition," Pettine once said, "was always a step above what it would have been with kids my own age."

At Conshohocken High School, Pettine, a lithe six-foot, 170-pound halfback, captained the varsity football team and led the Ches-Mont League in scoring his senior year, earning himself an audacious nickname: "The Conshohocken Comet." He was an all-league basketball player, a pitcher on the varsity baseball team, an honor student, and the president of his class. He married a cheerleader. After graduating from Villanova University, he took a job as a social studies teacher and assistant football coach at a Catholic high school in Pottstown, Pennsylvania, but stayed there only two years. A similar position for better money had opened up at Central Bucks High School, and Pettine and his wife, Joyce, already had two children by then. The financial demands of supporting a family on the salary of a Catholic-school teacher were too much to bear. The Pettines moved to Doylestown in 1965, and two years later, Pettine took over for Kracsun.

"They were wondering if he'd be able to do the job," Bob Schaffer, who served as the football statistician for Central Bucks High and West for thirty-three years, once said, "because he had only been an assistant coach."

It did not take Pettine long to dispel those concerns. Central Bucks High went 9–0–1 in 1967, his first season as head coach, and beginning in 1971, two years after Central Bucks split into CB West and CB East, the Bucks went 47–4–1 over a five-year stretch—and that was before the fifty-three-game winning streak that East ended in 1988. He won with teams that ran the ball. He won with teams that threw the ball. Entering the '98 season, he had won 296 games, meaning it was only a matter of time before he would become the second football coach in Pennsylvania high school football history to win 300 games in his career.

And so the stories spread—tales told by fathers to sons about what it took to play for Pettine, about what it took to have millions of people read about CB West in *USA Today*'s national high school football poll, about what it took to *win*. . . .

Here I am, going in for a touchdown, and he's hollering at the guy who missed the block. . . . He made me run the drill 17 times, until I did it just the way he wanted. . . . I drove past the school at 11 o'clock at night, and he was still watching game film in his office.

Even Doylestown's location and geography worked to enhance the West legend. Why drive an hour to Veterans Stadium, fighting traffic the whole way, to watch the Philadelphia Eagles when there was an unbeatable football team playing just around the corner? Why watch another team lose when you could watch those hundred Bucks, clad in black and gold, stalk out onto the War Memorial Field turf and win, when you could see the opposing players' hearts stick in their throats and practically read their lips? *Oh, shit. We don't have a chance.*

The common trait that all Pettine's teams shared was their exceptional play along the offensive and defensive lines, particularly after one of his former players, Mike Carey, returned to Doylestown in 1977. Carey had played center for Pettine and graduated from West in 1971, earning a football scholarship to the University of Pittsburgh. He had designs on forging a professional football career for himself—getting a tryout with the Oakland Raiders, then playing briefly in Canada—before a brutal car crash that almost cost him one of his legs ended those hopes. Having majored in education at Pitt, he taught at West for a year and volunteered to assist Pettine. He finished that year of teaching, opened the first of the four taverns he eventually would own in central Bucks County, and became Pettine's top assistant coach, drawing on his experiences at Pitt and his brief time in the NFL to make line play and weight training the foundations of the West program. Off-season attendance at thrice-weekly weight-room sessions became mandatory, and Carey implemented many of the Olympic lifts that he and other Pittsburgh players had used under head coach Johnny Majors. Through the 1980s and into the 1990s, the sophistication and intensity of their weight-training program gave the Bucks an advantage over nearly every team they faced, though Pettine's and Carey's football acumen and the amount of time each was willing to devote to coaching were no small factors, either. Once Pettine retired from teaching in 1996 and Carey arranged his business affairs to open up more free time for himself, it was as if West had two full-time professional football coaches.

The two of them made quite a pair on the sideline. Pettine was lean and leathery with silvery hair, wore thick bifocals atop his Roman nose, and had a voice that, when he was angry, exploded forth like a blast of buckshot. He broke clipboards over his players' helmets. Carey had a shock of red hair and arms like those of a pipe fitter who didn't need a wrench. He didn't need to scream to get a player's attention, but he sometimes did anyway. The first year that Pettine and Carey coached together, 1978, West won each of its eleven games by an average of nearly twenty-five points. Twenty years later, on the day before West's '98 season was scheduled to begin, the *Intelligencer* selected the '78 Bucks as the greatest Bucks County high school football team of the previous twenty-five years.

Saturday, September 5, 1998

The team was finally his. Bryan Buckley had been waiting to assume this role since the spring, since his friend Dave Armstrong had scribbled a note in Bryan's yearbook, telling him to take a strong leadership role on the team the following fall. The '98 West team, while talented, would be different from the '97 squad that had won the state title. For one thing, it would be inexperienced at two important skill positions. Armstrong and Corey Potter, two of Bryan's best friends, had combined to be the beating heart of the '97 Bucks, but as had two other players with whom Bryan was close, lineman Matt Volitis and backup tight end Ed Hillman, Armstrong and Potter had been seniors and had graduated. An all-America selection at fullback by *Parade* magazine, Armstrong had rushed for 1,970 yards and scored thirty-nine touchdowns, and Potter, in his first season as a starting quarterback, had emerged as the team's emotional leader and was first-team all-state, rushing for more than 1,000 yards and throwing for 718 more. Their departures— Armstrong to the University of Michigan, Potter to the University of Massachusetts—meant that two non-seniors, each of whom had little or no varsity experience, would have to replace them.

Mike Orihel would be the starting quarterback—a decision that had not been an easy one for Pettine, because Orihel would be the first sophomore to start at quarterback for West. There had been something of a "quarterback controversy" during the summer passing camp and the preseason, as Orihel competed for the job with senior Bill Stone and another sophomore, Phil DiGiacomo. But Stone and DiGiacomo were more versatile players, able to play other positions. Orihel, on the other hand, had been groomed to be a quarterback. His father, Paul, had spray-painted lines on the family's backyard lawn so that Mike could practice dropping back, and the Orihels had made it clear that Mike was at West for football. They did not live within the Central Bucks School District's boundaries; their home was in Solebury Township, closer to the Delaware River, and they paid a few thousand dollars in annual tuition so Mike could go to West and play for Pettine. Orihel was long and thin and ran with the loping, almost tentative strides of a fawn, but he had a strong arm, and Pettine believed that West had enough weapons on offense that a game's outcome probably wouldn't have to come down to his young quarterback.

The most dangerous of those weapons figured to be junior fullback Dustin Picciotti. At six feet three and 235 pounds, Picciotti was bigger than most linemen in the Suburban One League and faster than most tailbacks. He could run forty yards in 4.5 seconds and could dunk a basketball backward. As a sophomore, Picciotti had trouble mastering the West playbook, and with Armstrong entrenched at fullback, Picciotti played mostly at linebacker or defensive end. Initially, though, he had balked to Pettine about playing only on defense. He knew he was a transcendent talent, and he wanted the spotlight and attention that came with carrying the football, and as a junior, he would get his opportunity. During a preseason scrimmage, senior Chris Ortiz, who had been in line to be West's starting tailback, had torn the medial collateral ligament in his left knee and would be out of the lineup for at least a month.

Even with Orihel's and Picciotti's inexperience and Ortiz's injury, Bryan entered the season expecting West to win the state championship again. Nothing in the Bucks' first game, against Upper Darby, suggested they could not repeat. Picciotti had 113 yards on twenty carries. Orihel completed six of his ten pass attempts for 133 yards and a touchdown. West rolled, 59–7, and senior wingback Greg Kinzel said afterward, "We all know we could have played better than this." Still, perhaps the most vital element of winning another state title fell on Bryan's shoulders, and not merely because he would probably end up playing multiple positions—fullback, wingback, linebacker, defensive end, and defensive tackle—over the course of the season. Pettine had made it clear throughout the preseason that it was on Bryan, as one of the team captains, to keep the team free of dissention and drama, and upon hearing Pettine grant him such responsibility, such control over the locker room, Bryan couldn't help but reflect on how his relationship with Pettine had changed since the beginning of his sophomore season.

That first game . . . he had been so nervous on the bus ride out to central Pennsylvania, to Cumberland Valley High School. Ten thousand people had been there, and the Cumberland Valley players had swaggered onto the field with their school band playing "The Imperial March" from *Star Wars*, and Mike Carey had noticed how wide Bryan's eyes were. "You're going to be all right," Carey had told him. But then one of West's starting linebackers, Chris McNutt, sustained a concussion on the game's first series, and when Carey said, "We're sending Buckley in," Pettine's response hadn't exactly sent Bryan's confidence surging.

"If we send Buckley in, we'll lose."

Except they did not lose, and Bryan made nine tackles and forced a fumble in the victory, and he never left the starting lineup again. In fact, over Bryan's first two years as a varsity player, West had lost only once—21–16 to Plymouth Whitemarsh in the 1996 district playoffs. That defeat had been a crushing one, ending the season for a previously unbeaten West team that had been regarded as a state-championship favorite, leaving most of the players with tear-smeared faces. "I never saw so many grown men cry," Bryan said later. The players had been no older than eighteen, and he considered them grown men.

Still, Bryan had acquitted himself so well over the course of his sophomore season that the Bucks' coaches contemplated naming him a team captain as a junior—at least until he mouthed off to Pettine during a preseason scrimmage. Bryan had fouled up an assignment on defense, and Pettine had let him have it on the sideline, and Bryan, sporting a sore shoulder that would worsen as the season progressed, had yelled right back at Pettine. That was all it took for Bryan to end up in Pettine's doghouse. That notion of making Bryan a captain as a junior? Forget it. Didn't Bryan deserve the team's defensive player of the week award after another season-opening win over Cumberland Valley, when he made ten tackles, forced a fumble, recovered a fumble, and had a quarterback sack? Not in Pettine's eyes. The award went to someone else. It was only when Pettine saw that Bryan was willing to play the entire season with a shoulder that kept separating—Bryan kept popping it back into place so he could play—that he allowed Bryan back into his good graces.

As much as he had wanted to keep his starting spot, Bryan had continued to play, had put off having reconstructive surgery on the shoulder until the off-season, to spite Pettine. But the more Bryan thought about it, the more he realized that Pettine had been right—that he had been disrespectful and insubordinate; that their feud had been his, Bryan's, fault; that he had challenged the head coach when he simply should have shut his mouth. The victories, the state championship, the memories—for those reasons, he believed, the pain had been worth it. He also understood the rite of passage that Pettine was putting him through, and looking back, he could appreciate the process's evolution.

As a sophomore, he had feared Mike Pettine.

As a junior, he had hated him.

Now, as a senior, he respected him.

FOUR

Rituals and Sacrifices

Friday, September 11, 1998

Bryan Buckley's first touchdown as a CB West football player was neither dramatic nor climactic. It did not come in the closing seconds of a tight ball game. It did not embody the principles on which winning football was built. It did not set a tone. It was an ordinary three-yard touchdown run in the sort of game that was becoming ordinary for the Bucks. Six days after beating Upper Darby by more than eight touchdowns, they edged Abington, 56–7, at War Memorial Field. Bryan's score had given West a 35–0 lead late in the second quarter, and if there was any obvious significance to the touchdown, it was that Mike Pettine was looking to the long term as West destroyed its opponents in the short term.

Pettine's assistant coaches and former players often described his laserlike focus on *the next game*; that focus, they argued, was an overriding reason for his success. If Team X was West's next opponent, Pettine concentrated on beating Team X and Team X alone. Then, once a game was over, Pettine could step back and evaluate the value of that particular contest, turn it over in his mind, examine it for imperfections, however slight they might be. After the Abington victory, he noted that West's wide receivers were slowing down while running their routes. Against better competition, they would have to cut more sharply, follow their patterns more precisely. But in this game, he offered an overt acknowledgment that more difficult challenges lay ahead for his team, because Bryan's playing time at fullback, despite the presence and production of Dustin Picciotti, was increasing. Picciotti had played only the first half, which was still enough time for him to run 103 yards and three touchdowns, but Pettine also found room in the game plan to give Bryan four carries from the fullback spot, the most that Bryan had ever had in one game. And those four carries had netted thirty yards and that ordinary three-yard touchdown. Bryan had been productive, too.

"They're going to have to be happy sharing the load," Pettine said, "because we need them both on defense."

Pettine's purpose was clear: For the sake of keeping his fullbacks upright and reasonably fresh over what, potentially, could be a fifteen-game season, he would use both Picciotti and Bryan as ball carriers. Besides, there was a growing sense around the Suburban One League, given the 113 points that the Bucks had scored in their first two games, that the fifty-eight-year-old Pettine could tote the football behind West's monstrous offensive line and score a handful of touchdowns. "Tell me—who's better?" Doug Moister, Abington's head coach, said. "That could be the best West team ever."

So Bryan and Picciotti would share the carries and the spotlight that shone only on players who handled the football. It would be, presumably, the best thing for the team, and each could still collect a copious number of highlights to show college recruiters. Accumulating those highlights would be especially helpful to Bryan, who though a senior had not yet decided where he was going to college and was hoping that he might yet receive a Division I scholarship. Bill, his father, was hoping the same thing. He brought his video camera with him to every West game, taping each one in its entirety from the coin flip to the postgame handshakes. Somewhere, in all those hours of action, a college scout surely would see something impressive in Bill Buckley's son.

The first time Chris DiSciullo went to a CB West football game, in 1996, it wasn't the football itself that caught his attention. It was the people around him—his future mother-in-law, in particular. In fairness, Connie Buckley *was* wearing a black-and-gold hat styled after the one worn by Dr. Seuss's Cat in the Hat, a hat tall and striped and utterly fantastic. Chris did not say anything at the time; he had been dating Connie's eldest daughter, Kim, for less than a year, and when exactly did it become appropriate to poke fun at your girlfriend's mother? Besides, the entire atmosphere at War Memorial Field intrigued him. His high school, Holy Ghost Prep, didn't have a football team, and though he had played varsity soccer there, the intensity around this single football game eclipsed anything he had experienced. He scanned the bleachers. Connie didn't stand out for her hat. Chris himself stood out for not wearing the appropriate colors, for not cheering with the same fervor as the people around him. There were no empty seats, at least none that he could see. He asked himself an obvious question: *Is the whole freaking town here?*

Chris's initial wonder over the scene at War Memorial Field soon wore off as he and Kim continued dating and he attended more and more of Bryan's games. CB West football became a part of his life as it became a part of the Buckley family's, as it had become woven into the tapestry of Doylestown life. By Bryan's senior year, Bryan's Friday nights were Bill and Connie's Friday nights, were Chris and Kim's Friday nights. The time that Bryan spent working out, watching what he ate, staying in shape—to Chris, it was as if Bryan were a professional athlete and his family members' schedules revolved around his. Certainly, the program had a community, a web of relationships and roles, of its own.

Connie was now the co-president of West's football parents' club, mostly because she was one of the few team mothers who had over-come her fear of speaking with Mike Pettine. She had met him during a parent-teacher conference while her son Stephen was taking Pettine's Global Issues course. Connie had heard stories about Pettine from neighbors and friends whose sons had played football for West, stories about a dictatorial coach, a man so consumed with winning that he spent much of each game with his hand tangled in his players' facemasks, yanking their heads toward him so he could better berate them. "He sounded like he was just evil," Connie said years later. Stephen, who graduated from West in 1992, was struggling in the class, but Connie didn't want to cower before Pettine when they finally came face to face. He was the big, tough football coach. *Well, whoop-dee-do for him—* that would be her attitude.

"He started telling me, 'Stephen doesn't do this right' and 'Stephen doesn't do that right' and 'I guess he's doing lousy in all his classes,'" Connie recalled. "And I said, 'No, just yours.' That was the extent of my conversation with Mike Pettine then."

But as the parents' club president, Connie had to talk with Pettine regularly to coordinate team functions and events, and the coach she came to know was not an ogre. The more they spoke, the more Pettine opened up to her, so much so that he began telephoning her each Friday morning as part of his pregame routine. Whenever the phone rang and he happened to be home, Bill Buckley chuckled at hearing that deep rumble on the other end of the line: ". . . (first throat-clearing cough) . . . This is Mike Pettine. . . . (second throat-clearing cough) . . . Can I speak to Connie?" Their conversations consisted mostly of Pettine's talking about football minutiae or how the behavior of teenagers puzzled him. Connie just listened. She didn't know enough about the intricacies of the sport to discuss strategy with him, and she sensed that he wasn't looking for any give-and-take, anyway. He sought something simpler: a sounding board.

Pettine's calls, Bill's videotaping, Connie's hat, Bryan's retreating to his room and his cocoon, Chris's Friday night treks to stadiums in support of his girlfriend's little brother—these rituals were as intrinsic to the Buckleys' experience of West football as the games themselves. Others had their own habits. At every game, standing and sitting and cheering among her fellow students, Dana Cumberbatch wore a CB West jersey with the number 9 on it—Bryan's number, Bryan's jersey. They had been friends since they were seventh-graders at Lenape Middle School, going to West games then to walk laps around the perimeter of the field, socializing before watching what happened on the field. Bryan didn't have a steady girlfriend during his senior year, so Dana—blond, blue-eyed, the physical emblem of the girl who wore the team captain's football jersey—wore his uniform and cut out of the *Intelligencer* every photograph of Bryan and every article that mentioned him. She filed away those articles and photographs in a box for safekeeping.

She was impressed that so many of the friends she made in middle school were part of a nationally recognized football team. The same boys she hung out with at parties when she was thirteen, fourteen, fifteen years old were mini-celebrities now. Kids asked them for autographs. People recognized them around town. She felt pride in that. "It was cool to see our friends' names in the newspaper and see them play," she said later. She had remained close with a few of them, Bryan especially, because they had gone to West together. Colby Umbrell had been an acquaintance back at Lenape, too, a friendly face in the crowd, but Dana lost touch with him once he went to East. She didn't talk to Colby much anymore, if ever.

Friday, September 18, 1998

There was, Colby Umbrell sensed, too much swagger in the steps of the CB East Patriots, too much belief in the inevitability of victory as they began the third game of their season, against Harry S Truman, located in gritty Bristol Township in the lower part of Bucks County.

The Patriots had routed Neshaminy, 35–0, one week earlier, getting a glorious game from Bryan Scott, who ran for 211 yards and three touchdowns, and an opportunistic game from their defense, which forced five turnovers inside their 25-yard line. The win had imbued East's players with confidence as they prepared for the Truman game, their first away from War Memorial Field, but the early minutes concerned Colby. He recovered a fumble at the Tigers' 48-yard line on Truman's opening possession, giving East's offense terrific field position, but Scott immediately fumbled the ball back to Truman, a bad sign. Scott had tweaked his shoulder against Neshaminy, and enough pain lingered in his joint throughout the week that Larry Greene had limited Scott's practice time and considered not playing him on defense against the Tigers. East already was shorthanded along the offensive and defensive lines; senior center/defensive tackle Dave Bleam had suffered a season-ending knee injury against Spring-Ford. Now, here was Scott, at less than 100 percent, taking a clean shot and coughing up the ball.

East's play worsened from there. Twice, the Patriots advanced inside the Truman 25-yard line, and twice, they came away with no points. On one possession, the Patriots went from second-down-and-2 at the Truman 8-yard line to fourth-and-28 from the Truman 40 after committing a holding penalty and allowing the Tigers' defense to swarm Scott for negative yardage on back-to-back carries. The game was still scoreless at halftime, and Colby, like the coaches, was incredulous that the Patriots—whose best player was banged up, who had won only four games the season before—weren't playing as hard as their opponents were.

"Now, do you believe us?" Greene told his players in the locker room. "You're playing a good football team." Little else was said. Little else needed to be.

To open the second half, Truman head coach Galen Snyder called for a "squib kick," telling his kicker to knock the football firmly and low to the ground so that an East player might juggle it. The kicker didn't hit the ball hard enough, though, and the Patriots took possession at the Tigers' 49-yard line. They rode Scott to the Truman 24, where they faced fourth down. They needed seven yards for a first down. They were too far from the end zone to have their kicker, Tim

Becker, try a field goal, and they were too deep into Truman territory to punt. Steve Kreider jogged to the East sideline to find out what play Greene wanted to run.

They would gather, six of them during the school year, seven during the summer months, sometimes at the Umbrells' house, usually in Brandon Heath's basement, where they were surrounded by black sheets and strings of Christmas lights that hung from cinder-block walls—young men in their teens intelligent and conversant enough to discuss current events, politics, and the world around them, and comfortable enough with each other that their disagreements never threatened their friendships. They had met each other through each other. Colby Umbrell had met Dan Tamaroff and Steve Kreider because Dan lived down the block from Colby, and Colby, Dan, and Steve had met Brandon in middle school, and so on, until all of them—Colby, Dan, Brandon, Steve Kreider, Steve Gonzalez, Mark Reilly, and Rich Weber—had all but forgotten how they had met, because it felt as if they'd been born friends.

They did not all go to school together, which was why not all of them could gather together during the school year. Colby, the Steves, and Mark Reilly all went to East. Gonzo was the political liberal in the group. He and Colby would argue politics until dawn, never agreeing on anything, never giving an inch, never holding a grudge. ("I think we had the same vision," Gonzo said later. "We just had different ways of getting there.") Mark stopped playing football after his sophomore year, mostly because he was just too thin, his neck so long that his head seemed certain to teeter from one side to the other because of the helmet's weight. As a gag, Brandon was fond of superimposing a photo of Mark's head onto the body of a giraffe. Rich Weber attended Germantown Academy and was bound for MIT as a chemical engineering major. Dan Tamaroff, also a football player, lived in a dorm at Peddie School, near Princeton, New Jersey. Among the others, Colby made the most visits there to see him. Brandon boarded at Academy of the New Church, a private Christian school, and played football there, too, but he often spent his weekends at home. He and Colby were the jokesters in the group, Steve Kreider the go-getter. If some of the guys got together to help one of their fathers with some landscaping work in the yard, Colby and Brandon would stand around arguing about sports while Kreider mulched.

"Just the normal boys-being-boys kind of thing," Kreider recalled. "We always worked hard. That was the one thing that kept us all together—the work ethic, the quest for knowledge as we got older. I think that's what formed our ideals. When we were hanging out, they were probably conversations you didn't hear many sixteen-, seventeen-, eighteen-, twenty-, twenty-one-year-olds have. But we did talk about all those different kinds of things.

"By being a football player, you're in a competitive environment. It is a win-lose game. You learn there's a difference between winning and losing. These are valuable lessons in life. There are winners and losers in life, not the PC thing where everybody's a winner. I think we grew up with that determination and brought it into other aspects of our life."

Back to the huddle hustled Kreider, the play on his lips, the game in his hands. Bryan Scott with a tender shoulder, seven yards yet to go for a first down—Larry Greene wasn't going to do something so predictable and, in this case, perilous as have Kreider turn around and hand the ball to an injured superstar. He was going to give Kreider options. He was going to let his quarterback—who over two and a half games had completed eight of his twenty-three passes—throw the football.

Kreider dropped back, planted his right foot, and looked to the left flat. Scott was there, but he was covered. Still rooted in the pocket and, at only five feet eleven, straining to see over the linemen in front of him, Kreider turned his head back toward the middle of the field. Colby and

Gonzo and the rest of the East offensive line held their blocks, giving junior split end Jason Ware time to cut horizontally behind several Truman defenders and settle between the hash marks, eleven yards down the field. Kreider zipped him the football for a first down at the Tigers' 13-yard line. The drive extended, Kreider then burrowed through the center of the Truman defense for a two-yard touchdown run with less than six minutes left in the third quarter.

Truman threatened to tie the game twice, marching to the Patriots' 7- and 21-yard lines on consecutive possessions, only to turn the ball over on downs after East junior linebacker Anthony Greene truncated both drives by sacking Tigers quarterback Trevor Smith. Now, with an opportunity to put the game away, Greene went back to Scott. On third-and-1 from the East 39, Scott finally found a sliver of space, galloping up the middle for 46 yards. Five plays later, East was at the Truman 4. Colby lined up at right tackle, and Kreider ran a bootleg in his direction. Following a block from Colby, Kreider leaped headfirst, the fresh white and red of his uniform flashing against the black night sky, and sustained a hit, naked and vicious, from a Truman defensive back. The hit sent Kreider's body spinning like a helicopter blade, spinning until he landed in the end zone.

After the 14–0 victory, Colby said what his friend wouldn't. Kreider had run for 23 yards and thrown for 23 yards and completed only three of his seven pass attempts—modest numbers all. But the fourth-down throw to Ware and his two fearless touchdown runs had kept East undefeated. Kreider, more than anyone, had controlled the game. "Steve was awesome," Colby said. "He probably doesn't want to say it himself, but he's the toughest quarterback."

The Patriots now had not allowed an opponent to score in two weeks. When their team bus arrived back at East, they learned that CB West also had won again, shutting out Pennsbury, 41–0, at War Memorial Field. Their rival was 3–0, and their rival's coach was one more victory away from making history.

Friday, September 25, 1998

For Mike Pettine, the week had been long, with too much attention focused on him. It had begun with two lengthy newspaper articles that appeared on the same Sunday in anticipation that West would win its next game, at Norristown, and that Pettine would join Berwick's George Curry as the only two high school football coaches in Pennsylvania to win three hundred games. Bill Lyon, the lyrical sports columnist for the *Philadelphia Inquirer*, had written the first piece, and it encompassed more than two thousand words and almost a full inside page of the paper's sports section. "He has been called the Joe Paterno of high school football," Lyon wrote. "In fact, maybe Paterno ought to be called the Mike Pettine of college ball." Not to be outdone in terms of length, if not eloquence, the *Intelligencer* published a three-thousand-word profile of Pettine that was accompanied by six photographs and a chart that broke down his coaching record to the most insignificant detail.

As another layer to the story, the teams would play at Norristown's Roosevelt Field, only five miles from Conshohocken; Pettine himself had played his home games there as a high school running back. Media and spectators showed up at West daily for the rest of the week to watch practice and to talk to Pettine about the milestone. "Our practice field looked like a parking lot," Pettine told one reporter. The attention bothered him not only because people's focus, like sunlight passing through a magnifying glass, honed on him alone, but because the interviews and onlookers were a distraction. To football coaches at any level—high school, college, the NFL—the word *distraction* is an anathema, and every minute Pettine spent answering a question about what it would be like to win his three hundredth game was another minute he couldn't spend preparing for what was certain to be the Bucks' most challenging game of their season so far. Norristown, like West, was 3–0, and the Eagles probably had the most speed of any team in the Suburban One League. Their quarterback, senior Kris Blake, and tailback, senior Troy Swittenberg, had Division I ability. Yes, it definitely was the wrong week for a distraction.

Before kickoff, without the coaches in the locker room, Bryan addressed the team: "I don't care what you think of the man, whether you like him or don't like him. Tonight's for him. Let's go out and blow the doors off these guys so he can get his three hundredth. He wants to get it over with, and he deserves it." Outside, it was a dry, clear night, the temperature in the mid-sixties. Mark Schweiker, the lieutenant governor of Pennsylvania, was ready to present Pettine with a certificate commemorating the occasion. Rod Stone, West's principal, and Mike Gold, the school's athletics director, each had a plaque for him. Representatives from the Buck Club, West's booster club, were waiting with a bronze football. Pettine's mother, who still lived in Conshohocken, did not attend the game; instead, she went to Saints Cosmas and Damian Catholic Church, knelt down in one of the pews, and offered a more ethereal manner of support.

Eight minutes into the game, any prayers on the Bucks' behalf appeared unnecessary. Mike Orihel loped thirty-four yards on an option run for the night's first touchdown, and Dustin Picciotti chugged thirty yards for another score and a 14–0 West lead on the Bucks' second possession. A blowout seemed in the making. It was not. Blake led Norristown down the field, finally completing an eight-yard touchdown pass to split end Trey Hadrick after a roughing-the-passer penalty on West allowed the Eagles to run nine plays inside the Bucks' 10-yard line. A roughing-the-passer penalty—the sort of inexcusable mistake that West rarely committed and that Pettine could never stomach. *Distractions . . .*

In his column about Pettine, Bill Lyon had used a compliment that former NFL coach Bum Phillips once paid to Don Shula as a compliment to Pettine: "He can take his'un and beat your'un. Or he can take your'un and beat his'un." It wasn't that Pettine surprised opponents with his play-calling all that often; what made the plays work was that the Bucks ran them with such precision and out of so many different formations and with different players in different roles. Orihel, Picciotti, tailback Dave Edwards, and Bryan each had carried the ball at least once in the game by the time Pettine called a timeout late in the second quarter, with West confronting a fourth-and-10 from the Eagles' 31.

"Well," Pettine said as he huddled with Orihel, "we need a first down. What do you want to run?"

"It's up to you, Coach," Orihel replied. Before every game, the sophomore quarterback strutted onto the field singing "Leavin' on a Jet Plane" to himself. He combined enough free-spiritedness and cockiness to believe that any play would work in any scenario.

"Throwback X is there," Pettine said.

Roger Grove, Norristown's coach, had watched Pettine's teams run Throwback X for at least ten years. It was a staple of the West playbook: the quarterback rolled at a 45-degree angle to the left, stopped, pivoted, and threw the ball to a split end near the right hash mark. Through all the game film that Grove had seen of the Bucks this season, however, he had not seen them run Throwback X. They ran it now. Senior split end Sean-Michael Yonson was wide open, and after Orihel hit him in stride, Yonson dodged two Norristown tacklers and dashed across the goal line. Out of an impossible situation, West had regained its two-touchdown lead.

Norristown made it close again midway through the fourth quarter, as Swittenberg, whom the Bucks had bottled up most of the night, broke free for a twenty-four-yard touchdown on a draw play. Edwards charged in off the left side to smother the extra-point attempt, keeping the score 21–13, and when West's offense took the field at its 17-yard line with 5:44 left in regulation, the wisdom of Pettine's share-the-ball strategy was made manifest. In Picciotti, Edwards, and Bryan, Pettine had three reasonably rested backs at his disposal; none of them had more than fourteen carries.

Pettine had begun the game with two handoffs to Bryan that netted eight yards, and on the drive's second play, Pettine gave him the ball again. Surging through a hole along the left side of West's line, Bryan took a step to his left as if he might swerve toward the sideline but instead cut back toward the middle of the field past two Norristown defenders, sliding to a stop after a twenty-six-yard gain. It took six more plays before Picciotti hurled himself into the end zone from the 2-yard line with 2:14 to go. When Bryan, who had provided the lead block, jogged to the West sideline, Mike Carey greeted him with a hug. The final score of the three hundredth victory of Mike Pettine's career would be 28–13. The celebration could commence.

Trailed by television cameras, his head tilted downward, Pettine walked briskly across the field to shake Grove's hand. "Nobody deserves it more than you," Grove said to him. An amoeba of people—players, coaches, fans, media—encircled Pettine. Schweiker handed him the certificate. Stone and Gold presented him their plaques. Pettine hoisted the Buck Club's bronze football. From behind, Bryan and Justin McDonnell, West's punter, dumped a yellow bucket of ice water over Pettine's head and down his back.

Bryan was the last West player to leave the field, answering questions from reporters until there were no questions left to ask. Roosevelt Field had been empty of spectators for more than thirty minutes before Pettine finally trudged toward the West team bus. Beyond the back of the stadium, dots of light from living room lamps twinkled in the row houses of the neighborhood he had known so well long ago.

"Everybody gets excited around me but me," he said. "I tried to downplay it as much as I could. Glad that it's over."

Later that night, back at the offices of the *Intelligencer*, Jeff Saukaitis, the paper's assistant sports editor, rummaged through files of CB West football clips. A man with a quiet, bookish demeanor, Saukaitis had covered West football throughout the early to mid-1990s, and his assignment was to write a column about Pettine for Sunday's edition. (The *Intelligencer*, at the time, did not publish on Saturdays.) Saukaitis said nothing as he leafed through those old articles, many of which he had written, in search of an illuminating anecdote or quote to drive home the point of his column: that there really was no secret to Pettine's success, that winning was merely his and his players' reward for their willingness to work hard, that the work ethic Pettine instilled would make his players better men.

Finally, Saukaitis found what he was looking for: a quote from Pettine from 1991, the year CB West won its first state championship. Saukaitis wove it into his column.

"If I teach a guy here," Pettine had said, "and all he had in five, ten, twenty years for a highlight up to that point is his yellowed scrapbook clippings and he's done nothing else, that's not a good situation. The most enjoyable thing for me is seeing the kids go on and be successful, not just in football."

Though Pettine insisted on near-total devotion to the West program from his players, he also hoped that they would, to a certain degree, leave their football careers behind them when the time was right. He framed his tough-love approach to coaching as a valuable apprentice-ship for the "real world," as a springboard to a satisfying career and personal life as these teenagers matured. There were certain kids who he knew, because of their desire and effort, would welcome the message he was trying to send through those arduous, repetitive practices and his harsh, sometimes dictatorial methods. Bryan Buckley was one. Pettine admired him for it. For too many ex-athletes, being the big man on campus, the letter-jacket jock, was as good as it ever got, and he trusted that Bryan wouldn't turn out to be one of those guys. For that reason, he also trusted that Bryan would accept and understand a difficult, football-related decision that Pettine didn't want to make but, more and more, believed he must.

Saturday, October 3, 1998

If sustaining a perfect record was serious business for the Bucks, it was becoming all the more lighthearted and enjoyable for the CB East play-ers, thanks in large part to Colby.

The Patriots' fourth victory of the season, 32–14 over Pennsbury, had been a nail-biter compared to their fifth. Against the Council Rock Indians—a team similar to Norristown in that it featured a Division

I–caliber quarterback and tailback—the Patriots had coasted, 36–13. Once again, Bryan Scott was the locus of East's offense, with 159 rushing yards, three receptions, and two touchdowns, but it was clear now that Colby was having an all-league season at defensive tackle, and he had been the difference this day. Council Rock's primary running back, Alex Wade, a senior who would play for Duke the following year, had rushed for 104 yards, but 42 of those yards came on one carry. More important, East had sacked Matt Verbit, the Indians' quarterback, three times, and Colby was involved in all three of the sacks, teaming with defensive end Troy Lavinia for the first before taking Verbit down twice on his own.

To observe Colby throughout the Council Rock game and during the victory's aftermath was to see the young man in full. He had dominated the game on defense, yet while talking to a reporter afterward, Colby let the questioner in on a secret: He didn't know which Council Rock player was Alex Wade. When Colby's quote appeared in the *Intelligencer* the next day—"As a matter of fact, I don't even know what his number was"—it could have been construed as a haughty kid suggesting that the best player on the losing team was overrated. That wasn't Colby's intention at all. He really didn't know who Alex Wade was, and it didn't matter much to him to know. "I just go to whoever has the ball," he said. This was the part of Colby's personality that Bryan Scott appreciated most. He did whatever was asked of him, never allowing outside matters (*Isn't Alex Wade going to an ACC school?*) to distract him. If Larry Greene asked Colby to lose sixty pounds and play wide receiver, Scott believed that Colby would do it.

Once their team bus arrived back at East, the Patriots headed into their locker room to shower and change . . . and dance. Following each of their previous four victories, the East players would pop their jerseys in laundry bags, turn on a radio, crank up "I'm Not a Player" by Big Punisher, and have a few of the seniors shake their way around the room. One by one, they would bump and thump down a conga line, some of them oh-so-smooth, some of them exaggerating their overbites, the whole scene a display of pure delight, no one relishing the moment more than Colby. There he was, shirtless and gyrating to a rap song in front of all his teammates, certainly the most uninhibited defensive lineman in the Suburban One League. At that moment, maybe the best, too.

The meeting, held in Mike Pettine's broom closet–sized office, was brief and direct, for there wasn't much for Pettine to say and even less that Bryan Buckley could or would say to change his coach's mind. Over his last two games—West's victory at Norristown and its latest win, 42–14 over Neshaminy—Bryan had rushed for 113 yards on fourteen attempts. Pettine had to do something about this.

"I have to cut your carries," Pettine told him, "to keep Dustin happy."

Neither Picciotti nor his parents were pleased with the way Pettine was spreading the ball to his various running backs. Through West's first five games, Picciotti had seventy-four carries, Dave Edwards thirty-five (he sat out the Neshaminy game with a hip pointer), and Bryan twenty-two. But Picciotti had rushed for more than 100 yards four times, including a 183-yard performance against Norristown, so why shouldn't he get the football more often?

Throughout his coaching career, Pettine had prided himself on never putting a player on a pedestal. The first-string quarterback and the third-string tight end? He hoped each of them, after leaving the program, would say, *He treated me like everyone else, made no special allowances. Everyone was equal in his eyes. He was tough but fair.* The problem was, Picciotti tended to sulk if he, in his mind, wasn't getting the ball often enough. Pettine rarely had encountered a player so openly defiant of West's team concept, but he also never had encountered a player who could match Picciotti's pure athleticism. Maybe West could and would win a state title even if Picciotti was unhappy, even if Picciotti quit the team, but Pettine didn't want to chance it.

Bryan was disappointed in Pettine's decision—not only because it meant Bryan would have a more limited role in the offense, but for what it said about Picciotti. Dustin's older brother, Paul, had been a starter for West in 1996. Paul and Bryan were friends, and Dustin considered Bryan something of an older brother as well, but to Bryan, Paul and Dustin Picciotti were opposites—Paul totally focused on his job and the team's success; Dustin too statistics-driven, too intent on being the center of attention. To an extent, this was the nature of Dustin's relationship with Pettine, as well. He was forever testing Pettine, growing his facial hair long and wearing gold, hoop-shaped earrings just for the sake of irritating an authority figure.

"I was young and stupid," Picciotti would admit years later. "I did a lot of stupid stuff."

Still, even coming from an immature teenager who couldn't help but see himself as a burgeoning superstar, Picciotti's was a mentality that Bryan couldn't comprehend. West was 5–0, and its next game, against North Penn, was an important one, for reasons that went beyond just the quality of the opponent, and this was what Dustin was worried about? That he wasn't getting the ball enough?

Bryan shook his head.

"I just want to win," he said, and he left Pettine's office. The subject never came up again.

FIVE

Shelter from the Storm

Friday, October 9, 1998

As storm clouds settled over Crawford Stadium and the rest of the sprawling, hilltop campus of North Penn High School in Lansdale, Rod Stone could chuckle, knowing that Mike Pettine must have been thinking about the weather. They couldn't have been good thoughts.

In the fifteen years that he had spent as Pettine's boss—ten as CB West's athletics director, five as its principal—Stone had come to expect the coach's near panic over a pregame weather forecast. Sometimes, finessing Pettine's fears over the condition of a given Friday night's playing field, be it War Memorial Field or a road-game site, seemed the most challenging part of Stone's relationship with him. Whenever the weather promised to be less than perfect, Pettine would slyly lobby Stone to try to get the game rescheduled. Rain, in Pettine's mind, never helped West, though the reason he thought so changed from year to year, depending on the makeup of the Bucks' roster. If Pettine had a big, bruising team built around a power-running game, he worried that the rain would make a slow team even slower, and West's opponent would have an advantage. If he had a small, quick team, he worried that the rain would rob his offense of its precision, and, well, West's opponent would have an advantage. "I think his bottom line was, rain hurts the better team," Stone recalled years later. "But each year, I would just say, 'What is it this year? Are we big and slow, or are we small and fast'?" Such were the idiosyncrasies of a coach with 301 career victories.

AccuWeather initially had predicted a temperate evening for Bucks and Montgomery counties—65 degrees with a 30 percent chance of precipitation—but those clouds that Stone could see suggested that showers were a certainty. Ordinarily, the prospect of playing through a steady rain would have been enough to worry Pettine, but there was more to concern him this night. There was the opponent, the 5–0 North Penn Knights, and there was the opponent's head coach.

Michael Pettine, Jr.

His father called him "Junior." Always had. Michael was the youngest of Mike and Joyce Pettine's three children and their only son, and he and his father had such similar temperaments—each stubborn, fiery, unwilling to surrender a single inch to the other—that when Michael entered his junior year at CB West and became the starting varsity quarterback, the Pettine family almost fell apart. The dynamic between Mike and Michael was one that so often plays out when a parent coaches one of his children: Mike Pettine—by nature a benevolent tyrant, reluctant to be perceived as playing favorites—was tougher on and more demanding of Michael than he was of any other player on the roster. In the middle of one practice, after another berating from his dad, Michael walked off the field, stripping off his uniform and pads, and didn't stop walking until he arrived home, two miles away. They talked about game plans during their morning rides to school and over the dinner table, the discussions often rising in volume the longer they went on. The fights over football between father and son were so fierce that Joyce Pettine, during Michael's senior year, finally told the two of them: "This is it. I'm leaving. I want you to leave the football outside when you come home." They did. From that point forward, every day after practice, they stayed in the family car after Mike had parked it in the driveway, getting everything off their chests before entering the house. Joyce's ultimatum was so effective, in fact, that after West lost to East, 7–6, on Thanksgiving Day 1983—Michael's final game at West—Michael neither spoke to his father nor ate a bite of turkey. He stayed in his room all afternoon and evening. Better to sit in that silence than to have the mother of all blowups ruin the holiday for the rest of the family.

From an individual, statistical standpoint, Michael was among the finest players to suit up for Mike Pettine. He ended his career with the fourth-highest number of passing yards in school history, and in a 22–14 senior-year victory against Archbishop Ryan from the Philadelphia Catholic League, he rushed for 176 yards, a single-game record for a West quarterback. He earned a full athletic scholarship to the University of Virginia to play defensive back. But by the standard of team success that Pettine had set at West, Michael's two seasons were a disappointment. The Bucks lost their first three games in 1982—their first three-game losing streak in twelve years—before winning their final six, then got off to a 7–0 start in '83, only to suffer two one-point losses in their last three games, including the Thanksgiving heartbreaker against East. At UVA, he lettered twice as a safety, led the Cavaliers in interceptions as a junior, and graduated in 1988 with a degree in economics that he could have used to get as far away from football as he wanted.

He chose, instead, to coach . . . at CB West. "I did it just to fill a void," Michael once said. "It was like I was going through withdrawal. For the first time in a long time, I wasn't playing football in the fall." So while working full time at Prudential Insurance in nearby Fort Washington, Michael spent five years on his father's staff. In 1991, as colleagues, the two of them shared the undefeated season (and state title) that they had never achieved during Michael's playing days. Their innate competitiveness remained. The West football coaches played regular pickup basketball games in the school's tiny, greenhouse-hot gymnasium, and "you'd think it was the Super Bowl," Michael told the *Philadelphia Daily News* in 1997. "I'd rather win fifty cents from him than a hundred dollars from someone else." Still, their relationship had changed, growing deeper with time. The father had mellowed. The son had matured. Now that Michael had passed through the West program and into adulthood, Pettine felt freer to express the pride that he always had carried for his son. Together, they had, perhaps, filled another void.

When his apprenticeship under his father ended, Michael served as a graduate assistant at the University of Pittsburgh—under Mike Carey's old college coach, Johnny Majors—for two years, then became the head coach at William Tennent High School in 1995. Over its three previous seasons, Tennent had gone 3–29. In Michael's first two seasons, Tennent won fourteen games, including a school-record nine in 1996. (In his first two seasons as a head coach, Mike Pettine had won fifteen games.) More than six feet tall, Michael looked like his father, especially during a game—the same slow stride to and from the sideline, his shoulders hunched forward at the same angle, one hand in the front pocket of his khakis. He looked like him, and he sure seemed to coach like him, too.

Edward Bowes noticed the similarities. Bowes had been hired in 1996 as the superintendent of the North Penn School District. In his previous superintendent job, in suburban Indianapolis, he had built Ben Davis High School's football program into a four-time state champion, hiring a new head coach, a new strength coach, and nine additional coaches for the district's three junior high schools. Now, here he was, in charge of a high school of more than 2,700 students. In parts of the North Penn School District, which abutted the Central Bucks School District along the CBSD's southwestern border, one literally could walk across the street and enter CB West territory. The same sorts of student-athletes were attending both schools, and Bowes's district had more of them. Yet North Penn's football team, somehow, had lost more games in 1996 than it won. The Knights had gone 5–6 under coach Joe Shannon, who also had suspended thirty players for attending a beer party, forcing the cancellation of the Knights' traditional Thanksgiving Day game against Lansdale Catholic. It was hard to tell what Bowes considered the greater stain: the players' suspensions or the team's losing record. Immediately after the season, he fired Shannon and, in the same press release, announced that he had hired Michael, who was assigned the task of turning one of the largest high schools in the state into a football juggernaut.

"I've been in coaching a long time," Pettine said after Michael's hiring, "and I can't remember a guy going into a job with any more pressure than this."

Bryan Buckley knew how much Pettine hated coaching against his son. Rod Stone knew it. Everyone affiliated with West's program knew it. Pettine was a competitor nonpareil. Be it high school football or a backyard game of horseshoes, he came to crush all comers, but there was a level of loyalty to his own flesh and blood that Pettine couldn't cast aside. During a passing-league game in the summer of 1997, weeks before the start of Michael's first season at North Penn, Bryan knocked down a Knights player, who stood up and threw a punch at him in retaliation. Michael started screaming at Bryan. So did Pettine. In the heat of the moment, Bryan was incredulous that his coach would align against him to any degree. "You want to take your son's side, or you want to stay with us?" Bryan shouted back at Pettine. "The guy's punching me. I'm going to knock him on his ass." Then, on October 3, 1997, in what was believed to be the first time in Pennsylvania high school football history that a father and son had faced each other as opposing head coaches, the Bucks pounded the Knights, 35–14, at War Memorial Field, and on the sideline, Pettine struggled to stop his tears as the game's final seconds ticked down. As Bryan sprinted across the field to congratulate Michael, telling him it was an honor to play against his team, Carey tapped Pettine on the shoulder, wrapped his arm around him, and told him, "He'll have his time." Competing against Michael had summoned something from within Pettine that his players rarely saw: a softer side.

Carey's words had consoled Pettine a bit, but that was a year ago now, and if that reassurance initially had made it easier for Pettine to cope with beating Michael, there still seemed something different about him during practice as his second head-to-head meeting with his son approached. To Bryan, the stress had been plain on Pettine's face during the week of workouts and film sessions. The practices, Bryan noticed, had been more intense and intensive, dragging later into the evenings. After all, as difficult as it was to coach against his son, Pettine would be damned if he would *lose* to him.

And he might. The possibility was real this time. North Penn was coming off an 8–3 season under Junior and was now ranked fourth in the *Harrisburg Patriot-News*'s state football poll. (West, of course, was ranked first.) Junior had just turned thirty-two two weeks earlier. He was the brightest young coaching mind in the state, let alone in the Suburban One League, and he and his top assistant, Dick Beck—another alumnus of Pettine's program—were as familiar with West's playbook and tendencies as any opposing coaches could be. On Thursday night, less than twenty-four hours before game time, Carey was poring over film of North Penn, and he called Bryan at home to confirm several defensive audibles, to make it clear how West's defense ought to react to the Knights' various offensive sets. "What stinks," Carey said to Bryan, "is that I know he's going to change everything for tomorrow night anyway, so half these calls aren't going to matter." Now, the matter was at hand. As Bryan led the West players through their pregame calisthenics, Crawford Stadium continued to fill up—parents in slickers, girlfriends in their boyfriends' jerseys, older men with wrinkled faces and baseball caps set on the backs of their heads, teenagers who had painted their faces either black and gold or white and blue. Crawford held 6,528 spectators, and there was no room in the bleachers; the place was sold out. Two radio stations, WNPV and WBUX, would broadcast the game live. Five television news stations from the Philadelphia and Allentown areas had sent correspondents to cover the game. To double the size and, presumably, the enthusiasm of the North Penn cheerleading squad, the junior varsity girls joined the varsity. Both West and North Penn had been unbeaten when they played each other in 1997, just as they were now, and Bryan certainly respected Michael, Beck, and the rest of the Knights' coaching staff, if for no other reason than their CB West pedigrees. Nevertheless, Bryan had regarded that game as little more than a dog-and-pony show for the local press, an easy story line ("Father vs. son!" . . . "Pettine vs. Pettine!") that didn't reflect how far apart the teams really were then. That '97 North Penn team, though improving, wasn't ready to dethrone West. This one, based on what Bryan had seen on film, might be. An additional year under Michael had made that much of a difference.

Complicating West's pregame preparation was Michael's fondness for calling trick plays: reverses, flea flickers, strange alignments that caused confusion for opponents. Michael liked to practice such gadget plays once every couple of weeks, just to break up the monotony of his players' daily routine, but once the next Friday night rolled around, he often didn't need to use those unusual formations. He had junior tailback Hikee Johnson, who already had made a verbal commitment to UVA and had rushed for 802 yards in the Knights' first five games. He had a pair of two-way linemen, senior Dave Costlow and junior Chris McKelvy, who were bound for Penn State and who already had the size and strength of Division I players. Costlow stood six feet four and weighed 260 pounds, and at six feet four, 295 pounds, McKelvy was even bigger. With that core, Michael didn't have to fool anyone; the Knights could line up against most teams and dominate them at the line of scrimmage. West presented a more formidable challenge. The Bucks could match or surpass the Knights' bulk along the offensive and defensive lines, and as well as Michael and Dick Beck knew the Bucks' playbook and tendencies, Carey was a quick study when it came to breaking down film. For all of Pettine's preaching to his players and coaches about the need to concentrate only on the next opponent, Carey had been collecting and studying tape of North Penn since the third week of the season. To beat West, Michael believed, the element of trickery was essential, and throughout the week, Pettine made certain to warn his players, Bryan in particular, to be ready for something out of the ordinary from North Penn's offense.

Regardless of what Junior had in store for him, what Pettine couldn't prepare for was how heavy rain might change the course of the game. That West wasn't playing fifteen miles away at War Memorial Field was, at least, a small comfort to him. Because CB East and CB West shared it, War Memorial was in constant use every fall and, from mid-September until early December, constant disrepair. West's and East's football teams played their home games there. West's boys' soccer team practiced and played all its home games there, and East's boys' soccer team played many of its games there, too. What little grass there was in the rectangular area between the 20-yard lines stood in small, pathetic patches or as single blades in a sea of brown. On a dry day, the ground was chewed up, pocked with cleat marks, hard, and pebble-strewn and gravelly. The key to playing on it, to surviving it, was learning how to fall on it: flopping straight down, no sliding. Sliding scraped a player's exposed skin. When temperatures dipped below freezing, the field seemed a lumpy, icy sandlot, and when War Memorial was wet, it was a pit of mud. Yes, all things being equal, Pettine would have preferred to take on his son and North Penn at home, just for the emotional edge, but he could live with playing such an important game in a hostile, unfamiliar setting. On this night, the slop that War Memorial Field was sure to become would be someone else's problem.

Just a month earlier, a group of CB East alumni and administrators had presented a proposal that would have gone a long way to alleviating the problem of War Memorial's thirty-year history of overuse. A nine-person steering committee had taken up the task of raising funds to build a football stadium on CB East's campus, and on a Thursday night in early September, the committee had made its proposal public.

The notion of East's having its own stadium had been a pie-in-the-sky suggestion at school board meetings and in the community since Central Bucks High's split in 1969. Sharing War Memorial Field was fine for a while, but for many of those affiliated with East's football program, the twenty-minute commute from Buckingham to Doylestown had come to symbolize the almost inherent advantage that the West program seemed to have. In 1989, as War Memorial underwent extensive renovations to its grandstands and lights, the Central Bucks school board debated whether, once the renovations were finished, the high schools should move their annual matchup back to War Memorial after ten years of playing each other at Delaware Valley College. During a meeting that year, Susan Heckler, who then was a member of the CB East Football Parent's Club and who lived in Doylestown, told the board that War Memorial was "emotionally linked to West" and that the East-West game should remain at DelVal's neutral site (which it did, until 1993). Regardless of the outcome of the meeting, Heckler wasn't alone in her opinion. She had tapped into a sentiment that others around Doylestown shared: that the school district should build a stadium at East out of fairness and equality and, as an added benefit, because it would cure a collective inferiority complex.

All of those factors had compelled about eighty people—parents of East players, alumni, area residents—to file through East's main lobby and into the auditorium, past a three-foot-long diorama that captured the committee's vision of what the stadium could be, to hear what the committee had to say. Mike Wallis, East's athletics director, had built the model in 1997, with the help of an East student, right around the time that Central Bucks School District set aside $2.6 million in its budget for the construction of a stadium at East. If the committee could come up with enough donations, the stadium project at last appeared viable. Costing between $3.5 million and $4.2 million to construct, the stadium, according to the committee members, would seat 4,500 people, a figure close to War Memorial Field's capacity; would feature light standards and a state-of-the-art irrigation system; and would be built on the plot of land at East that the football team used as its practice field. Scott Stankavage, an East alumnus and former member of the NFL's Denver Broncos, flew in from Charlotte, North Carolina, for the event, pointing out to the attendees that now that East had been around for thirty years, its alumni were in better, more stable financial positions to contribute to the campaign. In addition, more than 1,400 students attended East now. "The actual need, the overuse of War Memorial Field," Stankavage had said, "is there."

Mark and Nancy Umbrell had attended that presentation. If they could help build a weight room, why not a stadium, too? In fact, Colby and Mark had paid to have their names engraved on two of the bricks in the new stadium, whenever the district got around to erecting it. Until then, the Umbrell family would settle for enjoying Colby's terrific senior season. He was on his way to being an all-league lineman. The Patriots were 5–0 and hosting winless Abington. It was Senior Night; each of the twelfth-graders on the team would be introduced before the game and would escort his parents to midfield amid an ovation. It would be a special night for that reason alone. Hell, West might lose to North Penn, and wouldn't that be something—the Bucks looking up at the Patriots for a change? Hours before kickoff against Abington, Colby and his teammates went through their Friday afternoon routine. They taped themselves up and got dressed. Wearing sneakers, their jerseys, their football pants, and their helmets, they did their pregame walk-through on East's practice field. Then they carted their shoulder pads with them as they boarded their yellow team buses. The Patriots trundled south along Route 202 to their home field, though this time, the ride from Buckingham to War Memorial Field didn't seem so long, even if those clouds above were darkening.

The overt trickery would wait. Michael Pettine wanted something subtler at the start. He began the game by calling six consecutive running plays to the right side of the field, hardly surprising considering that Costlow was lined up at right guard and McKelvy at right tackle. The first five plays gained twenty-eight yards, giving the Knights a first down at West's 43-yard line. Throughout the game, Bryan would line up at either linebacker or nose tackle, depending on what Carey was signaling to him. It was up to Bryan, though, to recognize North Penn's offensive front and shift West's defenders accordingly before the ball was snapped—to "man over" the defense so that the Bucks had as many tacklers on each side of the line of scrimmage as the Knights had blockers. Sure enough, on North Penn's second play, the Knights came out in an unbalanced set, stacking their tight end and wingback to the left side of the field, and after the Bucks adjusted, Hikee Johnson ran off *right* tackle for ten yards. So Bryan made what he later called a "command decision": no more shifting. On the sixth play of that opening drive, he shot through the middle of the line on a blitz from his linebacker spot and dropped Johnson for a two-yard loss. The tackle restored a measure of equilibrium to West's defense. After allowing one more first down, the Bucks stopped North Penn on fourth-and-4, stuffing Johnson for a one-yard loss and taking possession at their own 24-yard line.

"You're not manning people over," Pettine shouted as Bryan came off the field.

Carey interrupted. "No, it's a good call. They're running away from the man-over."

The chess match was on. Now, it was the father's turn. If Michael and Beck presumed that Pettine would pound away at the Knights' defense with Dustin Picciotti, they were wrong, at least for the first two plays. From an I-formation, with Picciotti as the blocking back, Dave Edwards took a quick pitch for thirty-five yards; in his white uniform and standing-straight-up running style, he seemed a ghost as he surged down the right sideline through the thick cloud of mist that now covered the stadium. Edwards then went for four more yards on his next carry to the North Penn 37. Picciotti bulled up the middle for another five, setting up a third-and-1 at the 32. Given how easily the Bucks had moved down the field, there was little reason to think Picciotti wouldn't get the first down, provided he held on to the football.

He did not.

Mike Orihel stuffed the ball into Picciotti's belly, and Picciotti took one step forward. Mike Kapusta, who played fullback on offense for North Penn but now was manning his left outside linebacker spot, came hard off the corner and drove his helmet into Picciotti's midsection. The ball popped out of Picciotti's hands like a piece of bread from a toaster, hung in the moist air for a moment, and landed in the arms of North Penn defensive lineman Dan Chang. There was no West player close enough to Chang to stop him from chugging sixty-eight yards for the game's first touchdown. *You've got to be kidding me*, Bryan mouthed to himself as he watched the sequence unfold from the sideline. Wes Heinel, North Penn's kicker, pushed the extra-point attempt to the right, but the Knights, out of nowhere, had taken a 6–0 lead.

West responded on its next possession with a typical West drive: fifteen plays, sixty-seven yards. On fourth-and-7 from the North Penn 30, Orihel rolled right and, in his only pass completion of the game, connected with Edwards for seven yards and a few inches, earning the Bucks a fresh set of downs. Four plays later, Picciotti scored from the 6, and West kicker Bob Tumelty put West up 7–6 when he nine-ironed the extra point through the uprights.

Still, a one-point lead was hardly calming, and as the mist thickened into a steady drizzle, strange things started happening. Johnson fumbled the ball out of bounds on North Penn's next possession, and when West forced the Knights to punt, the snap sailed over the head of punter John Corson, who smartly covered up the ball as several West special-teams players piled on top of him at the North Penn 22-yard line. With terrific field position, West was poised to blow the game open, except that Picciotti couldn't hold on to the football. On third-and-6, the Bucks caught a break after Picciotti dropped a handoff from Orihel; the ball rolled forward five yards, where tackle Ben Carber recovered it. Instead of turning the ball over, the Bucks faced a manageable fourth-and-1. But for the second straight play, Picciotti and Orihel couldn't carry out a simple handoff, the ball thudding to the ground between them, and with two minutes and seventeen seconds left in the first half, North Penn's offense took over at its own 16.

Clay Kuklick, the Knights' junior quarterback, hadn't thrown a pass in the game yet, let alone completed one. On first down, Michael sent wide receiver Evan Fitzpatrick on a fly pattern down the center of the field and had Kuklick heave it in his direction. Kuklick overthrew Fitzpatrick, which was almost irrelevant. The true intent of the call was to soften West's defense, a strategy that worked. Two running plays ripped off twenty-eight yards, and Kuklick found Fitzpatrick wide open on a seam route for nineteen yards to the West 23. Three plays and six more yards later, Michael called his final timeout of the half with less than a minute left on the clock, gathering his eleven offensive players around him in a circle. It was fourth down. The field was becoming a swamp. A field goal of at least forty yards was out of the question.

Michael told his players to run a play called Sneak Attack.

The Knights broke their huddle with Michael and came out in a tight formation, nine of them bunched together along the line of scrimmage. Fitzpatrick lined up as a tight end on the left. Kuklick was under center. Three yards behind Kuklick, Johnson, the only player in the backfield, stood in a slight crouch, his hands on his knees.

Before the game, Michael had made sure to meet with the referee and other game officials, describing this formation to them, asking them not to make a mistake and blow the play dead after the ball was snapped. It would be natural, he said, to do that.

Chang, who also started at center for the Knights, snapped the ball, and Kuklick lunged and wriggled forward, as if he were running a quarterback sneak. Several Bucks, Bryan among them, converged on him, tackling him near the 15-yard line.

There was one problem.

Kuklick didn't have the ball.

Chang's snap had sailed through Kuklick's legs directly to Johnson, who caught the ball and, for a heartbeat, didn't move. Meanwhile, Fitzpatrick pretended to throw a block, then sprinted for the end zone.

Johnson squared his shoulders, lifted his right arm, and threw a flawless spiral toward Fitzpatrick. Playing free safety and realizing too late what was happening, Dave Edwards was a stride behind Fitzpatrick when Fitzpatrick hauled in Johnson's pass in the back of the end zone.

Forty-seven seconds remained in the half. The two-point conversion attempt failed. No matter. North Penn led, 12–7.

"Got to take some chances, baby," Michael told a television reporter as he charged off the field at halftime.

His father was furious. *Watch the trick plays . . . Watch the trick plays . . .* Pettine had said it all week, and there were his players, raising their fists, thinking they had stopped Kuklick short of a first down, while Fitzpatrick was celebrating in the end zone. For the first time all season and only the third time in two years, West was trailing a game at halftime. A couple of times during the half, Bryan had caught Pettine glancing at the North Penn sideline, at Michael, with a look on his face that said, *What are you thinking now?* Bryan had never seen that look from Mike Pettine before, had never seen him so uneasy. It was more disconcerting than the five-point deficit. Maybe Junior really was in his old man's head.

As one Pettine tried to outfox the other, Steve Kreider lifted his cleats out of the sludge of War Memorial Field and looked down. Two inches. Kreider swore that's how deep the mud was. Two freaking inches. It was bad enough the seniors' mothers and fathers had to carry flower bouquets and try to maintain their dignity while tiptoeing through such a mess before the game. Playing in it would be dreadful. Throughout pregame warm-ups, Larry Greene and his assistant coaches reminded their players to take short, choppy steps and to keep their shoulders aligned directly over their feet. Taking a longer stride or leaning too far forward while running would make it harder to maintain balance on such a slick, squishy surface. Lateral movement was going to be a challenge anyway, and Abington ran the Wing-T, an offense characterized by multiple ball-fakes and by an offensive line that used trapping and pulling blocking schemes. East's defenders would have to move from side to side.

East's offense players, meanwhile, would do everything they could to avoid having to move from side to side. Greene wanted to lessen the workload of Bryan Scott, who was averaging almost twenty carries a game and was nursing several bruised and sore body parts, and feature more of senior Mark Notwick, who was starting at fullback for the first time all season. That strategy meant more running between the tackles, more running behind Colby.

Neither team controlled the line of scrimmage, but Abington, as 0–5 teams are wont to do, made two early, costly mistakes. Kreider scored on a two-yard sneak after one of Abington's running backs fumbled on the game's second play, and the Galloping Ghosts' second possession ended on an interception by East senior defensive back Ryan Callahan. Notwick, who started because Larry Greene wanted Phil Laing to play middle linebacker exclusively, went twenty-nine yards up the middle to set up a two-yard score by Scott. By the midpoint of the first quarter, the Patriots had a fourteen-point lead, but certainly not because they were pounding a hapless opponent. Anthony Greene, East's junior outside linebacker, was convinced that the weather was equalizing the game, that the Patriots' defense was, on the whole, a step slower for having to slosh around the field, and a winless team can be a desperate, dangerous team. "Abington was tough, scrappy," he recalled. "They weren't going to lie down."

Though he felt like he was playing in slow motion because he was concentrating so much just on not fumbling each snap, Kreider was having enough success running quarterback keepers that, in the second quarter, the Patriots freed Scott for his only big play of the night. Kreider offered a token play-action fake to Scott on third-and-10 from the East 39 and, as Colby held a block at right tackle, rolled to the right. Abington's defense shifted toward Kreider. But instead of tucking the ball away, he stopped, turned, and threw the ball back to Scott, who had drifted toward the left sideline. Scott caught the pass, eluded two defenders, and cut back across the field, past three more Abington players, for a sixty-one-yard touchdown. In four days, Scott would announce that he had accepted a full football scholarship from Penn State. The play made clear why Joe Paterno offered him the full ride in the first place.

There was still a buzz over Scott's touchdown among the East players and coaches and in the War Memorial bleachers, where Mark and Nancy Umbrell sat soaked to the bone, as Abington's offense embarked on its first sustained drive of the half. Those Wing-T traps and counters were starting to work, their deception neutralizing the quickness that Colby brought to East's defensive line and that Scott brought to the secondary. Finally, on one counter, senior Jim Johnson, Abington's most talented back, broke clear of the first wave of East tacklers and surged into the middle of the field. Anthony Greene came forward toward Johnson, but one of Abington's guards blindsided him with a clean block. Junior free safety R. J. Hamlin tripped up Johnson by the running back's shoestrings for a touchdown-saving tackle, but Greene, flat on his back, didn't see it.

What he saw was another East player on the ground.

What he saw, and heard, was Colby Umbrell, moaning in pain.

No one had touched him. No one had blocked him, chop-blocked him, pushed him, clipped him, or bumped into him. Colby simply fired out of his defensive-tackle stance, planted his left foot—in the two-inch-deep mud—and twisted his left knee. His foot didn't move. He went down and stayed down.

From the stands, Colby's parents could see the entire sequence unfold. They raced down the bleachers, their feet clanging against the metallic steps, the sound echoing on the mostly quiet East side of the stadium. Nancy didn't go out on the field—*What would it look like*, she thought, *to have his mommy run out there?*—but Mark did. He rushed down from the bleachers to his son. Joseph Jennelle, East's principal, was out there, too, holding an umbrella over Colby. Squatting next to Colby's legs, John Reading, East's trainer, conducted Lachman's test, a common method of checking for damage to the anterior cruciate ligament. Reading gripped Colby's thigh, near the top of his injured knee, and held it steady as he pulled the tibia, the lower bone in Colby's leg. If it was still healthy, Colby's knee would move no more than four millimeters because the intact ligament would restrict the knee's range of motion. But when Reading pulled down on Colby's lower leg, the knee moved farther than a few millimeters.

Mark knew exactly what had happened. The same thing had happened to him when he was a younger man. Colby had torn his ACL. His senior season, his last East-West game, the possibility of playing football in college—all of them appeared in jeopardy now, if not already out of the question.

Colby draped his arms over the shoulders of two of his teammates, defensive backs Jason Ware and Scott Benham, and let his left foot dangle above the ground as they carried him off the field. Nancy approached Jennelle, who was still holding his umbrella, and said, "Thank you. I wanted to do that." Colby's teammates and parents helped him take his pads off, and then Mark and Nancy took him home.

"Oh, well." Colby sighed during the drive home. *We're more disappointed about this than he is*, Mark thought. *My kid isn't the type to cry in his soup.*

Mark and Nancy helped him through the doorway.

"Get me in the shower," Colby said.

Whenever a sophomore entered the West program, Pettine assigned him a "buddy," an older player who would show the neophyte the ropes.

Usually, the upperclassman would initiate the younger player by having him perform a series of minor tasks, such as carrying his buddy's helmet and pads off the field after practice each day. When Bryan was a sophomore, his buddy had been Dave Armstrong. Dave didn't make him carry equipment. "You're a player," Dave had told him. "You're one of us." Bryan had remembered that when Pettine assigned him his buddy: Phil DiGiacomo.

Bryan didn't make DiGiacomo carry any equipment, either. Instead, the two of them carpooled to each preseason passing camp session. It wouldn't have felt right to Bryan to haze DiGiacomo, and not just because Bryan had appreciated what Dave had done and wanted to give his understudy the same measure of respect. Even as a sophomore, DiGiacomo possessed a confidence that bordered on cockiness. When he smiled, his mouth curled into a knowing smirk. One day at practice, Pettine needled DiGiacomo about how high he wore his socks, and DiGiacomo went right back at him about the clothes the coach wore. A sophomore, riding Pettine? This simply wasn't done, but DiGiacomo could get away with it. Through West's first five games, he had rushed for 158 yards and two touchdowns on only eighteen carries for a gaudy average of 8.8 yards per attempt, and he was the Bucks' primary punt and kickoff returner. He had an uncle and a cousin who had played under Pettine, and his father, Phil, had been an all-state defensive end for Archbishop Wood High School, just eight miles south of Doylestown, in 1973. From the first day of the '98 season, DiGiacomo was "one of us" in Bryan's eyes, and in Pettine's eyes, as well.

North Penn ran six plays on its first possession of the second half before Corson lofted a thirty-one-yard punt to DiGiacomo, who fielded the punt cleanly and steamed straight ahead for a fourteen-yard return to the West 47. Pettine noted how well DiGiacomo had negotiated the muddy field. After that thirty-five-yard burst on his first carry, Dave Edwards had managed only twenty yards on his next nine attempts. He had run gingerly, slipping to the ground twice. Pettine gambled on fresher legs and firmer footing. He removed Edwards from the game and put in DiGiacomo at tailback.

DiGiacomo dived forward for a three-yard gain on his first carry, and as he picked himself up, the sky opened in a fury of rain, fat drops landing with tiny thumps on the players' helmets and on the people in the stands. West's white uniforms were blotched brown from the mud. The television camera crews wiped down their lenses after each play. One newspaper reporter, covering the game from the West sideline, had been keeping his game notes and statistics on a yellow legal pad covered in a clear plastic bag, but the pad was useless now. It was so wet that he couldn't write on it. He took his microcassette recorder out of his pocket, pressed the record button and, for the rest of the night, narrated each play into the machine.

His team unable to throw the ball downfield because of the weather, Pettine called 55-I Post, a play whose design was fit for Vince Lombardi's great Green Bay Packers teams of the 1960s. Wingback Greg Kinzel sealed off North Penn's strong-side linebacker. Picciotti, leading the way for DiGiacomo, rubbed out the strong-side cornerback. DiGiacomo burst through the tunnel that those two blocks created; he had covered forty yards before Hikee Johnson knocked him out of bounds at the Knights' 10.

Bryan jogged back on to the field. It was now his turn to be the blocking back for Picciotti, who surged for seven yards on first down. On second down, Bryan cleared Kuklick out of Picciotti's path, opening a huge hole through which Picciotti reached the end zone. Again, the storm prevented a successful extra-point try, but with 2:46 left in the third quarter, West had retaken the lead, 13–12.

The storm, in fact, had rendered any play other than a basic handoff—a pass, a kickoff, a punt, a field goal, an extra point—treacherous and unpredictable. Whether they were trying to field a kick or catch a snap, players had a difficult time following the football's flight, the sheets of rain like a thin strip of gauze that blindfolded them. When West's first possession of the fourth quarter stalled at its own 36, Pettine had no choice but to send out punter Justin McDonnell to try to swing field position back in the Bucks' favor. But McDonnell dropped the snap and, after scooping up the ball, had his punt blocked. The Knights recovered the ball at the West 16. The home side of Crawford Stadium throbbed with sound. A twenty-game unbeaten streak, the number-one ranking in the state, and coaching supremacy in his own family potentially could vanish for Pettine if his defense didn't make a stand.

West still had an advantage, though. The poor field conditions robbed North Penn's offense of the aspect that most concerned Pettine, Carey, Bryan, and the rest of the Bucks: Michael's creative play calling. There was no double-reverse coming, no option pass from a running back, nothing that would surprise anyone. The situation was just too risky, the field too slippery, to try such a play, which left the Knights only one option: running the ball into the maw of the West defense. "We always felt good about our plans, but it got to the point where our biggest trouble against West was our inability to run the football," Michael recalled later. "We always felt like we were a lineman or two short against them because their defensive fronts were so good. We couldn't get on track because of the inability to block one or two guys up front." After back-to-back running plays netted the Knights only three yards, Kuklick stood in a shotgun formation on third down. Carey called a blitz. The one guy North Penn couldn't block was Bryan. He broke through the line and drove Kuklick into the muck as the quarterback released the ball. Kuklick's sickly pass fell harmlessly to the ground. From the sideline, Carey strode onto the field, pumping his fist.

It was fourth down. Michael now had no choice: he sent out Wes Heinel to attempt a thirty-yard field goal. Considering Pettine's pregame worries about the weather, the result was ironic. Kuklick, the holder, couldn't catch the snap; he recovered the ball and was tackled at the West 34 with 6½ minutes left in regulation. The Bucks melted away more than 5½ of those minutes with a drive of thirteen plays, eleven of which were handoffs to Picciotti. He finished with 134 yards on thirty-three carries. DiGiacomo intercepted Kuklick on the game's final play. *Rain hurts the better team.* Not this time. The rain had saved West's streak.

Mike and Michael Pettine met at midfield and embraced. It was still possible for their teams to meet again in the district playoffs. As Bryan and Carey walked to the visiting locker room, Pettine approached Bryan, shook his hand, and said simply, "Good game."

"I know you don't like hearing it," Bryan told him, "but we're going to see these guys down the road."

In response, Mike Pettine didn't smile, didn't stop walking, and didn't say a word.

After Colby left the field, Abington completed its final drive of the first half by scoring a touchdown, cutting East's halftime lead to 21–7. Behind War Memorial's south end zone was a white bell tower, the bottom of which was as big as a one-car garage, that served as the Patriots' locker room, and Kreider stormed in. The coaches weren't in the room yet, but Kreider started screaming at his teammates.

"This is pathetic!" he said. "How can we play like this? We're playing like shit."

Truth be told, though, he wasn't as furious over the Patriots' first-half performance as he was upset about Colby's injury. The two friends had spent most of the off-season together in the weight room, and all that hard work seemed pointless in light of losing Colby. More than any other player on East's team, even Bryan Scott, Colby had come to be regarded as indestructible. "It was a psychological shock to us to see him go down," Anthony Greene would say later, and maybe Kreider's rant inspired enough of the Patriots to focus on the task at hand. They held Abington scoreless in the second half and won, 28–7. Kreider had run for two touchdowns and thrown for one. Scott had gained only forty-six rushing yards, but with sixty-two tough yards on just nine carries, Notwick had been a godsend. Those silver linings, though, weren't enough to minimize the damage done to the Patriots' lineup. First, there was Colby's injury. Then, in the second half, Brandon Scott had to be carried off the field; he, too, had torn a knee ligament. East was now 6–0, but the cost of the victory—the team's best lineman and its second-best running back—had been steep.

Without Colby, the Patriots boarded the buses after the game. The players returned to East, where they cleaned up and changed, and their parents rejoined them in the cafeteria for a postgame pizza party. The mood in the cafeteria was somber, most of the attendees staring at their slices of pizza or at the floor, and it remained that way even as Mark and Nancy helped Colby limp into the room. They hadn't taken him to a hospital yet. A doctor's visit could wait. Colby wanted to be with his teammates and coaches first.

They approached him quietly one by one, patting him on his shoulder. This was a good team, Nancy said years later, a good group of kids, and there was a sense in the cafeteria that they had just seen their season go down the drain.

"What do you think?" Larry Greene asked Mark.

"He tore his ACL," Mark said. "He's done."

As much as Mark admired Colby's desire and commitment to his teammates, there was no other conclusion he could draw about Colby's future in football. Colby had decided to play at East, at least in part, because Mark had played there, because Colby considered it an honor to continue a family tradition that his dad had begun, and thinking about those gestures made Mark's heart swell with a fierce pride that only another father could appreciate. It was why, for a long time, Mark Umbrell considered the sight of his son lying in the mud, unable to walk on his own, the worst moment of his life.

SIX

Crises and Comebacks

Saturday, October 10, 1998

The day after his son's high school football career apparently had ended, Mark Umbrell took a lonely drive in search of a cold beer. He and Colby had just come from an appointment at Doylestown Hospital with Dr. Kieran Cody, a 1981 Central Bucks East graduate and an orthopedic surgeon who specialized in treating sports-related injuries. After examining Colby, Cody had confirmed what the Umbrells already knew: Colby had torn the anterior cruciate ligament in his left knee. At some point, he would need surgery; Cody, in fact, had the paperwork ready.

The course Colby had charted for his future would have to change. His hope of entering the U.S. Military Academy had vanished. West Point required of all its candidates a qualifying medical examination overseen by a Department of Defense review board, and there was no way that the board would clear Colby now. Also, because of the nature of an ACL injury and the standard six months of rehabilitation that lay ahead for Colby—a rehabilitation that, Colby and Mark presumed, would have to begin immediately—the likelihood that a college coach would offer him any sort of football-related financial aid was slim. Who would take such an expensive chance on a kid with a bum knee, no matter how many tackles he'd made in the first game of his senior season?

More than anything, though, it was the sheer shock of Colby's injury, the jarring shift from the joyful atmosphere of Senior Night to the expectation that Colby would never play for East again, that most bothered Mark. The entire high school football experience—the Friday nights, the sense of togetherness, the connections between past and present—had been so much damn *fun*. Mark didn't want any of it to end. So that afternoon, he drove along State Street through downtown Doylestown. The fence that guarded the north end zone of War Memorial Field passed across his driver's-side window, and he continued south on Route 202, past Delaware Valley College and a 7-Eleven and a country store and a series of shops and small businesses and a barbecue joint called the Duck Deli, right on out of town, to the New Britain Inn.

There is a universally accepted truth regarding American small towns: For every high school football team, there is a corresponding watering hole where the patrons are all intimately familiar with the team's past and its prospects, where the people of the town gather to cherish that past and laud the star player and complain that the coach ain't calling the plays the way he used to.

Berwick, in the anthracite region of northeastern Pennsylvania, was as gaga over coach George Curry's Bulldogs as any hamlet in the state was over its hometown team, and with good reason. Over the thirty-five years that Curry coached there, Berwick won 364 games and six state championships in Class AAA, the second-highest enrollment level in Pennsylvania football, and if you were visiting on a fall Friday night, the best spot to be, aside from the school's Crispin Field, was the Villa Capri Bulldog Lounge, which offered steamed clams and buffalo wings and was kitty-corner from the stadium. In the 1983 film *All the Right*

Moves—shot in Johnstown, Pennsylvania—Tom Cruise played the star cornerback for fictitious Ampipe High near Pittsburgh, and his character drank Iron City lager (underage, presumably) and rumbled with mustached townies at the American Carpatho Citizens Club. There's a template to these bars and others like them. The walls are wood-paneled and festooned with photographs of football players. Pinball machine lights flicker from a corner. No one drinks wine.

The New Britain Inn was one of those places. It was Central Bucks West's place. More accurately, it was Mike Carey's place. He bought it in 1979—eight years after graduating from West, two years after his brief professional career as an offensive lineman ended, one year after he became an assistant coach under Mike Pettine. The New Britain Inn wasn't located in Doylestown; it was just three miles southwest of the borough. But its stark gold-and-black sign, impossible to miss if you drove down Route 202 away from Doylestown, left no doubt as to the owner's allegiance. The New Britain Inn was as closely aligned with the tradition and culture of CB West football as Pettine's mystique or the school's weight room or the West alumni who still wore their corduroy Bucks jackets around town. During weekdays, a cross-section of central Bucks County filled the NBI for lunch: lawyers, teachers, local politicians, many of them sidling up to Carey for some inside information about what he, Pettine, and the coaching staff had in store for the next Suburban One League sacrificial lamb. After West games, Pettine, his coaches, and those closest to the program (the players' parents, for instance) often headed to the NBI to decompress, and the players themselves often worked there during their summers. Carey would throw them a few bucks for helping to clean up the kitchen or sweep the floors after a busy Saturday night. Just inside its front door, the NBI had a "Wall of Fame" covered in framed newspaper clippings, preserved behind sheets of glass, and framed photos (many of which were autographed) of former CB West players (some of whom had struck poses styled after the Heisman Trophy). At the New Britain Inn, a football aficionado could sit at the bar, sip a pint, and let the legend of CB West football seep into his psyche, yet the New Britain Inn was where Mark Umbrell—CB East alumnus, CB East booster club president, CB East football father—was headed.

Mark and Mike Carey had known each other for years. As boys in the late 1960s, Carey, his younger brother Pat, and Mark had played midget football together for the Warrington Athletic Association. Mark and the Careys had remained friends since. When Colby was in middle school, Mark had asked Mike Carey's advice on starting Colby on an age-appropriate weight-training program, and in a way, Mark was calling on Carey for counsel again. He wanted to talk to someone who would lend an understanding ear, and with the connections he had made over his years of coaching at West, Carey might even be able to do something more than just listen to Mark unload.

Carey had not heard about Colby's injury yet, and as Mark was explaining what had happened and what Cody had said about the need for surgery, Carey stopped him in midsentence.

"Hold on," Carey said. "Let me call Pat."

While Mike, two years older than Pat and Mark, was playing college football in western Pennsylvania, starting on the offensive line at the University of Pittsburgh, Pat was quarterbacking CB West to two unbeaten seasons in 1971 and 1972, throwing for close to 2,800 yards in his three-year career. Like his big brother, he played college football, for Temple University. Unlike his big brother, Pat did not become a coach. He became an orthopedic surgeon.

Over the course of the twenty-three years Mike Carey would spend as a coach at CB West, there was no opponent he obsessed over more than CB East. Yet whenever he got the opportunity to meet or coach East players in a Bucks County All-Star Classic, he always came away respecting them. They were the same kinds of kids—from within the same geographic boundaries, with the same accents on work ethic and academics—as those he coached at West. When Mark Umbrell sat down at the New Britain Inn's bar that day, Carey would explain years later, he had no second thoughts about helping Mark and Colby. "Number one," Carey recalled, "I thought the world of Mark Umbrell, and his kid was just a character kid." Here was the nature of the East-West rivalry, the camaraderie that invigorated the competition, distilled to one player's prognosis. Here was Mike Carey, a West coach, working to make sure Colby Umbrell, East's best lineman, would have the chance to play in the East-West game—and that East, in turn, would have a better chance of winning.

After Pat answered, Mike put Mark on the line. Over the phone, Pat explained that surgery wasn't Colby's only option, that his season wasn't necessarily over. With a few more phone calls, the Careys arranged an appointment for Colby the following week with another Bucks County–based surgeon, Jim Bumgardner. There was no harm, and nothing to lose, in getting a second opinion.

Another cloudy autumn afternoon was giving way to nighttime as Larry Greene, wearing a navy-blue Windbreaker, interrupted an extra-point drill. Something had gone wrong. The snap was too high. Someone had missed a block. And this was just a drill during practice. In a real game, especially against an opponent such as Norristown, the whole sequence would have been doomed to fail.

"It's got to be perfect," Greene bellowed at his players. "This game could come down to one play."

When practice ended, a reporter approached Greene and thrust a sheet of paper at him before the coach could even walk off the practice field. Printed on the paper were the PIAA Class AAAA District One football standings, freshly updated after the season's sixth week. At the top of the list, tied with forty-eight district-playoff points apiece, were two of the only four undefeated teams left in the district. At the top of the list were Central Bucks West and Central Bucks East.

Greene glanced at the sheet, then made a face as if he had just tasted a small spurt of bile.

"You know, honestly, this list gets put in my box at school," he said, "and I don't even look at it. I just know that, if you focus on that, you're going to lose the next game."

Greene had a right and a reason to be so cautious. The Suburban One League National Conference had two tiers in 1998. More than halfway through the season, four elite teams—CB West, CB East, 5–1 Norristown, and 5–1 North Penn—had separated themselves from the rest of the conference. None of the bottom six teams—Council Rock, Neshaminy, Bensalem, Pennsbury, Harry S Truman, or Abington—had beaten any of the top four teams, and Norristown and North Penn's losses had come against the same opponent: CB West. By contrast, the combined record of East's first six opponents was 12–23, and the Patriots still had to play Norristown, North Penn, and West over the regular season's final four weeks, a brutal stretch that would start with a game early Saturday afternoon at Norristown.

West did not face so rigorous a schedule. Before closing their regular season against East, the Bucks had back-to-back road games against Bensalem and Truman, then hosted Council Rock. As far as Bryan Buckley was concerned, these teams weren't much more than something at which to sneer. West hadn't lost to Bensalem, for instance, in eleven years. Once, as he was walking out to the field before a game, Bryan overheard a Bensalem player mutter, "Please, don't beat us too bad." The Patriots didn't have the luxury of such a pregame psychological edge. Truth be told, they didn't have many luxuries left. Steve Kreider was playing well at quarterback; over his last five games, he had completed 64 percent of his passes and rushed for five touchdowns, more than any other quarterback in the National Conference. Bryan Scott was an ever-present threat. And Greene had transformed the phrase that he had used in the postgame huddle after East's season-opening win over Spring-Ford—"Nobody's talking about us"—into a rallying cry. "To tell you the truth," middle linebacker Phil Laing said to a reporter, "I don't mind being an underdog. It makes us better. We don't overlook teams we think we're better than. Keeps us sharp."

Still, the Patriots had the hardest road of the four potential district-playoff teams in the Suburban One League National Conference, and they wouldn't have Colby, they assumed, for the rest of the season. In fact, as the Norristown game approached, Colby's injury forced Greene to shift East's defense from a 4–3 alignment to a 4–4. Because Colby had demanded a double team from an opposing offensive line, the linebacker on his side of the field often went unblocked and found a free path to the ball carrier. Without Colby, the Patriots would need more run support from their linebackers, especially against the likes of Troy Swittenberg, Hikee Johnson, and Dustin Picciotti—Division I–caliber backs all.

"He's our most valuable offensive and defensive lineman," Greene said before leaving the practice field. "We'll miss him."

Mike Pettine was well aware of the volatility that accompanied coaching teenagers. At some stage of every season, there would be a natural lull for the players, a week or two where practices and daily obligations would feel rote and Pettine's admonishments about failing to stay focused would fall on deaf ears. The lull was, to a degree, understandable, because football filled so many of the players' hours outside the classroom, because fifteen-, sixteen-, and seventeen-year-old boys generally bore easily, and because Pettine had constructed a system of preparation from which he didn't dare deviate. Each week was exactly the same.

Sunday: Pettine met with his coaches at his home in the evening to break down the previous game's film, vote on the weekly individual awards (offensive and defensive players of the week, etc.), and make tentative suggestions for any adjustments on offense or defense.

Monday: A light practice commenced at 3:15 P.M. The linemen worked the blocking sled. The coaches installed new wrinkles into the game plan and walked the players through those changes. Each player went through a short workout with Joe Hallman, the strength coach, lifting heavy levels of weight. At five, Pettine dismissed the players for dinner. Many of them grabbed a bite to eat at Nat's Pizza, just a few blocks east on State Street. All of them were due back at the weight room at seven to review game films.

Tuesday: The first of the week's three full-contact practice days, Tuesday was for the defense. Because West employed multiple defensive formations, Pettine and Carey ran the Bucks through every adjustment of every defense to every offensive set that an opponent might use. The practice time would vary from two and a half hours to more than three, depending on how quickly the players picked up and carried out the adjustments and how important the upcoming game was. Hallman's postpractice weightlifting session worked the players' lower bodies through dumbbell lunges and leg presses.

Wednesday: As they had with the defenses, Pettine and Carey had the players run through every offensive play and repeat it through the three to five sets that West might use. An upper-body weight-room workout followed: bench presses, bicep curls, seated dumbbell presses.

Thursday: Pettine would rerun anything from Tuesday or Wednesday that required fine-tuning, then spend the remaining 80 percent of the practice on special-teams play. The team was usually off the field by 5 P.M. The players didn't lift weights on Thursdays, but Pettine would meet with them as a group to review various administrative details: when and where to report for the game, what to wear if the weather promised to be hot or cold or wet.

Friday: For a 7 P.M. home game, the players would report to West by 4:30; for a road game, they would report earlier. Once more, the players would walk through the various sets. Each position coach would conduct "committee meetings" with the players he oversaw. In the final team meeting, Pettine used a chalkboard to emphasize the most vital aspects of the game plan before delivering his pregame speech to the team.

Saturday: Everyone—players, coaches, parents—had the day off.

To combat complacency, Pettine and Carey wielded the power of potential embarrassment during the Monday night film sessions and the Thursday team meetings. In the sessions, the coaches provided cutting critiques of players' blocking, tackling, and knowledge of plays and formations. ("That's not CB West football," was perhaps the most common one. "Jesus Christ!" was a close second.) A CB West player who thought himself to be hot stuff after having a good game often found himself punished with extra conditioning drills the following week because of what Pettine and Carey had seen from him on the game film. On Thursdays, Pettine would select players at random and quiz them on their scouting reports. ("DiGiacomo, if Neshaminy comes out in a double-tight set, who's probably going to get the ball?") The fear of looking foolish motivated the players to study the playbook and to commit themselves to playing with the precision that Pettine expected of them. When it came to evaluating a player's performance, it didn't matter what the *Intelligencer* or the *Inquirer* had printed in their coverage of CB West's latest game, or what the local fans had shouted from the stands, or what the player's parents had told him once he had come home. In fact, the final score didn't matter all that much. What mattered, to Pettine, was what the film said and whether the player had done what the coaches had commanded of him, and there was always something imperfect on the film, something Pettine and Carey could demand that the player correct. And if they didn't demand it, Bryan Buckley would.

With the graduation of Corey Potter and Dave Armstrong, the nuclei of the '97 state-title team, and because of the trust he had engendered from Pettine and Carey, Bryan had established himself as first among equals on the team. Dustin Picciotti was the offensive star, with the astonishing statistics and his freakish athleticism, and Mike Orihel had the Hollywood looks and the relatively glamorous role as The First Sophomore Starting Quarterback Ever at West, but Bryan was the bridge between the coaches and the players. He was spokesman, sheriff, inspirer, interpreter. He had the authority, for instance, to approach a teammate who hadn't put forth a full effort in practice and say, "You're pissing me off, so you've got two options: I can go sit with Pettine and talk to him about you and how you're pissing me off, or you can do five hundred bellies right now." Over his more than two decades of coaching at West, Carey had considered Corey Potter the best leader he had encountered at the high school level, and from what he could see, Bryan had modeled himself after Potter. As had been the case with Potter, when Bryan spoke, the players listened to him, and, in Carey's words, Bryan was willing to "jack someone up" to accentuate his point, be it an opponent during a game or a lackadaisical teammate during a scrimmage. His method of leadership was to cultivate cachet by performing on the field at a higher level of ferocity and emotion than anyone else, by delivering the hardest hit or the biggest block. He carried himself with an intensity his teammates couldn't ignore. Orihel, for one, appreciated that. Bryan had won a state championship. He had credibility. Plus, Orihel figured, even if Bryan started screaming at you, it was a respite from having Pettine scream at you.

"Buckley was one of a kind," Pettine said later. "When you talk about peer-pressure leadership, there were a lot of problems I didn't have to deal with because he would settle them. He had high standards for himself, and when people around him were not responding, he didn't hesitate to get in their faces. He got frustrated when practice wasn't going well, when people around him weren't working hard, and he didn't hesitate to speak up, always from the heart, sincere. His buddies knew he meant business."

But his buddies were still teenagers, and after that one-point victory over North Penn in their most ballyhooed game of the regular season, the Bucks surrendered to human nature the following Friday against lowly Bensalem. They had a letdown. They were sloppy throughout the first half, committing three turnovers, missing tackles, blowing assignments. They led 21–0, mind you, but such a performance simply would not do. Pettine was not given to blistering halftime speeches; he generally saved dressing-downs for one-on-one moments. This time, he did not. If they didn't start playing better, he told the Bucks, "the next week of practice will be the worst week of your lives."

West scored thirty-three points in the third quarter, winning the game 62–7, setting the school record for points in a game. Picciotti rushed for 137 yards and four touchdowns on only thirteen carries and, while playing defensive end, added a quarterback sack. Bryan's assignment for the game was to key on Carlos Hernandez, Bensalem's best running back. Hernandez carried the football sixteen times for a net total of –1 yards.

After the game, Leo Carey, Mike Carey's father and one of Bryan's middle-school coaches, approached him.

"What do you think?" Leo said.

"I don't think we played too well, Coach," Bryan replied.

It was obvious that Larry Greene and his offensive coordinator, Bart Szarko, had to do something different. Their best lineman was standing with his teammates on the visiting sideline at Roosevelt Field in Norristown, but Colby Umbrell wore no helmet or pads. A pair of crutches kept him propped up, and across his face was that stern, square-jawed look that he got when things turned serious, and his voice was exploding forth from his mouth in bursts of "COME ON, EAST!" Katie Armstrong, one of the team managers, liked seeing that side of Colby. He was so quiet in the hallways at school during the week; it was as if he were holding in all his words and emotions from those five days, just so he could release them during a game, like a shaken bottle of seltzer. His exhorting was more urgent now, surely, because this was the Patriots' most important game so far and because there was nothing he could do to help East win except stand there in his white road jersey and scream out his support. He felt helpless. For things were serious now for the CB East Patriots.

They had begun wonderfully. Senior defensive back Ryan Callahan intercepted Norristown quarterback Kris Blake's first pass of the game, deep in the Eagles' territory. But on East's second offensive play, junior Chris Butts, one of the Patriots' starting guards, tumbled to the ground as he blocked a Norristown lineman. The fall broke Butts's right collarbone. With senior Gary Conover already filling in for Colby and with center Dave Bleam still out with *his* knee injury, Butts's absence meant that of the five linemen who were supposed to start for East when the season began, the Patriots were down to two. Norristown then blocked a thirty-six-yard field goal attempt by Tim Becker, the East placekicker, and later in the quarter, Swittenberg dashed thirty-one yards for a touchdown, giving Norristown a 6–0 lead. So yes, this was serious, and Greene and Szarko had to do something different. East was so shorthanded up front that the run blocking needed to free Bryan Scott wasn't likely to be there. The Patriots—Steve Kreider, actually—would have to throw the football to beat Norristown.

Entering the game, Roger Grove, Norristown's head coach, had anticipated that the Patriots might use Scott as often at flanker as they would use him at tailback. He told his defensive backs to play press coverage on Scott, to jam him at the line of scrimmage so that he couldn't run his routes. On the first play of the second quarter, though, with East at its own 37-yard line, Scott lined up wide to the right, and the Norristown cornerback charged with covering him failed to bump him as Scott started his route, a quick slant. Six yards downfield, Kreider hit Scott in stride, and because he had been facing single coverage, Scott had the middle of the field to himself, sprinting for a sixty-three-yard touchdown. Becker drilled the extra point. Fourteen seconds before halftime, he added a twenty-one-yard field goal to extend East's lead to 10–6.

Had Colby been healthy, had Dave Bleam been healthy, had Brandon Scott been healthy, had Chris Butts not ended up with his shoulder in a sling just seconds into the game, a four-point advantage would have seemed far more secure for the Patriots. After attempting thirteen passes in the first half, Kreider threw only three times in the second, but with their makeshift offensive line, the Patriots created little space for Scott to run and couldn't sustain a drive in the third quarter. Worse, a Norristown defender blindsided Scott on a draw play late in the period, jarring the ball loose, with the Patriots at their own 34. Perhaps Colby would have shielded Scott from that defender. Perhaps . . .

Norristown recovered Scott's fumble, and Swittenberg scored on a seven-yard run on the first play of the fourth quarter to put the Eagles ahead again, 12–10. On its next possession, East summoned one more march, moving to the Norristown 22-yard line, where on fourth down, six yards away from a first down, Greene confronted a choice that could change the Patriots' entire season. He could elect to go for it, or he could have Tim Becker, who hadn't made a field goal of more than thirty-five yards all season, attempt a thirty-nine-yard field goal. Four minutes and eleven seconds remained in the game. Even if they got the first down, the Patriots might not score. Even if Becker missed the field-goal attempt, the Patriots might get the ball back if they forced Norristown to punt.

One play to win the game.

Greene sent out Becker.

The snap was perfect.

The kick was short.

Colby dropped his head. That was it. That was East's last shot. Blake would have a subpar game, completing only five of his eighteen passes for forty-seven yards. Nevertheless, despite knowing that the Eagles would continue feeding Swittenberg the ball, East was no longer stout enough to stop him. With twenty-five carries and 177 yards in the game, the Syracuse recruit was applying death slashes to East's undefeated season with every handoff. Five yards . . . Four yards . . . Three yards . . . Five yards . . . He ground East's defense down to dust. Standing on the sideline next to Colby, Kreider shared his friend's feeling of helplessness. The previous season, Kreider had lost the starting quarterback competition to senior Justin Habel, in part because Kreider could start at linebacker and Habel couldn't and Greene wanted to maximize his talent on each side of the ball. Kreider wanted to be back out at linebacker now, to do something, anything, to stop Norristown's offense, but he hadn't played linebacker all year. East's backup quarterback, Josh Felicetti, was just a ninth-grader, and after all the injuries the Patriots already had sustained, the risk of losing Kreider was too great for Greene to send him out there. Steve Kreider stayed just a quarterback, stayed there next to Colby, as Troy Swittenberg and Norristown ran those final four minutes off the clock and broke the Patriots' hearts.

In the skeletal set of bleachers behind Roosevelt Field's visitors' bench, Kreider saw a group of high-school-aged guys descending the creaky steps as the game ended. The guys were wearing lettermen's jackets, black with gold lettering. There was Phil DiGiacomo. There was Matt Carey. There was Bryan Buckley. They had come to check out CB East, wondering if the team they regarded as second-best in their school district might also be the second-best team in the state. They admired East's effort, but they weren't afraid of the Patriots, not when East was so shorthanded. That was the most galling part to Kreider: He and his teammates had laid themselves bare, had lost by two lousy points, and in his mind, the game hadn't come down to one play. It hadn't come down to Scott's fumble or Becker's missed field goal. It had come down to what John Marmor, an East assistant coach, said to him as the two trudged off the field together.

"If we have Umbrell," Marmor said, "we win that game."

When determining whether a patient needs surgery to repair a torn anterior cruciate ligament, an orthopedic surgeon—perhaps literally, perhaps only in his or her mind—draws a graph. The horizontal axis plots the level of instability that the injury has caused to the knee. Damage to the ACL can lead to what doctors call *pivot shift episodes*, in which the patient feels as though the injured knee is slipping out of place or will give out, but that slippage varies from person to person and from knee to knee. If the collateral ligaments, menisci, and muscles around the torn ACL are strong and tight, the knee may remain stable enough for an athlete to continue participating in his or her sport.

The vertical axis plots the demand on the injured knee—that is, the amount of stress placed on the knee each day. Once a surgeon—for instance, Jim Bumgardner, who was now examining Colby in Bumgardner's office in Sellersville, a town set in the pastoral upper part of Bucks County—is familiar with the severity of a patient's injury and the knee's reaction to stress, the surgeon weighs the knee's instability and demand against each other in judging whether to recommend surgery. If a businessman's knee shows minimal instability, and if the greatest demand he places on his knee is his five-minute walk from the train station to his office, he may never require an operation to repair his ACL. But for a football player—whether one in high school or in the NFL—who undergoes two hours of strenuous practices and workouts each day and who can't plant his foot without feeling that his leg will crumple, surgery is a necessity.

With his injury, Colby fell between those two extremes, into an area where a doctor has some leeway in making a diagnosis and recommendation. Cody had taken a cautious tack in suggesting that Colby needed the surgery right away; Bumgardner saw another alternative. None of the other ligaments or musculature in Colby's knee had sustained any trauma, and because Colby was in such fine physical shape—240 pounds with 5 percent body fat—his knee, protected by a brace, could withstand the stress of playing football. Colby had torn his ACL completely; it would be painful for him to play, and his mobility and the knee's range of motion would be limited, but he couldn't damage the ligament further. Had Colby been a collegiate or professional football player, or if the injury had occurred earlier in the season, Bumgardner would have insisted on immediate surgery. Playing in East's next game, against North Penn, was still an impossibility, but if Colby could put up with the pain, Bumgardner saw no reason, provided he rehabilitated the knee with vigor, that he couldn't suit up for CB East's final two games: at Bensalem on Saturday, October 31, and, of course, against CB West on November 7.

This was what Colby and Mark had hoped to hear. On their way home, they had another stop to make, had to elicit the assistance of one more former CB West football player. Eric Bass had been the starting fullback for Central Bucks High in 1967, Mike Pettine's first season as a high school head coach. That team went 9–0–1, and in the years since, Bass, after playing under Joe Paterno at Penn State, had coached CB West's and Delaware Valley College's track and field teams and remained a loyal follower of West football and devotee of all things Pettine. Bald, wearing a thin black mustache, Bass was fond of saying that he would "go run through barbed wire" for Pettine—he said it, as a matter of fact, the night that Pettine won his three hundredth game—and West players were always welcome at the business he now owned, Doylestown Aquatic Therapy. In the early 1980s, Bass had invented the Aqua Ark—a hydrotherapy tank seven feet deep in which patients were strapped into a harness and suspended in water heated to 98 degrees. (He sold his first ark to the Philadelphia Eagles.) Doctors and trainers already used hydrotherapy to treat sports injuries, but Bass's ark allowed athletes to maintain their cardiovascular conditioning while getting an earlier start on the rehabilitation process. A long-distance runner who had sustained a stress fracture in his foot, for example, no longer had to sit around his house for three weeks, waiting for the fracture to heal, before he could begin running again. He could simply lower himself into Bass's tank and, in a matter of speaking, walk on water.

Mark and Colby asked Bass if Colby could carry out his two and a half weeks of rehab at Bass's therapy center in town. As a freshman at Penn State, Bass had traded reps in a backfield that featured Franco Harris and Lydell Mitchell before a broken ankle sent him to the bench. "The biggest thing I learned," he said years later, "is not to make football your whole life. You can't put your hopes and dreams in one basket." Now, he had a chance to give this kid sitting in front of him—even if it was a CB East kid—a second shot at the sport and the rivalry Colby treasured so much. Bass understood. He said yes. When the time was right, Colby would have to persuade only two more people that he could indeed play in East's last two regular-season games—and in any postseason games, should the Patriots knock off North Penn.

In retrospect, Anthony Greene would admit, it was silly for the CB East players to be so confident as they entered the game that could effectively end their attempt to reach the district playoffs. That close Norristown loss, though, had filled them with a false sense of optimism, a belief that if they could push Norristown to the brink even when they were without so many key components, then they certainly could upset North Penn at War Memorial Field. After all, "on film, Norristown was a hundred percent better than North Penn," Greene said years later. "We had the sense that those guys didn't hit as hard as Norristown."

They were wrong. North Penn never completed a forward pass against East—and never needed to. The Knights piled up 392 rushing yards against East's depleted defensive line, had a three-touchdown lead by halftime, and rolled to a 28–6 victory. Michael Pettine had devised a series of box-and-one-style defenses to stymie Bryan Scott, to prevent him from breaking the sorts of big plays that had been his hallmark all season, and the defenses worked: Scott had ninety-seven rushing yards but didn't score until midway through the fourth quarter. "They bulldozed us," Anthony Greene said, and there wasn't surprise in the Patriots' eyes after the game as much as there was resignation, an acknowledgment that they were unable to match their effort against Norristown and that it had been unrealistic to expect themselves to do so. Now 6–2, the Patriots were sixth in the District One Class AAAA standings, and only four teams constituted the District One tournament. To have any hope of qualifying for the playoffs, not only did the Patriots have to beat Bensalem and West, but the teams in front of them had to start losing games, too. In the span of two weeks and two excruciating losses, the playoffs had become a pipe dream.

That the Patriots' season was likely to end after they played West did nothing to lessen Colby's desire to return to the lineup. Less than twenty-four hours after the North Penn loss, he, Mark, and Nancy met Larry Greene and John Reading, East's trainer, at the school to discuss the prospect of Colby's playing again, and if anything, the two-game losing streak might make it easier for the Umbrells to sell Greene and Reading on the idea of Colby's coming back. It was only two games, and they meant so much to him, particularly that second game, against West, and already there had been a buzz around the team that Colby might try to play. Bryan Scott had told Colby that he wasn't sure such a quick return was a good idea. "If I can walk," Colby told him, "I can play." Phil Laing, the Patriots' senior middle linebacker, had missed the final six games of the '97 season after tearing the ACL in his right knee. He had spent eight months rehabilitating it. *If Colby comes back from this*, Laing told his teammates, *he's a freak of nature*. Even Colby himself didn't count on his performing at his pre-injury level. He wanted only to play as well as the players who had taken his place, and he thought his return might serve as some inspiration for his teammates.

At first, Reading was apprehensive. In his previous five years as East's trainer, he had never known a student-athlete who had torn his or her anterior cruciate ligament and attempted to play before having surgery. He reminded Colby and his parents what the worst-case scenario was. Without an ACL, the bone in Colby's knee could slide around and damage the cartilage, which could lead to arthroscopic surgery.

Greene, meanwhile, simply couldn't believe that Colby could play on one and a half legs.

"Has this all been cleared by a doctor?" he asked.

Wielding a note from Bumgardner, Colby, Mark, and Nancy explained that the musculature around Colby's knee was preventing that sliding and that his murderous two-hour sessions in Eric Bass's ark were keeping that musculature strong. Once he heard that a doctor had green-lighted Colby's return and that Mark and Nancy supported the idea, Greene wasn't going to stand in the way. He and Reading agreed that Colby could practice with the team and suit up the following week against Bensalem.

While Colby was rehabbing and East was slipping out of the postseason picture, Bryan Buckley was starting to lose patience with his teammates. The lethargy with which the Bucks had played against Bensalem had lingered like a cold into their next game, a 35–0 victory over the Harry S Truman Tigers. Bryan hated playing against Truman; he always seemed to leave the field sore and feeling as though he hadn't played well—feeling as though, for once, his opponent had been the aggressor. The scoreboard suggested that West had dominated the game, but the Tigers, as they had earlier in the season against CB East, played with an edge, a nastiness, that seemed to shock the Bucks. Truman forced two West fumbles in the first half, and early in the second half, Tigers defensive back Mike St. Martine delivered a thunderclap hit on Chris Ortiz, who was seeing his first game action since his preseason knee injury. St. Martine's helmet collided with Ortiz's chin, knocking Ortiz out cold and sending him to a nearby hospital with a concussion. The Tigers were tough kids from tough neighborhoods, and what they lacked in talent and innate football instincts, they made up for in sheer guts. That didn't bother Bryan. He respected such an attitude. What bothered him was his teammates' reaction to it.

More and more, Bryan heard players moaning about Pettine, muttering under their breath how tired they were of the coach and his grueling practice schedule. Some of them said that they might turn in their uniforms and quit. Bryan had heard similar complaints throughout his two previous seasons and had dismissed them, so though he considered addressing the team about his concerns in the days leading into West's October 31 meeting with the Council Rock Indians, he never did. Besides, Pettine often could defuse such discontent with a colorful aphorism cut with a warning: "You guys have been eating filet mignon so long that maybe you need a piece of crud thrown in your face." This was a longtime tactic that Pettine used whenever he sensed complacency settling in. As with the film critiques, Pettine's goal was to scare his team straight without sacrificing a long winning streak, and he usually succeeded. Still, it was a fine line for him to walk. The fear of losing was a hellacious motivator, but how could Pettine make his players understand how much it hurt to lose just one game when most of them hadn't experienced that hurt yet? Bryan understood, of course; the memory of that Plymouth Whitemarsh playoff loss his sophomore year had never left his mind. That loss was, to a certain degree, *his* loss because he had been a starter in 1996. Most of his fellow seniors now hadn't started that game, and none of West's sophomores and juniors was on the varsity team then. Over more than a season and a half, no mistake that any of them had made had cost West a victory, so it was natural that such a winning streak would cultivate a measure of collective arrogance. At times, Pettine felt like a parent dealing with disobedient children who kept holding their hands over a hot stove, who learned their lesson only after their skin was singed.

And here was the heat, against Council Rock. A victory would clinch a district-playoff spot for the Bucks, yet they played as if the game had no importance to them at all. They committed eight penalties, most of them illegal-motion infractions, in the first half. A muffed punt in the second quarter led to a Council Rock field goal, and Rock scored its first touchdown after a snap sailed over the head of West punter Justin McDonnell early in the third quarter. When the Indians pulled off a successful two-point conversion, West's lead was down to 14–11.

After an interception by sophomore defensive back Dave Camburn, Pettine showed how deep his trust for Bryan ran. The Bucks had fumbled four times in the game, and with West at the Rock 1-yard line midway through the fourth quarter, Pettine sought a ball carrier who, above all, would protect the football. He lined Bryan up at fullback and had Mike Orihel hand off to him. Bryan plunged into the end zone for his third touchdown of the season, giving West what seemed a comfortable 21–11 lead.

That lead appeared even more comfortable with two and a half minutes left in the fourth quarter and Rock pinned at its 14-yard line, until it wasn't so comfortable anymore. Matt Verbit, the Council Rock quarterback, fired a pass twenty yards downfield toward Camburn's waiting arms. His second interception of the game and another West win were mere formalities; all he had to do was catch the ball.

He didn't.

Camburn tried to bat the ball out of bounds, but the ball skimmed off his fingertips, deflecting to Rock wide receiver Chris Mahony, who was behind the entire West secondary. Mahony zipped down the right sideline for an eighty-six-yard touchdown. The Indians were within a touchdown, 21–17, and could tie the game with a field goal, assuming Rock coach Mike Ortman elected to kick an extra point.

He didn't.

Ortman had coached at Rock for more than a decade, was as familiar as anyone with West's dominance of the Suburban One League, and he wanted no part of an overtime period against the Bucks. This was what West's reputation did to other coaches: it removed logic from their strategy, shattered the play-it-safe approach. "They can kick the stuffing out of us in overtime," Ortman would say after this game, so if there was a way for his team to beat West in regulation, he would take it. One way or another, the Indians would attempt an onside kick, so why not set up a scenario in which a field goal could win the game? Ortman decided to go for two.

Verbit's pass was incomplete. The Bucks retained their four-point edge. All they had to do to win the game was recover Rock's onside kick.

They didn't.

Alex Wade, the Indians' standout running back, fell on the football at the Bucks' 39 with two minutes, twenty seconds left in regulation.

For the first time since his first loss as a varsity player at West, Bryan allowed an unnerving thought to seep in: *Holy crap, we might lose this game.*

Needing a touchdown to win instead of a field goal to tie, Ortman called a screen pass on third-and-7. Verbit's pass caromed off the hands of running back Corey Jones. West defensive end Damien Smith intercepted it.

Afterward, Pettine wasn't so much angry as he was dazed, telling reporters that the win "was one of those abstracts, with the chimp throwing paint on the canvas." He wasn't so pithy with his players. This time, there was no rainstorm to foul up a game plan, no potential playoff opponent on the other sideline. Rock was a middle-of-the-road team in the National Conference, and West had come within a couple of deflected passes of giving a game away.

"What the hell was that?" Pettine asked in the cramped weight room. "Does anyone have anything to say?"

Amid the silence in the room and the odors of dead grass and dried sweat, Bryan stood to speak.

"A lot of you guys are saying, 'I don't want to do this anymore. I want to quit.' Then be a man right now. Give me your pads and walk out, because I don't want to be around guys like that. If you have any doubts in your mind, get out."

He turned to the coaching staff, lined up to his left.

"You want to yell at someone? From now on, just yell at me. I don't care. These guys are being prima donnas, getting their feelings hurt? That's their problem. This is my team, and I'm not losing."

Saturday, October 31, 1998

His knee was weak, wrapped in a heavy brace to keep it stable, but the rest of Colby Umbrell felt fresh and free and strong again, out on the football field at Bensalem High School. He played only offensive tackle in his first game since his injury; there was less risk in having him know where he was supposed to go on the field than in having him play defensive tackle, a more reactive position. It was safer for him to act on an opponent than to be acted upon. Colby was, at best, half the lineman he had been before tearing his ACL, Larry Greene guessed, but half of Colby was enough to throw a key block to spring Bryan Scott for a forty-six-yard touchdown run, to pave the way for Scott's thirty-carry, 214-yard night, to ignite a 21–7 East victory.

"It brought morale back up," Colby said after the game.

The confidence boost came at a welcome time. Yes, reaching the district playoffs was out of the question now—Norristown and North Penn had won the night before, eliminating East from contention—but the Patriots would settle for the satisfaction of upsetting West. The Bucks were reeling—as much as a 9–0 football team could reel, that is—and beating them seemed more likely now that East was coming off a win instead of three consecutive losses. Hey, anything was possible. Colby Umbrell had come back in three weeks and played pretty much on one leg.

"And I'll play against West," Colby said.

In the upper bleachers, a sense of calm came over Mark and Nancy as they looked down at Colby, mingling with the other East players after the game. For a night, their worries over what Colby was going to do about his knee and his football career and his life after high school had receded. They saw him playing. They saw him happy. For a night, that was enough.

SEVEN

Traditions

From the time she was a tot, Casey Umbrell recognized the exalted place that football, particularly the rivalry between Central Bucks West and Central Bucks East, held in her family, even if she herself wasn't enamored with the sport. Three years younger than Colby, she was a fan first of the Flyers, Philadelphia's professional ice hockey team, just as a matter of preference, and as a ninth-grader at Lenape Middle School, she rarely saw her brother play football. Casey was a member of CB West's marching band, so whenever and wherever the Bucks were playing on a Friday night, she was, too, and her clarinet kept her from attending most of Colby's games during his senior season.

When these obligations of their eldest children conflicted, Mark and Nancy usually went to watch Colby play. Casey also swam for West's varsity team; swimming was "her thing" in the way football was Colby's thing, and because swimming season didn't begin until after football season had ended, Mark and Nancy were as diligent about attending Casey's meets as they were about attending Colby's games. But in the fall, East football came first, as it had for Mark while he was still in high school, as it had on Friday nights while Colby and Casey were growing up. Casey understood that, and if at times she wished her parents could get to a few more of her marching-band performances, her close relationship with Colby undercut whatever resentment she might have felt toward him.

Teenage boys often consider little sisters embarrassments, annoyances to be tolerated. Colby did not. He picked Casey up after she finished her swimming practices and band rehearsals. (West did not have a pool on its campus. East did. So West's swimming team held its meets at East, just as East played its football games at West, though the Umbrells and the rest of East's football boosters didn't exactly consider it an equal trade-off.) He invited her and her friends to hang out with him and his friends. In ninth grade, Casey began to grow into a woman, and her slender swimmer's build and outgoing nature caught the attention of a West senior. His attention caught Colby's attention. Believing that any twelfth-grade male who was interested in a ninth-grade female could not have the best of intentions, Colby one day waited in the West parking lot for the prospective gentleman caller, his fists balled, until a mortified Casey shooed her overprotective brother away, assuring him the senior's advances weren't working. She couldn't stay angry at Colby for anything, really. Once, as the Umbrells relaxed at their resort during a family vacation to Disneyworld, Colby began teasing Casey, pushing things a little too far, delivering one punch line after another until she became upset. He knew what he had done. How could he make her smile? So five minutes later, with the whole family looking on and laughing, there was Colby in the middle of the hotel room, singing Michael Jackson's "Thriller," reenacting the movements of those line-dancing zombies from the song's famous video, the expression on his face one of utter concentration, as if he were Baryshnikov performing in *Giselle*. Casey took one look at him and laughed, too. She considered him her best friend. That dance, that expression, was why.

This upcoming game left her with conflicted emotions. Between her preseason swimming practices at East and her band rehearsals at West,

Casey could see how the rivalry and the game gripped the students at each school—the confidence of the kids at West, the hope of the kids at East. In her heart, she was praying for the Patriots to pull off an upset, just so her brother could celebrate it. For almost a month now, Colby's torn ACL and the cumbersome brace on his left knee had made him as stiff-legged as Frankenstein's monster. Just climbing the flight of stairs to his bedroom was a chore for him, and though she knew Colby could function with the injury, Casey winced whenever her brother had to get up and get around the house. She'd love to have him rewarded for, as she put it later, "being such a trooper." She'd hate to see him hurt himself worse in this game, of all games.

There were responsibilities and rituals throughout the week before every East-West game, both for those who played and coached and for those who were on the periphery of the rivalry. After decorating their respective hallways in their school colors, the students traded pranks. In 1997, for instance, some East students infiltrated West's Friday afternoon pep rally and released mice into the gymnasium. The cheerleaders stopped kicking and started shrieking. The following year, Mike Orihel received a few phone calls at his home from anonymous voices telling him he was too young and too scared to be a varsity quarterback. "They were trying to psych me out," he would say later. Each school's campus featured a large, beige-gray boulder on the lawn of its front quadrangle, and each rock was a prime target for good-natured graffiti. Jenna Menard, East's senior class president, lived just two minutes from East and kept a supply of red, white, and blue paint at her house year-round, just in case a group of saboteurs had sneaked into Buckingham in the dead of night and slathered the word *WEST* onto East's rock in black and gold. (Both sides also often wielded honey and feathers as aesthetic weaponry.) Twice in the days leading into the '98 game, Menard arrived at school only to see the rock, turn her car around, and drive back home to pick up her cans of paint.

On the Wednesday before the game, the teams' coaches, their seniors, and the seniors' families gathered to have dinner together, a sort
of pregame peace offering over rubbery chicken and mealy green beans.
In the earlier years of the rivalry, when East and West played on Thanksgiving, the dinner would be held at the Doylestown Moose Lodge, on
the eastern side of the borough, but once the game was no longer necessarily the season's bookend for both teams, the dinner's site alternated
annually between the schools' cafeterias. This time, the dinner was at
West, and it was the last place that Bryan Buckley wanted to be. He
was not in the rosiest of moods. For one thing, he was fighting a fever,
spending much of his time during the week in the office of West athletics trainer Sean Kelly, wrapped in a blanket. For another, he had decided
two days earlier that he had something more to say to the Bucks' seniors, something beyond his postgame address after West's victory over
Council Rock, something best said out of the earshot of the team's juniors and sophomores. Despite winning their previous three games by
an aggregate score of 118–17, the Bucks, according to the yardstick
by which Mike Pettine measured them, were in a slump. The number
of unforced mistakes that West had made against Council Rock had
served as a conclusive signal that the players' concentration was slipping, and Bryan believed that the seniors had not done enough to
shake the team out of its collective complacency. During the players'
two hours of free time Monday between practice and the weekly film
session, Bryan called the seniors into the weight room, and he called
them out.

Their play over the last three weeks? Soft, he said.

Their work ethic over that time? Lazy, he said.

"We should blow the doors off East," he told the seniors. "They
shouldn't hang with us. But when we get to the playoffs, we're going
to have some tough games."

His disregard for East was borne out of his belief that the Patriots,
aside from Bryan Scott, barely posed a threat to the Bucks, that Pettine
and Mike Carey would devise a scheme to render Scott—and, in turn,

the rest of East's one-dimensional offense—irrelevant. The most concerning matter to Bryan was whether the Bucks would play with the same alacrity and emotion that they did during the first five games of their season. The result, he believed, was predictable: West would win; East would lose. That outcome had repeated itself twenty-six times in twenty-nine years, and Bryan was certain that it would happen again. He liked the guys at East. He had gone to middle school with many of them, including Colby, and he counted one of them, defensive end Troy Lavinia, as a good buddy, but the notion of having the players dine together just rubbed him the wrong way. Why bother with the kabuki theater of shaking hands and breaking bread with the opponents you planned to pound in three days? Oh, and as an added irritant, the East players and coaches were twenty minutes late for the dinner.

"Do you believe this shit?" Carey asked him.

Carey's indignation was rather convenient. After all, the Bucks could practice at War Memorial Field if they wanted. They could practice longer than East. They could practice under *lights*. The Patriots didn't have that luxury, and because the scouting report and preparation for West were so much more detailed and complex, Larry Greene needed every last available glimmer of daylight. Every night that week, he drilled his players until they left the practice field amid pitch blackness. It was an advantage West had long enjoyed. In the run-up to a couple of Thanksgiving games in the late 1970s and early 1980s, former East coach Chuck Rocconi would order his players, once the sun had gone down, to park their cars so that the headlights were facing the practice field. Then he told them to leave the headlights on and return to practice. Given that East's practice field was set on a hill, those cars couldn't have cast much helpful illumination, but Rocconi was desperate. He presumed, apparently, that the players would remember to carry jumper cables.

Greene and the Patriots did what they could in the darkness. The defensive starters made up the scout team's offense, so as to best simulate what West's offense might do. "We were overloaded with information,"

Anthony Greene recalled. "They ran the same plays out of every formation. They had no tendencies. It was like, 'Out of this formation, fifteen percent of the time, they run this, and fifteen percent of the time, they run that.'"

Reasoning that Pettine and Carey would have West's defense keying on Bryan Scott, Greene and his offensive coordinator, Bart Szarko, planned to use Scott as a decoy as much as possible. They would still feed Scott the football, of course, but fullback Mark Notwick had emerged as such an effective weapon since entering the starting lineup that Greene and Szarko hoped to have him carry the ball enough to keep the Bucks off balance. To that end, Colby was taking reps almost exclusively with the first-team offense. Having Colby, on one good leg, try to fight off one or more of West's linemen just to tangle with Dustin Picciotti didn't seem to make much sense.

Since Mark Umbrell's visit to the New Britain Inn, Carey had come to marvel over Colby's return to the lineup. In the early 1980s, Carey's cousin Frank Naylor had played a short while for the USFL's New Jersey Generals before an ACL tear ended his career. Naylor never had his ACL repaired and still walked in constant pain from the injury. From what they could see of Colby on East's game films, Carey and Pettine knew that he didn't have the same quickness that he had displayed earlier in the season. Nevertheless, the two kings of West's program couldn't help admiring Colby for the courage he was showing simply by suiting up.

"This would have been a whole different season for you guys," Pettine told Nancy Umbrell during the dinner, "if he hadn't gone down."

Saturday, November 7, 1998

By 7:30 P.M., kickoff time, eight thousand people had filed into War Memorial Field, most of them squeezing themselves into bleacher seats, the rest snaking around the stadium and leaning against the fence that encircled the football field. As a member of East's homecoming court,

Jenna Menard had ridden to the stadium in the annual East-West parade. Each extracurricular organization at the schools entered its own float, and the procession of cars snaked along Main and State streets through downtown Doylestown, out Court Street to War Memorial. She had considered wearing a sweatshirt and jeans and painting her face as a show of school spirit for the parade, but she opted for a dress and a warm coat instead, which, if nothing else, pleased her mother.

On a night when the temperature hovered in the high thirties and a slight rain earlier in the day had left War Memorial's remaining grass dewy, five male students from East stood in the stands, each of them shirtless, each of them with a letter painted in blue on his chest to spell out *Y-O-U-N-G*. They were the personal fan club of junior Chris Young, one of the Patriots' starters on the offensive line, and they ejected vapor from their mouths as they cheered in the chill. Bill and Connie Buckley took their customary seats in the center of the home stands; Bill had his video camera at the ready.

Her white vest crisp, her black-and-gold sash a hypotenuse from her right shoulder to her left hip, eye black smeared above her cheeks, Casey Umbrell high-stepped in with the West marching band. The scene reminded her of how Hollywood depicted high school football in the movies—the fans dressed in their teams' colors, the bands blaring those stadium staples "Gimme Some Lovin'" and "Rock and Roll, Part 2," local pride on the line. Her parents strained to see her from East's side of the stadium.

On the field, each player and coach paused, however briefly, to consider the magnitude of the moment. A ninth-grader, Bobby Hulmes, East's backup fullback, had not begun playing football competitively until he was in seventh grade at Our Lady of Mount Carmel School, the Catholic elementary school in Doylestown Borough. Hulmes was barely aware that the rivalry had existed until coaches from East and West started showing up at his CYO games, trying to coax him to come to their respective schools. The next year, Hulmes was on the East sideline for the 1997 game. Now, he was in uniform, and the Patriots' entire season had seemed to be built around this game. "I was really kind of in awe," he said years later.

Mike Pettine and Mike Carey waited to find out the effect of a major change that they had made Thursday to West's offensive line. As he had headed out to the practice field, Carey walked past senior tackle Chris Havener and, recalling that the Bucks had fumbled fifteen snaps from center in their first nine games, asked Havener if he ever had played center. Yes, Havener said, in middle school. So, at 6 P.M. on Thursday, two nights before West's tenth, and arguably most important, regular-season game, Chris Havener became the Bucks' starting center. The move was unusual for the Bucks, if only because Pettine wouldn't normally be inclined to take such a risk before the East-West game. Truth be told, Pettine didn't relish the pageantry and tradition of the rivalry. "I hated the game in the sense that we were in a no-win situation," he said later. "We could be 9–0, and if we lost that game, our season was a disaster." A football team, Pettine believed, got "super-piqued" for at most three games in a season, and he always felt that East-West would be a super-pique game for the Patriots but not necessarily for his team because West was expected to win. "I can just remember some of those East-West games," Pettine said later, "looking out at the level of play, and they're knocking our chin straps off, and I'm thinking, 'This is not the same team I scouted on film.' They had just raised themselves up to a level that was amazing."

Bryan Buckley was as relaxed as he allowed himself to be before a big game. The 1996 game, when East and West were each 9–0—that was stressful. That was *crazy*. He had stood on the field next to Dave Armstrong, who told him, "This will be your biggest East-West game—as a sophomore." Compared to that night, this was a vacation. His arms, pale and bulky, branched out from beneath his shoulder pads. He wasn't wearing sleeves. Neither was Colby Umbrell. Colby couldn't feel the cold or the ache in his knee, so excited was he to be out there for what, win or lose, would be his final high school football game.

The two of them joined their fellow team captains at midfield for the coin toss. West won the toss and elected to receive. Among the nine captains, Bryan and Colby were the last ones to shake hands.

Mark Mattern, the soccer player who served as East's kickoff specialist, booted the ball to the West 15, and Dave Edwards fielded the kick and found an open lane near the left hash mark. Only Scott and his speed saved the Patriots from surrendering a touchdown on the play. The last man for Edwards to beat, Scott knocked him out of bounds at the East 42. On second down, Pettine called a play-action fake and a downfield throw, a sure sign that the Bucks were bent on burying East quickly. But Orihel, rolling to his left, underthrew the pass, and East safety Nick Mellors dived to intercept it at the Patriots' 9-yard line. The Patriots' sideline and the people in the visiting stands, Mark and Nancy included, erupted in sound. Maybe, for the first time in fifteen years, it was to be East's night.

A false-start penalty on first down—not the way to begin your first offensive series—pushed the Patriots back to their 4-yard line. Scott was getting the ball now. Fifteen yards for a first down, and he could pick up all that and more just by slipping through the slightest crease. Colby lined up at right tackle. Injured or not, he was the Patriots' best lineman, and they were going to run behind him. Bryan lined up across from him. Former teammates and former schoolmates now sharing such similar roles on their respective teams—what collision could have better represented the rivalry?

Steve Kreider handed the ball to Scott. Colby fired out of his stance toward the inside of the line, lowering his right shoulder, cutting down Bryan with a perfect drive block. On his back, turtlelike, Bryan reached up at Scott but didn't touch him, the tailback gliding past him for an eight-yard gain.

The East fans roared again. Casey Umbrell didn't. She couldn't. West band members weren't supposed to cheer when something went right for East, and even if she had been allowed to, she was too nervous to cheer. She was afraid for her brother, checking after each play to make sure that he was upright again. Ten years later, as she spoke of this game, she said that she could feel her heart beating faster in her chest, just as it did that night.

The momentum that Scott's eight-yard burst generated was a mere flash fire. The Bucks gang-tackled him for a two-yard loss on the next play, and Bryan atoned for Colby's flattening of him by breaking through East's offensive line and dragging down Scott for a seven-yard loss on third down, forcing the Patriots to punt. That drive-killer began what might have been the worst four-play sequence of Scott's brilliant high school career, and Bryan Buckley would be the cause of half of Scott's misery.

After Orihel's interception, Pettine wouldn't be of the mind to throw the ball again immediately, and it was moments such as this that made Dustin Picciotti snicker. From Picciotti's perspective, Pettine liked to pay lip service to limiting the fullback's carries, but when the Bucks needed to score, the stubborn coach sure did lean on him a lot. From the East 40, Picciotti gained only two yards on first down. Second down was different. Scott charged in from the right side on a safety blitz. Bryan, at wingback, met him head-on. Appearing surprised, Scott pulled up as Bryan braced to block him, denying Bryan the chance to jack up a future NFL strong safety by taking himself out of the play, and Picciotti was gone, chugging thirty-eight yards for a touchdown.

On the ensuing kickoff, West employed a tactic that it used from time to time throughout the season. Rather than have kicker Bob Tumelty boom the ball deep down the middle of the field, giving the returner—in this case, the dangerous Scott—more room to run, the Bucks' coaches would have Tumelty chip a high, short kick toward the right sideline. For Scott to catch the ball, he would have to sprint forward fifteen yards, and if he did catch it, the sideline would force him to run back toward the middle of the field, where West's coverage team would be waiting. If another East player tried to catch the kick, West was in a win-win situaation. The player, slower and less sure-handed than Scott, was more likely to muff or fumble the kick, and even if he did catch it, he was virtually no threat to rip off a long return.

So Tumelty fluttered the kickoff toward the sideline, and for Scott, there was no alternative. Twice, he had played West. Twice, he had lost. He relished the idea that a team would shadow him, would commit so much of its strategy to stopping him. He would win this game by himself, if he had to.

He sprinted forward to catch the ball.

And dropped it.

Gavin Potter, Corey's younger brother and a sophomore special-teams player for West, recovered at the East 40. Nine plays later, Edwards dashed twelve yards off left tackle for West's second score. It was 14–0, and East had run all of three offensive plays. Three more, and East punted again, and the Bucks drove sixty yards for a four-yard Picciotti touchdown run. With eleven minutes left in the second quarter, West led 21–0. Half the stadium was silent. The game was getting away from the Patriots. Mike Dougherty, East's special-teams coach, stared across the field at Pettine, muttering, "You SOB" to himself out of admiration. During Dougherty's four years as a student at Bishop Egan High in Bristol, Pennsylvania, in the late 1960s, Egan had won three Philadelphia city championships, and Dougherty went to every one of those victories. But compared to West, those teams that Dougherty had treasured as a teenager might as well have been playing two-hand touch. The Bucks weren't doing anything that the Patriots hadn't seen them do on film. They weren't fancy. They weren't fooling anyone. They just didn't make any mistakes, and it frustrated the hell out of Dougherty.

Finally, East's offense started moving the ball on its third possession, mostly by falling back on the coaches' pregame plan to use Scott as a decoy. On the first play, Scott shifted out of the backfield and lined up as a wideout, and three West defensive backs followed him, allowing running back Mike Taylor to pick up four yards on an inside handoff.

From their 19-yard line, the Patriots advanced seventy-three yards in thirteen plays, and Scott touched the ball only four times. The drive set up the game's critical play: third down and goal for East from the West 8-yard line, less than four minutes before halftime. Scott was fresher now. Colby had been at right tackle every play of the possession, his left leg hardly a bother. The time for decoys had passed, Larry Greene and Bart Szarko decided. If the Patriots were to cut West's lead to two scores, if they were to get back in this game, they would do so with their two best players.

After all, it had been fifteen years.

Kreider pitched the ball to Scott, seven yards deep in the backfield, and at right tackle, Colby rose out of his stance to take on Bob Bowser, one of West's defensive tackles. At six feet two and 235 pounds, Bowser was of comparable size to Colby, but he had an advantage: two intact anterior cruciate ligaments. Bowser shifted his hands to the left side of Colby's upper body and pushed. The only way that Colby could have sustained his block would have been to plant his left foot and lock his left knee. He staggered backward, and Bowser lumbered forward. Colby tried to backtrack and block Bowser a second time, but it was too late. Scott had nowhere to go. Bowser wrapped him up for a twelve-yard loss. Colby hung his head.

Greene then sent out Tim Becker to attempt a thirty-three-yard field goal into a 15-mph wind. Becker's kick fell in front of the crossbar like a dying dream. West needed less than two minutes to score again: an eight-yard touchdown pass from Orihel to tight end Bryan Colahan.

Halftime: West 28, East 0.

"What happened?" Greene asked Tony Schino, one of his assistants. "Why aren't we able to play with these guys? How have they gotten so good?"

Small victories, as usual, were all that East was left with. The final score was 42–20, the Patriots playing West to a near stalemate in the second half. That took away some of the sting. Bryan Scott managed only fifty yards on seventeen carries, but Picciotti had the best night of his career to that point, rushing for 202 yards and two touchdowns on nineteen attempts. The players and coaches chatted on the field for a while, friends and foes, old and new.

Fifteen years had become sixteen.

"No matter what the records are, you can pretty much throw them out the window," Bryan Buckley told a reporter after the game, because it was exactly what he was supposed to tell a reporter after this game, even if he didn't entirely believe it to be true.

After the CB West band had marched to the school's visitors' parking lot, Casey Umbrell headed back to the field, still wearing her white uniform and her eye black, to find her parents and Colby. The three of them were standing near the south end zone, not far from the white bell tower with a stern sentence blazing across its wall in black capital letters: *THEY SERVED THAT WE MAY LIVE FREE*. Mark wanted a photo of his two children together, a memento to capture both halves of the rivalry within his own family, to preserve the first and only night that Colby and Casey participated in the same East-West game.

Colby had half-changed out of his football gear, replacing his shoulder pads and helmet with a white, hooded *CB EAST FOOTBALL* sweatshirt and a baseball cap he turned backward on his head, but what he wore would maintain the motif. He wrapped his right arm around his sister. Later, Casey would remember that moment, how snugly he gripped her shoulder, how he pulled her closer to him, how her big brother didn't just droop his arm around her for the sake of a nice pose in a photograph, that there was true affection in his gesture. Behind them, the light from the field's standards, still burning high above, bounced off the metallic bleachers on the home side of War Memorial Field, giving off a silvery glow. Brother and sister smiled. The camera flashed. They hugged. And Colby, for the last time as a Central Bucks East football player, walked off War Memorial Field.

Mark didn't, not yet. Just then, another CB East parent, Gary Conover, Sr., approached him. Conover's son, Gary, Jr., was also a senior lineman for the Patriots. He had grown up playing midget football with Colby, and he stepped into the starting lineup after Colby had torn his ACL. Like Mark and Nancy, the Conovers cheered at every game, assisted with every fund-raiser, involved themselves with the East program in any way they could.

Mark and Gary Sr. gave each other the same look. The look said, *God, wasn't this whole experience great?* Arm in arm, the two men walked back to the center of the field. The stadium lights remained on, creating a sense that only now, at close to 10 P.M., was dusk falling.

The men stood there, and they cried, sad to see it all end, a biting nighttime breeze at their backs.

EIGHT

Beyond the Game

Friday, November 13, 1998

Michael Pettine had a term for Bryan Buckley, for a certain category of CB West player. Bryan was a "Program Kid," and to Michael Pettine, Program Kids were the secret to the success of his father's football teams.

The irony was, Michael himself had not been a Program Kid. Michael had been a Division I-A prospect, one of the most sought-after recruits at West, when he played for his father in the early 1980s, and CB West usually had at least one such player on its roster each year. (In 1998, West had two: Dustin Picciotti and senior offensive tackle Ben Carber, who had committed to the University of Virginia before the regular season began.) The Program Kids made up the next layer of talent on West's roster; they didn't necessarily possess enough natural skills to play Division I-A football. In any given year, West had six to nine Program Kids, none of them all that big or fast. Each stood between five feet ten and six feet one and weighed no more than 220 pounds. Their real value lay in their attitude, their work ethic, their knowledge of the game. Program Kids were smart, tough, fundamentally sound. They understood and accepted why Mike Pettine coached in the manner that he did, and they made sure the other players understood and accepted it. They chewed out a teammate if they noticed him loafing through a drill or heard him whining in the locker room. Program Kids held things together.

They were also, at the moment, kicking Michael Pettine's ass all over War Memorial Field.

This was the first round of the District One playoffs—West the first seed, North Penn the fourth. Unlike the first time that these two teams had played, in October, this night was dry—no fat, cumbersome raindrops, nothing to equalize the teams, nothing to stop West. With fourteen seconds left in the first half, Mike Orihel feathered a beautiful, ten-yard fade pass to Dave Edwards for a touchdown and a 16–0 West lead; all Edwards had to do was turn his head, and the ball seemed to be suspended in the air, waiting for him. North Penn had turned the ball over on its first possession of the game and couldn't muster a first down on any of its next three. Picciotti and Edwards were running free, on their way to romping to a combined 268 yards in the game. This was the first round of the District One playoffs, and this was everything Bryan Buckley wanted.

He had entered the game angry—"tasting blood," he said. Pettine and Mike Carey had told Bryan that Dick Beck, North Penn's top assistant coach, had referred to him as a "blowfish" because, they said, Bryan puffed out his chest and talked a lot but didn't back up his words with his play. And according to West's coaches, several North Penn players, after their 13–12 loss to West, had said that they "ran all over" the Bucks and "really didn't respect them." The double-barreled bit of gossip infuriated Bryan at the time, but later, he would wonder whether the coaches were merely trying to get a rise out of him. After all, Bryan and Beck had what Bryan knew to be a respectful relationship. Pettine and Carey often mentioned to the team whispers and scuttlebutt that they claimed to have picked up from reading the newspaper or talking with people in the community, and whether those whispers were true was not the point, not the reason Pettine and Carey passed them along. To them, the slightest sign of disrespect toward West, even if they conjured it out of thin air, was fodder for motivation. Conversely, Pettine stressed to his players that they ought never to say anything remotely controversial to any reporter anywhere, lest an opponent use the same strategy against the Bucks.

Come the closing minutes of the game, though, Bryan's anger had dissipated. West had chewed up half of the third quarter with a six-minute, seventy-nine-yard touchdown drive and more than half of the fourth quarter with a seven-minute, eighty-four-yard march. The final score, 29–8, did not capture fully how dominant West had been, what little chance Michael Pettine and Dick Beck's team had of winning. Afterward, there was no trash-talking, nothing hostile. Michael Pettine and Beck shook Bryan's hand and wished him luck against Norristown in the district-championship game. You had to respect a Program Kid.

Nancy Umbrell was pleased and grateful when, not long after CB East's football season ended, her eldest son at last submitted to surgery on his left knee. To tease and torment his mother and get a laugh from people, Colby would say, "Look, my knee bends the other way," and then reach down, wrap his hands around his knee, and prove it. Nancy would shriek, "Stop it!" *That son of mine . . . what a character.*

The surgery would allow Colby to continue playing football after he had graduated from East. When and where he would play, he hadn't yet decided. For a high school football player with a real opportunity to play in a major college program—a player such as Dustin Picciotti or Bryan Scott, for instance—the recruiting period began during the player's junior year. For an athlete such as Colby, for whom the Division I-AA level was the highest at which he could hope to play, his play during his senior season mattered more because recruiting at college football's lower rungs wasn't quite as cutthroat. Schools had more time to mine talent. Nevertheless, the timing of Colby's injury had altered, irrevocably, the course of his college admission process. A Division I-AA school would likely hesitate to offer him a football scholarship until he had proven that he had completely rehabilitated his knee. A Division II school might be more amenable to trusting that Colby would return to full strength, but fewer football scholarships were available at the Division II level. And because Division III colleges and universities don't award athletic scholarships of any kind—only academic scholarships and grants based on financial need—Colby's indifference toward academics during his high school years made it more difficult for him to find an affordable option.

His apathy with respect to his studies frustrated both his parents and his teachers, especially in light of his 135 IQ and the 1200 he scored the first time he took the Scholastic Aptitude Test. "You're an idiot," Mark would tell Colby, with just enough seriousness to make his point. "Why aren't you applying yourself?" He had retained the same blasé attitude that had concerned Ann Kuntzmann, Colby's guidance counselor at Lenape Middle School. Cynthia Magnuson, who sat behind Colby in their advanced-placement statistics class, thought him funny. She did not know Colby well, but she looked forward to the class each day because, invariably, he would swivel his hulking torso around to face her and would say something to make her laugh. Getting a giggle from her seemed as important to him as his mastering any of the course's complex equations.

"As a student, he was very much a kid," recalled Paul Wilson, who taught the statistics class and, at the time, was also the head coach of East's boys' track team. "His grades were good. Were they outstanding? No. Something had to pique his interest to get him to do what he could do best. You had to catch his interest somehow, and sometimes you could and sometimes you didn't. If it was something he wasn't interested in, he wasn't disruptive. He wasn't annoying. He was just, 'I'll do as much as I have to do to get by, but I'm not going to knock myself out.' When you got hold of his interest, boom—he was all over it. He did everything he could do."

In spite of his girth, Colby did not stand out to Wilson in the classroom, but he didn't fade into the background, either. He didn't volunteer to answer questions or jump at the opportunity to join a class discussion of a given day's lesson, but he didn't recoil from interacting with Wilson or the other students. Wilson could see, from those interactions and from Colby's captaincy on the football team, that he possessed leadership ability. Wilson soon would spend more time with Colby and come to believe that the military would be the ideal channel for his energies and ambitions. It would reward Colby for his willingness to be physically adventurous, and it could provide enough of a mental challenge to appeal to him, could provide the discipline that could coax the flickers of his intellectual curiosity into a full fire. In his heart, Colby knew, too, that the military could develop that side of him, but he first had to find the right route there.

Friday, November 20, 1998

The wind on the night of Bryan Buckley's final football game at War Memorial Field blew cold enough and strong enough to turn exposed skin into frozen sandpaper, and it caught that familiar smell of popping popcorn from the snack bar at the stadium's south end and carried the aroma across CB West's campus. Bryan loved that popcorn smell, that instant of synesthesia that marked his first step out of the locker room before a game. That smell made him think of football, of *CB West football*, of an atmosphere that caused his body to tingle as if there were a pleasing electric current humming through him. That smell . . . the bracing autumn air . . . the marching band beating its drums . . . when he was a kid, he could hear those drums from his parents' house, and their thunder told him that it was time to head to War Memorial to bear witness to the Bucks' latest victory.

There wasn't much disagreement among West's players and coaches that Norristown had been and would be the best opponent the Bucks had faced all season. The Eagles had taken North Penn apart, 31–13, in the teams' regular-season finale, and their only loss of the season had been to West. "Respect," Dave Edwards said in the days before the district-title game. "We respect them. I truly think they're the most underrated team in the state." In a way, it was to Pettine's advantage that Norristown would pose such a threat to West's winning streak (now twenty-six games) and its state-title aspirations. All season, he worried that a sense of inevitability might settle in his players' minds, that they would regard another berth in the state-title game as a fait accompli. Even for Bryan, the prospect of a second consecutive district championship held no cachet; winning district titles was what West was supposed to do. Against Norristown, though, there was less of a chance that the players would take victory for granted. Because the Bucks were acquainted with Norristown's talent, its capability of striking suddenly on offense, Pettine's warnings were less likely to fall on deaf ears.

The most effective way to neutralize Norristown's offense, of course, was to keep it off the field, and with Pettine and Carey's reshuffling of the Bucks' offensive line before the East-West game, that task had become easier. The glitch that the coaches had sought to correct—too many fumbled snaps—was gone; Mike Orihel hadn't dropped a snap since Carey decided to make Chris Havener the center. Now, there wasn't a team in the district, and perhaps in the entire state, that could match West's size. Along a seven-man front—a center, two guards, two tackles, and two tight ends—West's linemen averaged 262 pounds apiece, and in the backfield were a 235-pound fullback in Picciotti and, depending on the formation, one of two 220-pound wingbacks, Bryan and Greg Kinzel. Behind a line of that mass and skill, it didn't much matter who was running the ball, but Pettine had stayed true to his promise to Picciotti to give him more carries at Bryan's expense. Over the six games since Pettine and Bryan's closed-door meeting, Picciotti had 133 carries, Bryan 10. The trend disturbed Bryan's parents more than it disturbed him. On those rare occasions when he stepped out of his self-constructed tunnel and concerned himself with questions apart from his next football game, Bryan remained confident that a college scout would look beyond sheer statistics and offer him a scholarship, but Bill and Connie weren't convinced. Pettine still telephoned the Buckleys' home every Friday morning to chat away with Connie, but neither she nor Bill ever betrayed their disbelief over what Pettine was doing: He was penalizing their son because Bryan was a team player.

As long as West kept winning, kept doing what it was supposed to do, Bryan couldn't be bothered doubting Pettine's instructions or decisions, and those moments of true trepidation—those few, fleeting seconds when it appeared as if West might actually *lose* a football game—were arising less frequently. Against Norristown, the first of those moments lasted two plays and two minutes' worth of game time.

Bent on preventing Norristown quarterback Kris Blake from riddling West's defense again, Pettine and Carey instructed their defensive ends not to worry about containing tailback Troy Swittenberg. The ends were to push up the field and pressure Blake on every play. The plan backfired fifteen seconds into the second quarter, when, with West leading 7–0, Swittenberg darted through the West defense for a sixty-four-yard touchdown to tie the game. Uneasiness wafted over the West sideline and the home-side bleachers . . . and wafted away once the Bucks got the ball back. On second down from the West 44, Edwards answered Swittenberg's up-the-middle touchdown with one of his own. Picciotti scored on a five-yard run later in the quarter, and the Bucks led, 21–7, at halftime.

The second moment was more forbidding. Early in the second half, Edwards fumbled, and Norristown defensive back Audley Stewart scooped up the ball and returned it fifty yards for a touchdown. It was a seven-point game again, 21–14. More uneasiness. More unpleasant memories for Pettine, for Bryan, for those who knew the Bucks' recent history. The district-championship game had bedeviled West; three times over the previous six years, the Bucks had reached the district final and lost, two of those defeats ruining perfect seasons. *You remember the losses*, Pettine often told reporters and his players, *longer than you remember the wins*—a lesson of competition that Bryan himself had learned as a sophomore, after that playoff loss to Plymouth Whitemarsh. That West team, like this one, had been expected to win a state title, but from that game's beginning, Bryan had perceived a "weird vibe" among his teammates, blank stares in the defensive huddle, a sense that Pettine and Carey knew they were impotent to inspire the players. The day after that loss, he and a teammate, Matt Carey (who was Mike Carey's nephew), had gone to McDonald's and wandered around Doylestown, munching on their cheeseburgers without saying much to each other. It seemed all the passersby had their heads down. *You remember the losses.*

West began its next possession at its 27-yard line. Four runs by Picciotti and two by Edwards advanced the line of scrimmage fifty-eight yards to the Norristown 15, the offensive line carving out enormous holes. On first down, Picciotti had the wind knocked out of him and sat out the next two plays, so on third-and-2 from the Norristown 7-yard line, Pettine called a fullback dive to Bryan. A hole to his right closed as quickly as it had opened, and three Norristown linemen dragged him to the ground after he had gained just one yard. It was his first carry of the game.

Having regained his breath, Picciotti trotted back on the field, replacing Bryan. Eschewing a short field-goal attempt on fourth-and-1, Pettine wanted his two-touchdown lead back. Bryan stood near Pettine on the sideline, watching West's eleven players on offense arrange themselves into a power-running formation—eight blockers along the line of scrimmage, Edwards just behind them and to Picciotti's left in a wingback position—and drop sharply into their stances, their right hands pressing into the clammy dirt.

Following a block from Edwards, Picciotti lumbered into the end zone. No Norristown player touched him.

The Eagles then stopped resisting. They fumbled the ensuing kickoff, and Picciotti scored again, his fourth touchdown of the game, this time from the 4-yard line. The score stayed that way, 35–14, to the game's end.

There was no raucous celebration in the aftermath of West's second straight district championship. The 4,800 people at War Memorial applauded politely and left quickly. His hands in his pockets, his shoulders slumped forward, Pettine walked across the field to shake hands with Roger Grove, Norristown's coach. After he was handed the PIAA District One Class AAAA Championship trophy—a thin, gold statue of a football player—Bryan lifted it up in his right hand as, around him, his teammates chanted, "C-B-WEST! C-B-WEST!" If he hadn't had to touch the trophy, he wouldn't have. When West had won the district championship the year before—by beating Plymouth Whitemarsh, fittingly enough—the victory had felt different to him. That West team had been younger. Less had been expected of it. There was more joy over the win. He had watched his friend Dave Armstrong cry that night. Dave's father had come down from the stands to the field, and he had held his arms out, and Dave Armstrong—six feet three, 255 pounds, all-American fullback, all-state wrestler—fell into his father's arms and bawled his eyes out because he would never play another football game at War Memorial Field. Now, the drums were silent. The snack bar was shut tight. And Bryan did not bawl. The state playoffs began next week. There was more to be done.

He walked off the grass, onto the track, through a gate in the fence around the field, never pausing as he headed back to the locker room.

Saturday, December 5, 1998

The thick rubber trash can thudded to the ground, culminating an outburst borne of Bryan Buckley's fury.

His anger had been building all week over what had happened in his previous game and what he had been reading about his next game. The Bucks had beaten Abington Heights, a team from the Wilkes-Barre area, 37–10 in the state quarterfinals the week before, but the score belied the day's difficulties. Bryan had overslept that morning and had almost missed the team bus, Pettine pulling him aside to ask, "Is everything all right?" The bursa sac on his left knee had opened early in the game, leaking fluid and blood on the joint; he would need to have the knee drained. The Bucks had produced seventy-four total yards, three first downs, and no points in the game's first twenty-four minutes, leading 7–3 at halftime only because sophomore Dave Camburn had returned an interception 101 yards for a touchdown. They had pulled away in the second half, burying Abington Heights under a barrage of big plays: a fifty-three-yard run by Edwards, an eighty-three-yard punt return and thirty-eight-yard reception by Sean-Michael Yonson, a thirty-yard run by Picciotti. Still, everything had seemed *off*, and that sluggish first half had provided Pettine with plenty of ammunition for the succeeding week of practice, as West readied for its state-semifinal game against the Parkland High School Trojans.

Then, Parkland's players provided some more. Always on the hunt for bulletin-board material, Pettine struck gold the day before the game. There was nothing that nestled more snugly into Pettine's motivational bag of tricks than an opposing player's suggestion that his team was capable of breaking West's winning streak, which was now twenty-eight games long. However innocent the player's intent, Pettine made sure that the Bucks would think there was no limit to the player's arrogance. This time, Parkland senior Nick Jarecke was the target.

"Their streak has to end sometime," Jarecke had told his hometown newspaper, the *Morning Call* of Allentown. "No one expects us to win, and that's good. We like to keep proving people wrong."

If Jarecke's quote hadn't succeeded in working Bryan and his teammates into a lather, Parkland's actions before the state semifinal did. The game site was Neshaminy High School—the PIAA held all its state-playoff games at neutral sites—and the officials would conduct the coin toss outside the teams' respective locker rooms before holding a purely ceremonial coin toss at midfield. As Bryan, with Mike Carey and a couple of West assistant coaches flanked behind him, met with

Parkland's captains, the rest of Parkland's roster marched past in a double-file line toward the field. Bryan and Carey could hear some of the Trojans mouthing off—"talking shit," as Bryan said. The hair on Carey's arms rose. After the Bucks won the toss, Bryan said that they wanted to receive the opening kickoff. Seething, he refused to shake hands with Parkland's captains, tossing aside that trash can before storming back into West's makeshift locker room in Neshaminy's gymnasium. Who did these Parkland players think they were, treating the reigning state champions like a bunch of punks?

"Teams that did this faced a whole different CB West team," Bryan said later. "We played at a higher intensity in those games. Take the CB East games. We never went out there to beat them up because we had respect for each other. We just played hard-nosed football and shook each other's hand afterward. Teams that disrespected us, we had a true dislike for them.

"They made it personal to me, and I was going to make sure the rest of the team took it personally."

He called his teammates out of the gym, telling them to stand outside and listen to Parkland's players and watch them make that long walk into the stadium. Sean Kelly, West's trainer, would later assert that "the game was over at that point." If not then, it was soon after. Edwards returned the opening kickoff sixty-eight yards, setting up a one-yard Picciotti touchdown run. Parkland went three-and-out and punted, and after fielding the kick, Yonson wormed and wriggled forty-three yards to the Trojans' 21-yard line. Again, Picciotti scored. For all his players' posturing before the game, Rich Sniscak, Parkland's head coach, knew that they were rattled now.

In the second quarter, Bryan charged in on a blitz from the left side and, in trying to make an inside move past the right tackle, slapped the tackle across the helmet with his left hand. The officials could have penalized Bryan for the head-slap had they seen it, but the play resulted in a different sort of punishment for him. Returning to the huddle, Bryan felt blood dripping off his hand. The edge of the Parkland tackle's helmet had sliced a deep gash from the webbing between Bryan's third and fourth fingers across the upper part of his palm. He squeezed his hand into a fist to hide the blood so that the officials wouldn't make him leave the game. During a timeout, Kelly hastily taped up Bryan's hand until it looked mummified, but by halftime, West had a 21–0 lead, and between Bryan's knee and his hand, Pettine felt he could afford to have him heal and rest on the bench for a while.

When Parkland opened the second half with a seventy-four-yard touchdown drive, Bryan's respite ended. Pettine reinserted him at wing-back, and Bryan set his sights on a defensive back who had been particularly mouthy before the game. On the third play of West's ensuing possession, a handoff to Picciotti, Bryan drive-blocked the defensive back to the ground. Rarely had any play in his high school career filled him with such satisfaction, and Pettine and Carey recognized that Bryan was jacking people up, was on that plane of intensity that only he seemed able to reach. They didn't dare sit him now. "Buckley was like a pulling guard," Carey said later. "He was going through the line, attacking those linebackers. It was just incredible, the hits he was putting on." West needed only three more plays—all runs, all of them with Bryan creating instant urban renewal—before Picciotti went nineteen yards for his third touchdown of the game and thirty-sixth of the season.

When the Bucks finally finished their 34–7 victory, they rushed to the center of the field in a mass of elation, Bryan the last to join the celebration. He dragged his still-stiff left leg. His left hand remained wrapped in tape. West would play for the state title again. He felt no pain at all.

While Bryan Buckley and CB West were taking their final step toward defending their championship, twenty-nine miles to the south Colby Umbrell was glimpsing—above him, below him, around him—what his future might have been, and what it still could be.

He sat in the 300 level of craggy Veterans Stadium in south Philadelphia, awaiting the opening kickoff of the ninety-ninth Army-Navy football game. Mark and Nancy had purchased ten tickets to the game for themselves, Colby, and several of his friends—a treat for their son after his abridged senior season. He was still rehabilitating his knee, putting himself through the aquatic physical therapy that had been so crucial to his rapid return to East's lineup, but with West Point out of the picture for him, more and more Colby regarded spending a year at prep school as his best option. The U.S. Coast Guard was willing to give him a medical waiver to play football, but only after he had taken a year to ensure that his knee was healthy again. Prep school would buy him that time and, perhaps, awaken his relatively dormant interest in academics. In the meantime, he had a more immediate objective in mind: playing in the Bucks County All-Star Football Classic in June. Despite missing those two and a half games because of his torn ACL, he had been a first-team all–Suburban One League National Conference selection; that was how highly the conference's ten head coaches thought of him, and he was honored. But playing in the county all-star game meant more to him. It would be a gift to his father, just as the Army-Navy tickets had been a gift to Colby.

Because the Umbrells' seats were underneath an overhanging section of the stadium's upper deck, Colby couldn't see the two Navy SEALs parachuting onto the Vet's billiards-table turf until they landed—one trailing yellow smoke and the other trailing lavender smoke from beneath their billowy yellow-and-blue chutes. He could take in the rest of the awesome sequence of the annual pregame pageantry, though: the Army attack helicopters thumping and the Navy F-18 jets shrieking during their flybys over the stadium, the men and women in uniform marching in lockstep, the sight of the opponents on the field who eventually would unite for a graver common cause. The entire scene lent a measure of majesty to the Vet—a venue that, although regarded with loyal affection by Colby and most of the parochial fans of Philadelphia's Eagles and Phillies, was quite literally falling apart.

As grim proof of the stadium's decrepit condition, later that afternoon four West Point cadets and five Army prep-school students were injured as they crowded in front of a TV camera when a railing collapsed and sent them tumbling fifteen feet to the ground. While the game officials halted play for more than thirty minutes, six ambulances roared onto the field to take the injured cadets and students to three nearby hospitals. The incident occurred on the opposite side of the stadium from where the Umbrells were sitting—they could watch the entire ugly sequence unfold—and was an unseemly blight on a 34–30 Army victory, but it didn't mar the day for Colby. Whatever job he held when he was older, wherever life led him, he wanted first to serve his country, and the spectacle and ceremony of the game had overwhelmed him, had reaffirmed his aspirations.

Only one element had been missing: the chance to see the president in person. In 1996, on the heels of his reelection, Bill Clinton had become the first sitting president to attend the Army-Navy game since Gerald Ford in 1974; but two years later, Clinton could not make it back to Veterans Stadium a second time. There were more pressing matters—foreign and domestic, personal and political—that he had to attend to.

NINE

Dominance

Sunday, December 6, 1998

Mike Carey parked in the visitors' lot at CB West High School at 9 A.M., fog curling around his car. The cloudy, drizzly morning was unseasonably warm; the temperature would approach 70 degrees by the afternoon. Carey, still a bit sleepy-eyed after a victory celebration at the New Britain Inn the night before, shuffled down the steps that led to Mike Pettine's office.

After West's win over Parkland, several of the Bucks' coaches, parents, and followers had retired to the NBI for dinner and drinks, but Pettine had to leave the party early. He had arranged to make a night-time ride west on the Pennsylvania Turnpike to rendezvous with a coach from New Castle High School, the Bucks' opponent in the upcoming Class AAAA state-championship game. The two coaches met near Harrisburg and exchanged game tapes, and though he was supposed to meet Pettine in the football office to review the New Castle film with him, Carey assumed Pettine had returned home and, before heading to bed, watched the film. Indeed, Pettine had done exactly that. It was in his obsessive-compulsive nature, of course, but there was also a practical purpose for the early preparation.

Without a winning season since 1988, having won only eight games over its previous three seasons, New Castle was 11–3 and had come out of nowhere to reach the state final, upsetting Erie Cathedral Prep, which the *Harrisburg Patriot-News* had ranked among the top ten teams in the state, in the western semifinal game. At a time just before the Internet had infiltrated every American home, just before the cornucopia of cable-television viewing options began to include high school football games broadcast nationally, Pettine and Carey couldn't learn much about a nonconference opponent unless they read about the team in the newspaper. They knew next to nothing about New Castle, located fifty-five miles north of Pittsburgh, until Pettine powered up the VCR. Then they learned everything that they would need to know.

Carey entered the office. Pettine was already there.

"What do you think?" Carey asked him.

"We're going to fucking kill them," Pettine said.

The legend of Pennsylvania high school football, of its status as a hallowed American institution that had spawned a litany of gridiron gods, was based mainly on the sport's history in the western part of the state. Johnny Unitas, Joe Namath, Mike Ditka, Joe Montana, Tony Dorsett, Dan Marino, Jim Kelly—all of them had come from the steel and riverside towns that ringed Pittsburgh. The Western Pennsylvania Interscholastic Athletic League grew into a behemoth, its tendrils reaching 156 schools by the 1981–1982 academic year. The WPIAL became so big, so fundamental, that to many high school football fans in the west there seemed no point in paying any mind to the teams that weren't affiliated with it. "Pennsylvania football from the 1910s to the 1950s had dominant football teams in the nation," Phil Gergen, a Pennsylvania high school statistician and historian, once said. "We've had great players come out of the Western Pennsylvania area"—and, apparently, none from the eastern area, or at least none whom Gergen could remember. The presumption for most of the twentieth century was that, compared to western Pennsylvania, the eastern half of the state regarded high school football as an afterthought. Put simply, the teams, the players, and the tradition there didn't stack up.

Mike Pettine resented that presumption. It was a toss-up as to which notion bothered him more: that his players were all hick farmers from a largely rural part of Pennsylvania, or that the Bucks couldn't compete with the best teams in the rest of the state. "We had to live with the image of the WPIAL, the 'Mecca of football,'" he recalled. Before 1991, three years after the PIAA's playoff system went into effect, CB West had never played an opponent from outside southeastern Pennsylvania, had never had the opportunity to test itself against a broader swath of competition. Once it did, it became the first eastern team to win the Class AAAA championship. From that point on, Pettine—and, to a lesser degree, his coaches and players—viewed a state title as a validation of the high quality of football not only in their program, but in the Suburban One League and throughout the region. His Bucks, whenever possible, would be the torchbearers for big-school football in the east, and more than anyone else, they were. With the state playoffs in their tenth year of existence, West was about to make its fourth appearance in the Class AAAA title game, the most of any program.

Yet if there was a slight drawback to West's success, it was that even its most fervid followers had come to assume that the Bucks would win every week—an expectation that, when combined with the affluence and culture of Doylestown, suggested a relative apathy around town in the days before the New Castle game. Yes, there were pockets where the game was a major topic of discussion. "People come in and talk about it every day," Patrick Murphy, who owned a bagel shop in the center of Doylestown, told the *Intelligencer*, and a handful of other small businesses throughout the central Bucks area displayed messages of support on placards and marquees. But the Doylestown community lacked the uniform excitement over West's prospective championship that the town of New Castle felt for its Red Hurricanes. "It's all anyone around here is talking about," Angelo Perrotta, New Castle's athletics director, said. "All the houses and storefronts are decorated. It's phenomenal." By the Wednesday before the game, New Castle fans had booked all 230 rooms at the Holiday Inn East in Harrisburg, not far from Hersheypark Stadium, the site of the state-title game, and the school had sold out its allotment of 2,000 tickets and was expected to sell another 2,500 by Saturday.

West athletics director Mike Gold, meanwhile, said that he doubted West would sell its 2,000 tickets by game day. This ambivalence was nothing new to Jim Benstead, the man so devoted to Doylestown and to Pettine that he had declined the opportunity to travel the world practicing international law just so he could coach middle-school football in his hometown. Across the street from the Bagel Barrel, where Benstead stopped daily for his morning coffee and where Patrick Murphy's customers couldn't stop talking about West football, were two elegant Italian restaurants, Paganini's and Domani Star, and no one was discussing the Bucks' prospects there. Benstead marveled at how Doylestown could balance its varied dimensions. This was still the town that James Michener could cite as a muse for his novel *The Fires of Spring*, with its castles and "wonderful, rolling hills," but now there was something there for everyone in the contemporary world—for shoppers, for local history buffs, for twenty-somethings who wanted to bar-hop on a weekend night, for those who had lived in Doylestown all their lives, for those who appreciated and were proud of the precision and excellence with which Pettine's teams played. In fact, Benstead believed that by the time the state playoffs had become a fixture of Pennsylvania high school football, Doylestown's sophistication and the ease with which West seemed to win had tempered the enthusiasm of the crowds at CB West games. That victory over Norristown in the district-championship game had been just the latest example of a trend that he had noticed: The opposing fans would go crazy during a game, but it was becoming rarer that an important or thrilling play would compel West fans to rise and make a loud, sharp sound.

"That, in a snapshot, was the difference," Benstead said. "In Doylestown, we're blessed with so many things that can compete for our time. In a coal-mining town, if they're lucky enough to have a team that does well once every forty or fifty years, that's unbelievable. The old-timers will talk about 'that team back then' that did whatever it did. Here, the West program was just one of many shining stars."

For Benstead, though, it was the one that came first. On the day of the state-title game, Benstead wasn't going to be touring the Mercer Museum or making a reservation at Domani Star. He would make the hundred-mile drive to Hershey. So would a father and son who wanted to see for themselves if New Castle really had any chance to beat big, bad CB West. So would Mark and Colby Umbrell.

There would be others, too. While she was selling bus tickets to the game one evening, Janet Bowser, the mother of senior lineman Bob Bowser and a member of the football parents' club, told a reporter that, though West fans might not seem excited for the game, "they are [excited] at games." The implication of her words was clear: When they were most needed, the people of Doylestown would be there for their own.

Bryan Buckley could not believe what he was seeing. Watching the New Castle game film, he had the same reaction as Pettine. *There's no way this team can beat us*, he thought. *None*. It was the only time that he lapsed into such haughtiness while he was at West.

What struck Bryan was the physical difference between the two teams. New Castle actually had more three-hundred-pound linemen than West—two to the Bucks' one, Ben Carber—but man for man, it was apparent that the Red Hurricanes couldn't match West's strength and technique up front. Over its last three playoff games, New Castle had beaten Erie Cathedral Prep, North Allegheny (which had been

10–2), and Woodland Hills (which had been 9–2), and all Bryan could think was, *How?*

That was Pettine's lone worry. Throughout the week before the game, in an attempt to give his players cause for concern, he mentioned to reporters that the Red Hurricanes ran the Wing-T offense, a wishbonelike alignment that had a history of giving West fits. (Plymouth Whitemarsh had run the Wing-T when it knocked West out of the district playoffs in 1995 and 1996.) But that was the best he could do. The gap between his team and New Castle was so great and so obvious that he wondered how much of the game film he should show to his players, for fear that they would grow overconfident. With the exception of the sloppy first half of the Abington Heights victory two weeks earlier, Pettine had been pleased with the Bucks' play since their win over CB East. The late-season team meeting that Bryan had called had worked, had snapped the team out of its slump. "It's such a long season, and you go through different emotions," Bryan told a reporter before the state-title game. "It's kind of hard to get up for those not-so-good teams."

The chances of the team's relapsing into its earlier funk dwindled on Wednesday, December 9, when the *Intelligencer* picked up and published a quote that New Castle quarterback Joe Cowart had given to the *Pittsburgh Post-Gazette*. In the euphoria of his team's 27–25 win over Erie Cathedral Prep, Cowart had said, "We're going to shock the world next week." Pettine slapped the quote on the wall of West's weight room. Little did Joe Cowart know what he had said and done.

Saturday, December 12, 1998

Hersheypark Stadium had not yet begun to fill by 3:30 P.M., so from high atop the stadium's stone bleachers, Bill Buckley and his video camera had an unobstructed view to the football field below, to a single CB West player who couldn't stand still. Some of the other players performed calisthenics. Some jogged to loosen up. Bryan did all those things and more, and he did them by himself. For five full minutes, Bill trained his camera on Bryan, tracking him as he tucked a football under his arm, twirled it in front of him, twirled it behind his back, tucked it back under his arm, high-stepped forward a few yards, leaned on a kicking net, grabbed his right foot, pulled his right leg up and back to stretch his thigh. He was restless, bouncy, like a hornet hovering and darting in the air. Kickoff in the PIAA Class AAAA title game was still an hour and a half away.

This was the first year that the PIAA held the championship games for its four enrollment classifications—back-to-back doubleheaders on Friday and Saturday nights—in Hershey, and Milton Hershey would have approved of the football extravaganza that the governing body of Pennsylvania high school sports now held in the shadows of the twin sepia smokestacks of his famous chocolate factory. Until the day in 1945 that he died, Hershey had loved sports, and he had built his sixteen-thousand-seat stadium in the 1930s as part of a construction spree that, according to author Gary Pomerantz, "made the Great Depression disappear" in the central Pennsylvania town. Aside from the hunger-inducing aroma that floated from the chocolate factory and sweetened the very air of the town—how many other places in the world smelled so good?—Hershey had another unique distinction: It was there, at the Hershey Arena, on March 2, 1962, that Wilt Chamberlain scored 100 points for the Philadelphia Warriors against the New York Knicks, setting the NBA single-game scoring record.

It would not be the last single-game scoring record set in Hershey.

Soon, more than six thousand people took seats in the stadium, and West's first drive would be all they needed to see to get a sense of what was to come. The Bucks went seventy-one yards in eleven plays, and Picciotti plunged into the end zone for a one-yard touchdown. New Castle managed two first downs on its first possession before punting, and Bryan, Picciotti, and the rest of the West offense took the field with the Bucks at their 14-yard line.

While he was coaching Picciotti at Lenape Middle School, Jim Benstead installed a new play into his offense, a play just for Picciotti: a fullback sweep. Fullbacks usually lumber, but Picciotti had the speed to run parallel to the line of scrimmage and then cut upfield after he had gotten outside the tackles. For Benstead, the best part of the play was that, if his linemen blocked correctly, the only defensive player who would have a shot at squaring up against Picciotti and bringing him down would be a cornerback—one of the smallest players on the field. There were few middle-school cornerbacks—and, now that Picciotti stood six feet three and weighed 235 pounds, fewer high-school cornerbacks—who wanted to tangle with him. But in this, Picciotti's first full season as West's fullback, Benstead hadn't seen the Bucks run a single fullback sweep, until now.

Bryan lined up as a wingback to Picciotti's right, then went in motion to the left. Mike Orihel accepted the snap while Bryan was still moving, giving Bryan a running start to batter New Castle's right defensive end, to unleash at last all that anxious energy that his father had taken such care to capture on camera. Picciotti went wide, then burst through the hole that Bryan had created. Benstead was right: For forty yards, no New Castle defender got anywhere near Picciotti until a defensive back caught up to him at the Red Hurricanes' 46-yard line.

Near the left sideline, the back dived at Picciotti's feet.

Picciotti jumped over him, stayed in bounds, and kept going.

The eighty-six-yard touchdown put West ahead by fourteen points. The lead might as well have been a hundred points. The Bucks forced two New Castle turnovers and scored three more touchdowns—two short-yardage runs by Picciotti and a seventy-yard draw play by Dave Edwards—to take a 35–0 halftime lead, setting up another indignity for the Red Hurricanes in the second half. According to what the PIAA called its "mercy rule," whenever a team led by thirty-five points or more in the second half, the game clock would run continuously.

The game, then, was all but over as Bryan met New Castle's four team captains at midfield before the start of the second half to review the terms of the pregame coin toss. He hoped to see a semblance of defiance from his opponents. Instead, what he saw offended him.

The New Castle captains had tears in their eyes.

Bryan sneered.

Shock the world.

Sure.

He trotted back to the huddle.

"They're crying," he said.

Years later, Pettine would recall telling Bryan, in a tongue-in-cheek manner, "Hey, Buck, show them a little compassion here." Moments after the game's conclusion, though, Bryan suggested to a reporter that Pettine hadn't been quite so kind: "He said, 'Well, don't have any sympathy for them.'" Whatever Pettine's response was, this much was certain: Bryan could barely contain his disgust over the fact that New Castle had seemed to surrender. He would have preferred a closer, more competitive game to cap his career. He would have preferred an opponent who made a stand.

The second half was a blur, the entire game anticlimactic. There is never drama in domination. In the most one-sided state-title game in Pennsylvania history, West won, 56–7, rolling up 492 rushing yards and establishing Class AAAA championship records with its point total and its margin of victory. Picciotti finished the game with 236 yards and five touchdowns and finished the season with 1,969 yards and a school-record forty-one touchdowns. Edwards rushed for another 134 yards in the game, putting him over the 1,000-yard mark for the season. Pettine was more relieved than he was ecstatic over the undefeated season, the second straight state title, and a winning streak that had now reached thirty games in length. "I can exhale," he told reporters after the game. "I can get a good night's sleep, hopefully. I'll have to go into some kind of decompression chamber, though." Such were the burdens and pressures that the pursuit of a state championship had created. More and more, at the end of each football season, Pettine contemplated retiring. He would have to think long and hard about how much longer he wanted to coach.

Bryan got the only thing he wanted. When it was time for Rod Stone, West's principal, to present the state-championship trophy to the

Bucks, he handed it to Bryan. The trophy looked a good bit like a desk set, but Bryan, interested only in what it represented, barely bothered to glance at it. He lifted the trophy above his head, a smile stretching across his face, allowing himself to be joyful at the end of a season that had felt more like a job. He performed his duties as the team's unofficial spokesman, and when there were no more interviews to be done, no more questions to answer, he stood outside the locker room, holding his helmet, for a moment talking to no one—the last player to take off his uniform. The games . . . the program . . . CB West football . . . they had been his whole universe, and now they weren't anymore. They had been his singular focus, to the exclusion of everything else. He really had no idea what had been going on in the world.

Mark and Colby Umbrell talked as they drove home from Hershey that night. Both of them were pleased that the Bucks had won. If not East, they figured, then West. Colby did not regret his decision in ninth grade to attend East when he could have attended West, even though the Bucks went 44–1 and the Patriots lost their only district-playoff game over the successive three years. Maybe Colby would have been a better football player had he gone to West, or maybe he wouldn't have played as much as he did at East. That sort of speculation, they agreed, was pointless now, anyway. It was the road ahead that mattered most for Colby now.

Three fire trucks rendezvoused with West's two team buses along Route 202, escorting them first to the New Britain Inn. Mike Carey, who had driven himself and his wife to and from Hersheypark Stadium, already was at the tavern and asked his deejay to announce that the state champions were on their way. The place emptied, three hundred people lining up along Route 202 to pound on the sides of the buses and reach up toward the open bus windows to shake the players' hands.

Carey then followed the caravan to West's campus, where another thousand parents and fans awaited the players' arrival. The crowd pressed toward the buses as Pettine, the coaches, and the players shambled out, the trophy still in Bryan's hands. The firemen invited Pettine, Bryan, and the four other team captains—Ben Carber, Chris Ortiz, and linemen/twin brothers Joe and Jon Wilson—to climb a short ladder and stand on top of one of the trucks. It was after midnight now. Bryan thrust the trophy and both of his arms skyward, and the red and white bulbs of the fire engines swirled, illuminating Pettine's and the captains' faces intermittently, allowing the trophy a golden glint in the darkness.

Someone yelled, "Speech!"

Pettine obliged.

"So much for those tough kids from the steel mill," he said from atop the fire truck. "The suburban boys whupped them."

And everyone cheered.

Wednesday, December 16, 1998

Bill Clinton had been back in Washington, D.C., for only a day following a brief trip to the Middle East, returning to a presidency in crisis and a conflict that had been simmering for months.

As Clinton was preparing to depart for Israel, the House Judiciary Committee, on December 11 and 12, had voted to approve four articles of impeachment against him. The articles alleged that Clinton had abused his powers as president and obstructed justice during his affair with White House intern Monica Lewinsky and that he had perjured himself both in the Paula Jones sexual harassment case and before independent counsel Kenneth Starr's grand jury. On the day of Clinton's return to the capital, he was met with two important pieces of news. The first was that eleven House Republicans who had been considered "moderates" and had been hedging on their impeachment votes announced that they would, indeed, vote to impeach Clinton.

The second was just as grave. Richard Butler, the chief weapons inspector for the United Nations, had reported to UN Secretary-General Kofi Annan that Saddam Hussein, the president of Iraq, had instituted new restrictions on Butler and his inspectors. A week earlier, the UN had renewed its investigations of Iraq's biological and chemical weapons program, and Hussein's restrictions were just his latest act of defiance, his latest test of Clinton's resolve. In September 1996, Hussein's forces had occupied the Kurdish town of Irbil in northern Iraq; the forces withdrew after Clinton ordered missile and bomb attacks on them. Two years later, in November 1998, Clinton had convened his national-security team at Camp David after Hussein once again had banished UN inspectors, and Clinton had been preparing to authorize air strikes against Iraq until Hussein relented and gave the inspectors access. Now, Clinton believed that Hussein's brazenness had left him with no choice but to take military action. His entire national-security team—Secretary of State Madeleine Albright, Secretary of Defense Bill Cohen, CIA Director Tony Lake, UN Ambassador Bill Richardson, and National Security Adviser Sandy Berger—agreed, as did Tony Blair, the British prime minister.

At 5 P.M. on December 16, the United States and Great Britain launched an attack on suspected chemical, biological, and nuclear lab sites in Iraq. In an address to the American people that night, Clinton said that "Iraq has abused its final chance" and cited Hussein's deployment of chemical weapons and Scud missiles against Iranians, Kurds, and Iraq's neighboring countries as justification for the use of force.

In all, the offensive lasted four days, the Americans and British lobbing 415 cruise missiles and more than 600 bombs at Hussein's weaponry and his means of delivering it. The initial strikes damaged eleven weapons of mass destruction (WMD) industry and production facilities and nineteen WMD security details, and several laser-guided bombs destroyed, among other targets, an intelligence-reporting post and a missile-storage facility in southern Iraq. But exactly how much the attack had wounded Hussein's capacity to use the weapons and how long it might take him to replenish his arsenal, no one yet knew.

TEN

Closure

For all the support that he had shouted and screamed from the stands during his son's career at Central Bucks East, Mark Umbrell did not fit the negative stereotype of the demanding football father. He was not the sort of parent who lived vicariously through his child's activities and accomplishments. Yes, Mark had dropped a small football in the crib when Colby was a baby, and yes, as Colby matured, he picked up on Mark's love of the game. But it irked Mark and Nancy when people presumed that Mark had pushed Colby into playing football. No one could push Colby into anything. He had played football at East because he had wanted to, not because Mark had wanted him to. Mark hoped only that Colby would have an experience with high school football similar to the one that Mark had at East. For those days offered nothing but warm memories for Mark, and those memories had nothing to do with how East's teams had fared or with any individual acclaim he did or didn't receive.

Mark had been one of the Patriots' better players during the program's early, harder years. While CB West was beginning its ascendancy under Mike Pettine, winning all twenty of its games over the '71 and '72 seasons, East was struggling to build and maintain some semblance of continuity. The Patriots had three coaches in a four-year span from 1970 to 1973, and after Mark's senior season, 1972, a group of parents petitioned East principal James Gallagher to replace head coach Vernon Young, who had been at East for only two years. Under Young, the Patriots had gone 3–6 in 1971 and 2–8 in 1972, and the specters of West's success and Pettine's presence had increased the parents' impatience with East's performance—a performance that, in truth, could have been worse. In fact, without Mark, the Patriots might have gone winless in 1972. A fullback and linebacker, he scored the team's first touchdown of the season in East's first victory, then returned an interception thirty-six yards for the winning touchdown in the Patriots' second victory. The following June, Mark was East's lone representative in the annual Bucks County All-Star Football Game.

As much as Mark savored those memories and moments, there was another anecdote, unrelated to anything that happened during one of his games, that gave him greater joy. In the early 1970s, West's players would herald their latest victory over the Patriots by climbing up to the roof of the white bell tower at War Memorial Field immediately after the East-West game and ringing the bell. A few days before the 1972 East-West game, Mark stopped by the fast-food restaurant in downtown Doylestown where Nancy worked to tell her of a grand plan that he and his teammates had concocted: Because they knew they were likely to lose to West anyway, they would sneak over to War Memorial the night before the game and steal the bell. If the Patriots couldn't beat the Bucks, at least they wouldn't allow them to rub it in again.

So Mark and ten of his teammates scaled the tower's walls, armed with a piece of foam rubber to muffle the clapper so they could disassemble the bell in relative quiet. But before they could finish the job, they heard someone yell out, "Hey, Umbrell!" Suddenly, the forms of ten West football players emerged from the darkness, and they were ready to throw fists if it meant foiling the Patriots' plan. Because Mark had gone to middle school with some of the players and had remained friendly with them, he was able to negotiate a peaceful settlement, but it didn't take him long to figure out how they had learned of the plot. Nancy might have been a loving girlfriend, but she was loyal to her high school, too. She had called West's captains and told them about Mark's secret mission. The next day, West beat East, 34–6. To Mark, the bell's clanging that day seemed as if it would never cease.

After Mark and Nancy had married, the foiled bell heist became a story that always made their family laugh, that cut to the core of the resemblance between Colby and his father. It was the sort of experience that Mark had wanted for Colby at East. Mark didn't get the satisfaction of stopping West from ringing that bell, didn't get to celebrate all that many victories, but he'd had a hell of a good time anyway. The experience itself of playing football, of competing, of developing friendships, had been the seed for those memories that he so treasured, and now Colby had collected his own remembrances: the chance to play alongside a potential pro in Bryan Scott, the moments of levity with Steve Gonzalez during practice, the gratification of returning to the lineup after the weeks that he had spent rehabilitating his knee. And there was the opportunity for another. Larry Greene would be coaching the North team in the Bucks County All-Star Football Classic in June. Colby was a cinch to be selected to the team, and as long as Colby's knee was strong enough (and there was no reason to think it wouldn't be), he would see significant action in the game.

It wasn't long after Colby had injured his knee that he and his parents had reached an agreement: He wasn't going to sit around the house for a year, waiting until it was time for him to join the Coast Guard. Once the football season ended, Colby would have more time to spend with his friends and his girlfriend, a brown-haired varsity swimmer at West named Anna Sommers, but he had to get on with preparing for his life after high school. He, Mark, and Nancy started searching through prep schools, finally deciding on Wyoming Seminary near Wilkes-Barre, Pennsylvania. That Wyoming Seminary was willing to award Colby a $4,000 athletic grant for his postgraduate year made the decision easier, but the grant also placed a responsibility on Colby to make sure that he was in good enough physical shape to play football there.

To do that, and to accelerate his recuperation from his November knee surgery in time for the All-Star Game, Colby told Paul Wilson, his statistics teacher and East's boys' track coach, that he wanted to be a part of the track team in the spring. More specifically, he wanted to throw the shot put, which was understandable for an athlete of his size, and he wanted to run the 100-meter dash, which would probably make him the biggest sprinter in the Suburban One League.

There were no tryouts, so Wilson agreed to have Colby on the team. The chance to play in one more high school football game had given him a goal toward which he could point himself, a tangible destination in the distance, and he knew that it meant even more to Mark. A father and son, playing in the same All-Star Game twenty-six years apart—the two of them appreciated that symmetry.

Paul Wilson spoke in the measured tones of an academic, of someone who had spent half his life in a classroom, imparting the importance of accuracy and exactness. Composed, bespectacled, skinny like a runner should be, he was the perfect coach for Colby's brief track career.

Wilson had taught mathematics and coached track and field in the Central Bucks School District for more than two decades, and over that time he had come to conclude that there were two kinds of kids who played high school sports. There were kids who were pure athletes, born to excel in a particular sport, and there were kids who wanted to be part of a team. Wilson considered it his job as a coach to meet the needs of each.

"There are goals for wins and losses and championships and all sorts of things," Wilson said after he had coached Colby, "and then there are goals in terms of something else. I would like my kids to know

it's important always to come to practice on time, always be at practice, and when they're there, always have a good attitude—to embrace
the activity for what it is, get as much out of it as you possibly can,
and realize that, in it, you may learn something about yourself in terms
of self-discipline, meeting challenges, achieving goals. All of those
things are ways to view aspects of coaching. Ideally, we embrace all of
them."

High school track and field, Wilson believed, represented sports at
its purest. It was rare for a runner, jumper, or thrower to earn an athletic scholarship, and most kids who participated in track and field did
so because gym teachers or coaches in other sports had suggested they
try it. Because of the individualized nature of track and field, Wilson
could focus his coaching on improving each athlete, and the entire
team, as a by-product, would benefit. (East's boys' team was a perennial
favorite to win its league.) To him, the runner who finished last in the
800 but who shaved a second off his time had achieved as much as, if
not more than, the first-place finisher who failed to lower his time by
even a millisecond. Like golf, like swimming, track and field pitted an
athlete against his toughest opponent: himself. In that self-competition,
Wilson found sports' true worth.

East had a large track team of sixty boys or more, and with each
team member, Wilson and his coaches did one of two things: Either they
assigned an event to the athlete based on the aptitudes or skills that
he displayed in practice, or, as in Colby's case, they allowed each athlete
to choose for himself the event or events in which he would compete.
Wilson recognized that, unlike in school, where a teacher had to catch
his attention, had to dazzle him a bit to get him interested, Colby was
self-motivated when it came to sports. He was not the sort of athlete
who would need much prodding to deliver his best effort. He was comfortable confronting a challenge, and his presence on the track team, in
and of itself, posed one. He was, after all, a 240-pound sprinter with a
brace wrapped around his recently reconstructed knee. So Colby would
stay after practice, after hours of honing his technique when putting the

shot, to work on exploding out of the starting block with more speed, to drop his time in the 40-yard dash, to push himself past the limitations that his injury had imposed on him.

"I love having Colby on the team, even though he's never going to score a point for us," Wilson told Mark one day at a meet. "These other guys whine and complain about everything, and here's a guy out there busting his tail on one leg."

Once a CB West season ended—state title or not—Mike Pettine spent much of his time on the telephone, talking up his players to prep-school coaches and college recruiters. He felt he owed it to his seniors to be a liaison between them and whatever opportunities might await them, and he felt that he especially owed those efforts to a player such as Bryan Buckley. The three years, the long hours, the leadership, the prioritizing of team before self—Bryan had given him a lot. Yes, Mike Pettine owed him.

Often, the hardest part of all those phone calls for Pettine was the expectations of his players' parents. Their logic was simple, if flawed, and they were usually unafraid of expressing it: *CB West players have received football scholarships in the past. My son was on a state-championship team. Therefore, my son should get a football scholarship.* Pettine knew that the recruiting process didn't work that way. It wasn't so linear. College coaches didn't always listen to recommendations from high school coaches, and though West's reputation as a state power may have given Pettine's players a small presumptive advantage over other recruits, it guaranteed them nothing. In the end, a scout or coach would rely on his eyes—by watching a player perform either in person or on game film—to judge whether a player was worthy of a scholarship.

These variables created a potential problem for Bryan, for it was difficult to appreciate what he brought to a football team just from watching him on film. A few Division I schools, including West Virginia, Massachusetts, and New Hampshire, had shown slight interest in him based on Bryan's recruiting tape and Pettine's pressing, but nothing more. Bryan had not been Dustin Picciotti. He had not been the center-piece of West's offense. Furthermore, his grades had slipped during football season, and he needed to boost his SAT score if he was to play football at a four-year college. All of these factors pointed toward his going to prep school for at least a semester.

While Pettine continued to work the phones, Bryan got a break. New Hampshire did not offer Bryan a football scholarship, but Chip Kelly, who was about to be promoted from offensive line coach to of-fensive coordinator at UNH, called his friend Mike Stubljar, the head coach at Worcester Academy in Massachusetts, telling him he had game tape of a kid from Pennsylvania who, according to Stubljar's memory of the conversation, "blocked the hell out of people." A recommenda-tion from a college coach Stubljar trusted was all he needed to hear; he didn't have to see Bryan's highlight tape to know he should contact him. He called the Buckleys' house. *Our offense is similar to West's*, he said to Bryan. *We could use a fullback like you. Come on up for a visit.* Bryan liked what he heard. So did Pettine. Bryan mailed Stubljar some game tapes, and they confirmed what Kelly had said: Bryan did indeed block the hell out of people.

One visit was all it took. Worcester seemed the right fit. Bryan had found what he believed to be his bridge to a Division I football scholar-ship. He could handle the months away from home; there was nothing tying him to Doylestown, anyway—no long-term girlfriend, no immedi-ate job prospects that he felt compelled to pursue. His friends Brian Spratt and Ed Hillman would remain there, but Dave Armstrong and Corey Potter already were off at college, and Corey was at UMass, just an hour or so away. There was just one loose end. He, like Colby Um-brell, had one more high school football game to play.

Saturday, June 12, 1999

CB East and CB West were scheduled to hold their respective senior-class commencement ceremonies in four days. But for Colby, Bryan, and the other players from East and West who had been selected to play for the North team in the Bucks County All-Star Football Game, a night of football in the late spring heat provided a more fitting moment of closure. Finally, after three years on opposite sides of the East and West rivalry, the players who had attended middle school together, like Colby and Bryan, were teammates again.

The game, held at Council Rock High School, was Larry Greene's third as a head coach, and from the first day of the week of practice he had with the North team, Greene intuited how easy coaching this team would be. For one thing, this team was more talented than either of the previous All-Star squads that Greene had coached; it featured Bryan Scott and Steve Kreider, Council Rock's Alex Wade, and four members of CB West's offensive line: Ben Carber, Jon Tor, Joe Wilson, and Jon Wilson. For another, there were "no 'me' kids on the team," as Greene put it. On the Monday before the game—a blistering 94-degree day, with the trees alongside East's practice field offering virtually no shade to the players—Greene had the players run some wind sprints. Most of them had not played a football game in at least six months, and the sprints left the players doubled over and sopping wet with sweat.

"You guys ready to be done?" Greene said.

"We've got to do more," Bryan Buckley said.

They kept running.

That was the Buckley whom Kreider and Colby remembered from their time together at Lenape Middle School—a boy "deadly focused on playing CB West football," as Kreider described him. The remainder of the week, Bryan was not so serious. "He was almost effervescent," Greene recalled. "He had a smile. You could see he was just a passionate kid. You could see that right away."

For Colby, being back on a football field was refreshing. By his own estimation, at least 90 percent of his original strength had returned to his knee. In East's final two regular-season games, Colby had been "probably half the player he was," Greene told a reporter before the All-Star game. The difference in him was apparent in the team's scrimmages. He had played well, and he had enjoyed the entire week, the relationships with the players and coaches. *He's never by himself,* Greene thought.

The game itself was never close. The North team scored on its opening possession as Kreider, who started at quarterback, completed passes of twenty-six yards to Wade and twelve yards to Scott to set up Wade's five-yard touchdown run. Bryan and Colby spent much of the game on the same side of the field in North's defensive lineup—Colby at tackle, Bryan at linebacker—doing their parts in a dominant performance. The South team managed only forty-seven yards of total offense, including an absurd –3 rushing yards, in North's 28–0 victory.

"We just 'outphysicaled' them," Bryan told reporters after the game. "We wanted to win convincingly."

Win convincingly. Save one game his sophomore year, it was all Bryan had known in his high school career. After the players had shed their uniforms and showered, Bryan shook Colby's hand and said goodbye. He was glad that they had gotten to know each other more in the days before the game, before they moved on from their lives in Doylestown. Colby worked hard, did what it took. That was all Bryan could ask of a teammate. That was what earned his respect. Maybe someday he'd cross paths with Colby again, and tell him that.

ELEVEN

Away from Home

Though Colby was unaware of it, his choice of Wyoming Seminary as the place to continue his education connected him, however tangentially, to one of the seminal nights in football history, and one of the strangest. Wyoming Seminary had played in America's first official night football game, against Mansfield State Normal School (now Mansfield University), on September 28, 1892—which was, fittingly enough for what the game's setting would portend, a Monday. In a valley deep within the Appalachian Mountains of northern Pennsylvania, the teams played to a scoreless tie on a field that was 110 yards long and covered in stones, butternuts, and manure from the cattle that idled around it. Adding to the odd game conditions, a power company wheeled in a 4,300-pound generator and plunged a light pole into the soil at midfield. The lights gave off so little illumination that the players—who had to dodge the large pole at the 55-yard line—often couldn't tell who had the ball, and the referee called the game at halftime.

That tidbit of trivia never came up during Colby's and his parents' search for the right prep school. It might have, had Colby made football his top priority, but his primary purpose in attending "Sem" (as the school's administrators, teachers, and students called it) was neither to play football there nor to assure himself of earning a football scholarship elsewhere. Had it been, the departure of Sem head coach Matt DiBernardo for an assistant coaching position at Hobart College in Geneva, New York, very well might have caused Colby to rethink his decision. Instead, he left Doylestown in August for the red brick buildings, the placid social life, the sheer isolation of Sem, bent on discarding the laziness and indifference that had characterized his entire academic career. At Central Bucks East, he had scored a 1200 on his SATs, well above average, but what good was his innate intelligence if he wasn't willing to apply himself? His torn ACL had taught him something about himself. It had taken West Point away from him, had cost him two games and perhaps cost his team a great season, yet it hadn't cost him his livelihood or his future. Football, he now realized, was a luxury. He loved it, but he didn't need it.

In truth, Wyoming Seminary's relationship with football wasn't much different from Colby's new regard for the sport's place in his life. The Methodist Church had founded the school in 1844, and Sem's mission was to maintain an accent on Christian values in its curriculum. Its four to five hundred upper-school students (grades nine through twelve) were required to take a course called The Bible and Western Culture, though they did not receive mandatory religious instruction. Its dress code provisions called for tucked-in collared shirts and full-length, hemmed slacks at all times; sneakers were verboten. Curfew was 11:30 P.M. In his first trimester, Colby took a "postgraduate experience" course taught by the dean of Sem's upper school, David Davies. The course was as much a group guidance counselor meeting for Sem's sixteen postgrads as it was an academic endeavor; it focused on the students' adjustment from public school to a private boarding school, their preparation for the SATs, and their college searches. But Davies, whose son Christopher was a senior at Sem and lived in Colby's dormitory, considered the course essential to a postgrad's adjustment to his new surroundings, his new rules, and this new phase in his life. From what Davies could tell, Colby's adjustment was easier than most. Davies wanted Colby and Sem's other postgrad football players to think of the sport as just one thread in their tapestry of experiences at the school. It shouldn't be their sole reason for being there.

"You're not playing under the lights," Davies told him. "You're playing for you and for your love of the game."

No, the postgrads weren't playing under the lights—because Sem's Nesbitt Field had none. It more closely resembled CB East's practice field than it did War Memorial Field. Its single grandstand, painted sky blue and white, accommodated at most three hundred spectators, and the field was so close to a street of modest two-story homes that if a quarterback happened to throw the football over a receiver's head and out of bounds, he ran the risk of shattering a window. DiBernardo's replacement, Corey Goff, would coach football at Sem for only the '99 season, Colby's season, and he described the atmosphere at those prep school games as "a lot more subdued than a Bucks County high school game with something on the line." But Colby, after suffering a high ankle sprain early in the season, was okay with subdued, okay with Wyoming Seminary's 3–6 record in 1999. He still possessed enough quickness that Goff and Randy Granger, Sem's running backs coach, relied on him as a pulling guard along the offensive line. (Instead of blocking the defensive lineman directly in front of him, Colby "pulled," moving laterally to block another defender on the opposite side of the formation.) Perhaps he was not quite the player he had been before the knee and ankle injuries, but the coaches at Lehigh University, a Division I-AA program, thought enough of him to track his progress from CB East to Wyoming Seminary. "They wanted him badly," Granger said, but to Colby, there were other considerations.

"He wanted a college where he could play football but also get a first-class education," Davies recalled. "He was not willing to trade down on the academic part for a bigger-time college football program."

That part of Colby's personality, of his self-confidence, struck

Davies. Colby was never unrealistic about his football ability. Over his twenty-two years as a teacher and administrator at Sem, Davies had known postgrads who regarded their time at the school merely as a means to their athletic ends. Many times, those students came away from the experience thinking they had made a mistake by going to prep school.

Saturday, October 16, 1999

Central Bucks West defeated Central Bucks East, 42–0, at War Memorial Field—the rivalry's largest margin of victory in twenty-eight years. The Bucks were now 7–0. The inexperienced Patriots—no more Colby, no more Bryan Scott, no more Steve Kreider—were now 0–7 and would finish the season with a 3–8 record.

West scored its final touchdown when senior Andrew Elsing, in one motion, blocked and caught a punt from East's Brian Davis and returned the ball fifty yards into the end zone.

Jail. That's what the whole damn school felt like. To Bryan Buckley, the seventy-two-acre campus of Worcester Academy—its Victorian columns and ivied walls, its gleaming green athletic fields, the very blending of the contemporary and the antique that was also characteristic of Doylestown—might as well have been a prison.

Because this was not Doylestown, and this was not high school. At West, he and his friends could saunter into a Saturday night party, their black-and-gold football jackets affording them status in the social strata of their peers, and they never felt the need to fit in, never minded that some of the other partygoers might have thought of them as meatheads. They could amuse themselves, crack each other up, give each other wedgies, and if they had a can or two of Budweiser at a party, that was okay, because having a beer at a party was part of being a teenager, and if some of West's younger players were at the party, Bryan could remind them that they had to be careful, that being a CB West football player carried with it certain responsibilities, that a night of fun could careen out of control and damage the players and the program. That was part of growing up, of becoming a man—having that freedom and learning how to handle it. But here, at Worcester, where the male students had to wear shirts and ties and everyone kept his dorm room door open while he studied and no one was allowed to have a television in his room and bedtime was 10:30, where was the freedom?

And the football . . . where was the football that he had known at West? He was going through what he and other alumni of the program called "the CB West hangover," a period in which he realized that nothing at his next level of football would equal the quality of coaching, the sense of community, and the success that he had experienced in high school. Once a week while Bryan was at Worcester, Mike Pettine would call to check up on him, and Bryan would pour out his frustration to Pettine. *It's not like West, Coach. It's not like West at all. I've got to get out of here.* There were things that were good. Worcester had a terrific '99 season, winning seven of its eight games, including its final four by a combined score of 107–13—a stretch that was CB West–like in its results. Bryan's roommate and his closest friend on the team was its quarterback, Gary Rockne, the great-grandson of Knute Rockne, the legendary Notre Dame coach. Rockne kept a photo of himself sitting on the lap of Heisman Trophy winner and NFL wide receiver Tim Brown, and he sometimes fielded phone calls from his "Uncle Lou": former Notre Dame coach Lou Holtz. And Bryan was becoming a better student because, in part, of his football coach, Mike Stubljar. Stubljar taught a postgraduate literature course, introducing Bryan and the other postgrad athletes to David Guterson's *Snow Falling on Cedars* and Tobias Wolff's *This Boy's Life*, closing the classroom door for some just-between-them bull sessions so that the students could vent. Those were the good things. They did not, in Bryan's mind, outnumber the bad.

Despite the lopsided victories at Worcester, the football wasn't the same to Bryan. The players, the coaches, the fans—no one seemed to take it as seriously as he did, as everyone at West had. Starting at full-back and linebacker, he'd come back to the sideline and try to jack some guys up, and they'd tell him to calm down. From Stubljar's perspective, Bryan had trouble acclimating himself to a setting where football was not supposed to be the most important component of his day-to-day existence. Stubljar had grown up in the town of Steelton, in central Pennsylvania, and he understood how intoxicating it must have been to be a CB West football player—and Bryan wasn't just any CB West football player. He was the captain of a team that went 15–0, that won a state-title game by forty-nine points, that might have been the best that Pennsylvania high school football had ever seen. "They were like gods," he said years later, and Bryan seemed to think that he could play at Worcester for a few months, get a football scholarship somewhere, and all would be well. "At CB West, he had all this to live up to," Stubljar said. "It was a lot of pressure on Bryan, more than I think he realized. I don't think he wanted to let anyone down." So Stubljar tried to seize the moment in those classroom bull sessions to persuade Bryan that earning a Division I scholarship wasn't so easy, that he had to broaden his objectives and goals. Sooner or later, he'd have to let the game go.

"Football's not everything, buddy," he told him.

It was to Bryan. While Stubljar was recruiting him to Worcester, Bryan had believed that Stubljar would make him the star of Worcester's offense, give him the opportunity to showcase his skills in a way that Dustin Picciotti's presence had prevented at West. But Stubljar ran a far different offense from West's, one that was much more pass-heavy. Ninety percent of his plays, he estimated, came out of a shotgun formation, and he wanted Rockne and the Worcester receivers, in the jargon of football, to "stretch the field vertically." It was not the ideal system for a fullback, and Bryan and his father felt a bit betrayed—that, for Worcester's annual tuition of more than $30,000, Stubljar had sold them an empty promise.

"You can't promise a kid anything," Stubljar said. "You can't promise you'll improve his SAT scores, can't promise you'll give him a scholarship. You tell him, 'If you work hard, I'll do everything I can to get you where you want to get to.' That's not a guarantee. When we reach a point that you're not getting what you want, we'll look at something else."

As the end of the fall semester neared, Bryan was getting closer and closer to that point. He returned home for a long weekend, discussing with Bill and Connie his doubts about Worcester and his future, wondering whether he could finish the term. Deep down, he still didn't know what he wanted to do with his life, what he wanted to be; football was all he knew, all he had known, and as strange as it might have sounded to someone else, the NFL was still on the periphery of his dreams. But he would not quit, would not let down his parents and Pettine. He would honor his commitment, finish the semester, but as soon as he got an offer from a Division I scholarship program—and he was certain it was only a matter of time—he was going, going, gone.

Saturday, December 11, 1999

He had told no one but his son that this game would be his last, so there was hardly anyone at Hersheypark Stadium who could grasp the irony of what was happening: Mike Pettine was about to lose the last game of his coaching career.

It was the Class AAAA championship game, 14–0 CB West against 12–1 Erie Cathedral Prep—the team that New Castle had upset in the western semifinal the year before, the team that now led West, 13–7, with three minutes left in the fourth quarter. The game had been as taxing to Pettine as the entire season had been. Once again, the Bucks had to beat Michael Pettine's North Penn Knights twice, but this year, the games' buildup and outcomes had been even more difficult for the elder Pettine to cope with. West and North Penn were each 9–0 entering the last weekend of the regular season, and their matchup drew national attention, as newspapers and television outlets couldn't resist the story: perhaps the two finest football teams in Pennsylvania, coached by a father and his son. To intensify the drama, two film crews, independent of each other, were documenting the teams' season—one crew that would produce a feature-length film on West, one that was following North Penn for ESPN's show *The Season*.

The two victories over North Penn—17–7 in the season finale, 21–0 in the district championship—had taken some of the pleasure out of the season for Pettine, as had the grind of maintaining the West machine. Unhappy over how Pettine was using him in the offense, Picciotti had quit the team briefly earlier in the season, only to return a day later after Pettine had accepted his apology. Now, Picciotti had sprained his right ankle in the first quarter and was gone from the state-title game, and Erie Cathedral was about to punt the ball back to the Bucks from its own 9-yard line.

Bill and Connie Buckley had driven out to Hershey for the game. While Bryan, trapped 350 miles away in his Worcester dorm room and anxious to find out what was happening, kept calling his brother-in-law Chris DiSciullo every twenty minutes or so, Bill kept his trusty video camera trained on the action and managed to capture a stunning sequence for posterity: Andrew Elsing's shooting through the line, blocking the punt—just as he had done two months earlier against CB East—picking up the football at the 2-yard line and staggering into the end zone. The extra point gave West a 14–13 victory, its third consecutive state championship, and its forty-fifth consecutive victory. In Doylestown, where a local cable network had broadcast the game on television, people screamed in the bars along Main Street, and car horns blared. In Worcester, Bryan Buckley wished that he could have been there to witness the Bucks' win, taking solace in a truth that he believed to be timeless: CB West was still CB West and always would be, as long as Mike Pettine was there.

Mark and Colby Umbrell walked through the cold, through the Hersheypark Stadium parking lot, to their car, still marveling over West's miraculous win. Mark had picked up Colby at Sem, and the two of them had driven together, down Route 81, to Hershey for the state-title game.

They got back into the car and kept heading south.

Thursday, January 13, 2000

The news of Mike Pettine's retirement had been winding its way like a serpentine stream through the Doylestown community for a week. Pettine had met with West principal Rod Stone to reveal his intentions, and out of that meeting, word trickled to other school officials, to CB West players past and present, to the players' parents, to the program's fans, and eventually to the media that Pettine was indeed stepping down after thirty-three years and 326 victories as a head coach. Stone had sent out a press release to announce that Pettine, in a 3:30 P.M. press conference in the West auditorium, would address the "future direction of the program," but there was no mystery as to what the conference's true topic would be.

Thirty minutes before the conference began, Pettine had gathered the West seniors and returning players in the weight room to tell them of his decision, and they entered the auditorium stone-faced. Among the 250 people on hand, Pettine's family sat in one of the front rows, and Bryan wasn't far behind them. Mike Carey, Pettine's presumptive successor, sat on an armrest a few rows back and to Pettine's left. Carey was by himself, his knees up close and his torso turned to face the podium behind which Pettine stood.

As Pettine officially made his retirement public and gave a brief address, it was impossible not to contemplate the stature of the West football program, the effort that Pettine had exerted to build it, and the toll that his immersion in its fortunes had exacted. He talked about the trade-offs that he had made since his promotion to head coach at Central Bucks High in 1967, the recurring question of how best to balance football and family, a million little choices over the years that—too often, he could now admit—tipped the scales in favor of football.

"I must have missed some of these beautiful fall days," he said. "You only get so many beautiful fall days in your lifetime."

His voice never broke, and he shed not a single tear. He conveyed calm throughout his speech, except for those moments that he would lift his hand and put it to his mouth, or when Stone presented him with a black CB West sweatshirt with Pettine's record—326–42–4—embroidered in gold on the left lapel. When Pettine made any sort of gesture, when he held up that sweatshirt for all to see, his hands trembled, his emotions leaking out of his fingertips.

Bryan sat at rapt attention, trying to process Pettine's words and their ramifications. Bryan had just begun to feel better about his situation, and Pettine had been part of the reason. Stubljar had contacted Don Brown, an old friend who was now the defensive coordinator at UMass. *I've got a kid who can play fullback or linebacker, who's bouncing off the walls, who doesn't want to be here anymore,* Stubljar said to Brown. *He's a great kid. Do anything you ask him to do.* In the course of checking into Bryan's background, Brown then called Pettine, who sang Bryan's praises to him. Finally, Brown talked to Bryan. UMass, he told him, couldn't offer him a scholarship, but he could walk onto the football team as a redshirt freshman and perhaps earn a scholarship by the time he was a senior. UMass also had two additional enticements for Bryan: One of his best friends, Corey Potter, played there (as did another CB West graduate, Greg Ward), and the Minutemen, under head coach Mark Whipple, had won the 1998 Division I-AA national championship.

Now, this. Just when Bryan's college situation was at last settled to his liking, he was listening to Pettine say, "I feel basically I do not have the energy it takes." What would his departure mean for West, for those kids who were part of the program now and the kids who would be in the years to come?

"He's probably one of the most caring guys you're going to meet," Bryan told a reporter after the press conference had ended, describing the weekly phone calls that Pettine had made to him at Worcester. "He was acting like a father to me. This is a horrible day. It's a dark day not just for CB West football, but for football in general."

February 2000

When Jim Margraff, the head football coach at Johns Hopkins University, had watched the highlight tape that Colby had sent him—Colby dragging down running backs and charging after quarterbacks, snippets of his CB East football career set to Aerosmith's "Back in the Saddle" and Steven Tyler's screeching vocals—he had been surprised that the football player on the screen would consider choosing a Division III program. *This kid, if he's 100 percent healthy, can be a star for us*, Margraff thought.

Colby and Mark had met Margraff face-to-face for the first time during the weekend of West's win over Erie Cathedral Prep, and Margraff had felt an instant rapport with Colby as they had chatted during their meeting. Margraff himself was a Hopkins alumnus, graduating in 1982 as the school's most accomplished quarterback, the program's career leader in pass completions, attempts, yards, and touchdowns, and since becoming Hopkins' head coach in 1990, he had not often encountered a recruit who seemed as comfortable around adults, as emotionally mature, as Colby. Later, Margraff was pleased when players who had gotten to meet Colby during his visit told him, *Coach, you've got to get this guy here.*

Colby had loved his visit to Hopkins, particularly the campus's location in Baltimore and its proximity to Washington, D.C. He was considering majoring in political science, after all. That Hopkins's football program was somewhat of an afterthought among its own students—the university had long been a Division I power in men's lacrosse—did not dissuade him from going there. The environment at Sem—the discipline, the collegelike class sizes and atmosphere, the time alone—had sharpened Colby's study habits. He had earned straight As.

He took the SATs a second time, and his score shot up to 1350. He was a student first now, and his original plan of applying to the Coast Guard Academy lost its appeal.

His college choice was down to Hopkins and Lehigh, and though he was leaning toward Hopkins, Lehigh needed his answer in February. So he and Mark had to give Margraff an ultimatum: Either Hopkins officially accepted Colby in February, or he would choose Lehigh. Margraff helped push through Colby's acceptance. When he learned that he had gotten into Hopkins, Colby found David Davies in Sem's cafeteria and high-fived him. Then he told Randy Granger.

"To be honest, I was shocked," Granger recalled. "But that was the kind of kid he was. He was a thinker."

With Sem's student guidelines limiting Colby's access to a telephone, Nancy offered to call the Lehigh coaches on his behalf and inform them of his decision. One of them called her back. She remembered their conversation this way:

"Colby has chosen Hopkins," she said.

"What? Why would he pick Hopkins over Lehigh?"

"Probably because it's a better school."

"Well, he obviously must not be the caliber of football player we thought."

Nancy hung up. That Lehigh coach sure didn't know her son.

TWELVE

Change

July 2000

Following those months at Wyoming Seminary, when he was sequestered from his friends and engrossed in improving his academics, here
at last was heaven for Colby Umbrell: floating in his family's swimming
pool, his parents and siblings away on vacation for a week, a Jack-and-
Coke in his hand, not a worry on his mind. That was how he spent
every afternoon of that week. His friends came over to the house each
night to hang out. The beginning of his freshman year at Johns Hopkins
University was still more than a month away. This was pure bliss, until
the telephone rang one day while he was relaxing in the pool.

"Whassssssuuuup!" Colby said into the phone, as if he were a character in a beer commercial.

The voice on the other end was somber.

"Can I please speak to Nancy Umbrell?"

"I'm sorry," Colby said, turning serious. "She's on vacation."

"This is Dr. Friedman," the voice replied. "Have her call me immediately. It's about her test results."

September 2000

Bryan Buckley had arrived at the University of Massachusetts with two endeavors on his personal agenda: to play football and to grow his hair long. For now, he could accomplish only one of them.

His hair was something to see. He had dyed it platinum blond, the color of a Southern California housewife's coif, and it was longer and thicker than it had ever been before. Those prep school shackles were off, especially now that he had a semester at UMass under his belt. The spring had been some fun. Everything he'd heard about UMass's reputation as one of the supreme party schools in the universe was true. There were five colleges and universities—UMass, Amherst, Hampshire, Smith, and Mount Holyoke—and more than 28,000 students within eighteen square miles. How could there not be parties aplenty? Plus, when selecting his courses, he could load up on electives; he could wait to take the core courses of his major, communication, until his junior and senior years. His favorite class that spring had been Abnormal Psychology, one of the most popular courses on campus. One day, the professor, Dr. Richard Halgin, shepherded the class through a psychological study of Charles Manson. Bryan was fascinated. Even if he was hungover, he would wake up by eight o'clock on a Friday morning to make sure he didn't miss that class.

Spring football practice was grueling. Grueling, Bryan could handle, thanks to Mike Pettine. During the Minutemen's indoor workouts in a gymnasium mat room, among the ninety players on the UMass roster, defensive coordinator Don Brown saw, for the first time in the flesh, that "tough-ass kid" he had recruited. "It was a very rigorous scenario," Brown recalled. "It's a very rigorous, high intensity process—a lot of up and down, a lot of rolling. It's roll right, roll left, slam yourself on the ground. We'd finish with 'Escape from Saigon,' where everyone's on the ground. They have to crawl, roll forward, and it's all elbows and knees. Usually, the guys who go into those things, you can tell they've got the deer-in-the-headlights look the first time. He loved it. I'm going, 'This guy's off his rocker 'cause he really likes it. He ain't afraid at all.'"

By September, though, Brown was no longer at UMass. Over the summer, he had accepted the head coaching position at Northeastern University. His departure disappointed Bryan. Brown had recruited Bryan as a fullback, but once Bryan arrived at UMass, Brown had told him, "I'm going to move you to linebacker because only one fullback starts, but three linebackers start." Moreover, Brown had telephoned Mike Pettine to explain why he had changed Bryan's position. Maybe he did it to maintain a good relationship with Pettine and West so that he could recruit other West players, but the gesture still meant something to Bryan. It showed that Brown understood that Pettine was a big part of Bryan's life.

It wasn't merely Brown's absence that made the fall a bit more difficult for Bryan. Because he was redshirting as a freshman, he hadn't played an official football game in more than a year, the longest he'd gone without the sport since he was in seventh grade. All he was, was a scout team linebacker, running the opponents' defenses in practice, a stand-in for a 7–4 football team. Thursdays before road games were particularly hard; after practice, he'd have to sit there and watch his teammates pack up their equipment to travel. On Thursdays, he said later, he felt "like a turd."

Hiding his homesickness from his new friends was easy. Colby could always play the comedian, could keep them laughing and smiling even as he agonized over his mother's health.

He turned his dormitory—Building B, on the north end of Johns Hopkins's campus—into a place that was part fun house, part pleasure dome. He and his roommates decided one night to light some rolls of toilet paper on fire and toss them out a window, just to see what would happen, and the smoky smell in Building B finally forced the dorm's resident assistant to ask them to stop. His favorite article of clothing was a black T-shirt that read *Crayola Rocks!* across its front; he wore it constantly, primarily because it seemed to have a talismanic effect on members of the opposite sex. On Sundays, Colby and Ben Stopper, a freshman kickoff and punt returner on the football team, would dash to a local supermarket to buy strawberries and daiquiri mix, don sunglasses and top hats and the shiniest shirts they owned, and sit on the lawn in Hopkins's quadrangle, sipping their daiquiris and dying for passersby to pay them some attention. At nine o'clock one Saturday morning, Colby bounded down the hall of his dormitory to the room of another freshman, Chris Said. He woke Said up, pulled out what appeared to be a full handle of vodka, and said, "Hey, Chris, watch me chug this." Before Said could move, Colby gulped down half the bottle and unleashed a belch that shook the dorm room's walls. "Colby!" Said yelled, but Colby told him that he just wanted to celebrate the fact that it was Saturday. He had Said convinced that the bottle had been full of vodka, instead of what it actually contained: tap water. Colby kept up the ruse a touch longer, got a sheepish laugh from Said, and moved on down the hall to pull the prank on another unsuspecting sleeper.

"He was pretty well known, and not just among the football guys," recalled Neil Bardham, who lived on Colby's floor in the fall 2000 semester. "There was a touch of crazy in him in a fun, adventurous sort of way."

The practical jokes were, in truth, a convenient cover for Colby's anxiety, allowing him to put aside the personal matter that most occupied his thoughts. Earlier in the summer, Nancy had gone to the Hospital of the University of Pennsylvania for a series of tests that, by the time Colby hopped out of the swimming pool to answer that doctor's phone call, had confirmed that cancer had infiltrated her mammary ducts. During Nancy's first bout with breast cancer, when she was thirty-one, radiation treatments and a lumpectomy had been sufficient to treat the disease. The doctors had caught this second cancer early, and they hoped that a lumpectomy would work again. They performed another. It did not. The only option left to save Nancy was a bilateral mastectomy; she had to have both breasts removed, or she would die.

Nancy tried to downplay the severity of her situation. She insisted to her family that she was not afraid, that she had survived cancer once and would survive it again, and she was fortunate to be eligible for a cosmetic procedure, to be performed immediately after the mastectomy, in which doctors would remove muscle tissue from her abdomen and use that tissue to reconstruct her breasts. But for Mark and the four Umbrell children, the fear of losing a wife and mother was fresh once more, particularly for Colby. Each week, he asked his parents to drive down to Baltimore for a visit. Then, when they did visit, he didn't want them to leave. Mark and Nancy couldn't understand why Colby was so desperate to see the two of them so often. After all, he had just spent a year away from home at Wyoming Seminary. It wasn't until the three of them went to lunch one day and Nancy left the room that the depth of Colby's anxiety—and his belief that his parents were hiding how grave Nancy's prognosis really was—became clear.

"Now," he said to Mark, "tell me the truth about Mom."

After the operation, Nancy wasn't up to attending Hopkins's 54–13 victory over Gettysburg on September 29. But Mark came to the game, and as a surprise for Nancy, Colby hitched a ride home with him, the two of them ducking into a rest stop along I-95 so that Colby could buy his mother a "Maryland" teddy bear. When he and Mark returned to Doylestown, Colby saw his mother for the first time since her surgeries. She was still groggy, and four tubes—two leading into her chest, two below her belly button—coiled in front of her.

To hide the tubes, she wore a maternity dress the following Saturday when she sat in the stands for Hopkins's 28–17 loss at Ursinus.

Still, the sight of her that day in Doylestown had shaken Colby. All he knew was that his mother was sick. Margraff, too, had picked up on Colby's distress and called him in for a one-on-one meeting. "It was easily visible," he said later. "His mom was ill, and that was devastating to him." Margraff had gathered, just in the course of recruiting Colby to Hopkins, how close he was to Mark and Nancy. As Margraff talked with him, Colby confessed that he couldn't get past his sense of guilt over Nancy's condition and his geographical and intangible distance from it. His mother was suffering, and he was off at college, enjoying himself, 130 miles away from her.

"Everything's going to be fine," he told Colby. "We want you to be here. We want you to excel. You've got to concentrate on yourself. You can't feel guilty about being at a great school, having fun, going to class, and playing football."

Long before, Margraff had learned to tailor his coaching style and his interpersonal approach to the typical student-athlete he encountered at Hopkins. He ran a complicated offense, knowing that his players had the intelligence to handle the various reads, shifts, and formation changes. "The smart," he often said to them, "take from the strong." He was not by any definition an authoritarian; it was his players' responsibility to get themselves in shape and mentally prepare themselves to play football, and if one of them wasn't prepared, another who was would replace him in the lineup. The way Margraff looked at it, the two hours that his players spent on the football field each day had to be the best two hours of their day. These were young men who were stepping out of organic chemistry labs and political theory lectures and the self-applied pressures of elite academia straight into football practice, and the last thing they needed was their coach screaming bloody murder at them. If any of his players couldn't make it home for a holiday, Margraff invited them to his house to have dinner with his wife and family.

"He was the kind of coach you could go to with any kind of problem," Ben Stopper said. "He really cared."

The meeting with Margraff reassured Colby. Hard as it had been for him to see Nancy in her postsurgery state, she was again clear of cancer—a blessing that, once Colby accepted it, lifted his guilt over being apart from her and should have freed him to play football with a clear mind. But his body didn't cooperate. At the start of the season, he had been a regular member of Hopkins's defensive tackle rotation, but he broke his hand after the loss to Ursinus. For a Hopkins team

State Street in Doylestown. The Art Deco style of the County Theater makes it a natural eye-catcher.
Photo by Kate Sielski

The Fountain House Starbucks, the epicenter of Doylestown.
Photo by Kate Sielski

The Mercer Museum is one of the most well-known and striking buildings in Doylestown. *Photo by Kate Sielski*

The Bucks County Vietnam Veterans Memorial, outside the county courthouse in Doylestown. *Photo by Kate Sielski*

This stone sign welcomes visitors to Central Bucks
High School West. *Photo by Kate Sielski*

Bryan Buckley (uniform No. 9) celebrates with his
CB West teammates after their 56–7 victory over New Castle in the
1998 state-title game. *Photo courtesy of Bill and Connie Buckley*

Colby Umbrell charges onto War Memorial Field during the CB East Patriots' pregame introductions. As a senior in the 1998 season, Colby was a team captain and started at offensive and defense tackle.

Photo courtesy of Mark and Nancy Umbrell

Colby Umbrell sacks Council Rock quarterback
Matt Verbit during CB East's 36–13 win during the 1998 season.
Photo courtesy of Mark and Nancy Umbrell

Two of Colby Umbrell's teammates carry him off the field
after Colby tore his anterior cruciate ligament on Senior Night
against Abington. *Photo courtesy of Mark and Nancy Umbrell*

Bryan Buckley (uniform No. 9) makes a tackle against Pennsbury during the 1998 season. *Photo courtesy of Bill and Connie Buckley*

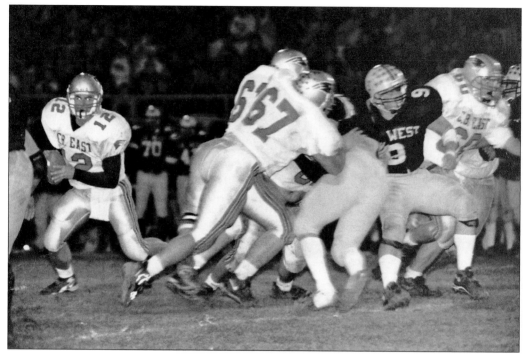

As CB East quarterback Steve Kreider (uniform No. 12) drops back to pass, Colby Umbrell (uniform No. 67) moves off one CB West defender to try to block Bryan Buckley (uniform No. 9). The Bucks won the game, 42–20. *Photo courtesy of Mark and Nancy Umbrell*

Bryan Buckley, Coach Mike Pettine, and Dustin Picciotti (l. to r.)
celebrate the Bucks' 1998 state championship. Earlier in that season,
Pettine had decided to make Picciotti the centerpiece of the West
offense. *Photo courtesy of Bill and Connie Buckley*

Colby Umbrell, at Johns Hopkins University.
Saddled with injuries, Colby played football for only three
years at Hopkins. *Photo courtesy of Mark and Nancy Umbrell*

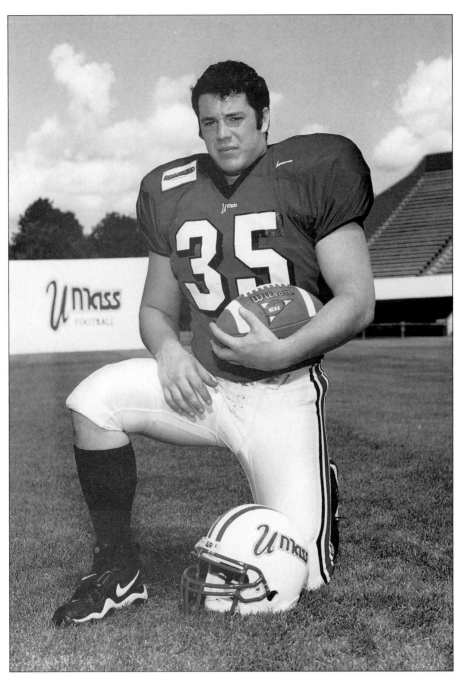

Bryan Buckley, at the University of Massachusetts. Bryan started
two games for the Minutemen during the 2001 season before deciding
to enter the military and transfer to Villanova University.

Photo courtesy of Bill and Connie Buckley

2nd Lt. Bryan
Buckley, United States
Marine Corps, in Iraq.
Photo courtesy of
Bryan Buckley

Bryan Buckley
communicates on
a radio in Iraq.
Photo courtesy of
Bryan Buckley

Bryan Buckley, in a rare
moment alone in Iraq.
The men in his platoon
respected him for his
willingness to participate
in their missions with
gusto.
Photo courtesy of
Bryan Buckley

ABOVE:
The Buckley family (l. to r.): Moey,
Connie, Bryan, Steve, Kim, Bill.
Photo courtesy of Bill and Connie Buckley

LEFT:
Connie Buckley shows off her
customary attire for a CB West
football game.
Photo courtesy of Bill and Connie Buckley

Colby's parents talk to him after a CB East football game at War Memorial Field. Mark Umbrell was the president of the school's football parents' club. *Photo courtesy of Mark and Nancy Umbrell*

The Umbrell family (l. to r.) on Colby's graduation day from Johns Hopkins University: Nancy, Casey, Colby, Bruce, Adam, Mark. *Photo courtesy of Mark and Nancy Umbrell*

After his death, Colby Umbrell (flag on left) was honored in a memorial outside the Bucks County Courthouse in Doylestown. *Photo by Kate Sielski*

that went 5–5, he played in only five games his freshman year, making three tackles.

Thursday, January 18, 2001

Before the turn of the millennium, Central Bucks High School West had not changed football coaches in its thirty-one years of existence. Now, Rod Stone was hosting another press conference to announce that, for the second time in a span of a year and five days, he had to hire a new football coach.

Mike Carey actually had decided to step down as West's head coach two and a half months earlier, while riding on a school bus in the dark. The Bucks had beaten North Penn, 13–7, for their fifty-fifth consecutive victory, moving them one win away from equaling General Braddock High's state-record fifty-six-game winning streak. Yet on the ride back to West, Carey was so physically and emotionally drained that he didn't care to celebrate the win. When he had accepted Stone's offer to succeed Mike Pettine, Carey had anticipated that he would last only one year as head coach, but the job's demands—from the parents, from the community, from himself—had been beyond anything he had envisioned. One night at home, he had sat down in a chair and could barely lift his arms, so tired was he from the hours and pressure that came with being the CB West football coach.

"I compromised every other facet of my life, and I didn't like myself for it," Carey recalled. "I wasn't really enjoying it."

The pressure to maintain perfection heightened as the season progressed. West won its fifty-sixth straight game, then its fifty-seventh to break Braddock's record, then its fifty-eighth and fifty-ninth to reach its fourth state-title game in a row. So when Erie Cathedral Prep—the team that West had beaten the year before on Andrew Elsing's timely blocked punt/touchdown—earned its redemption by outlasting the Bucks, 41–35 in overtime, in the Class AAAA championship game, the end comprised equal parts disappointment, exhaustion, and relief for Carey.

"Getting to the top is easier than staying there," he said at the press conference, "without a doubt."

The man who would replace Carey was Randy Cuthbert—a thirty-one-year-old math teacher at West, an assistant coach under Pettine in 1999 and Carey in 2000, and one of the few alumni of the West program to have played in the NFL. The Bucks had gone 33–0 from 1985 to 1987, Cuthbert's three seasons as a high school player, and he had been a standout running back at Duke University—under a brash, innovative coach named Steve Spurrier—before playing eleven games for the Pittsburgh Steelers over the '93 and '94 seasons, then pursuing his teaching degree. He had a laconic, generally easygoing personality, a contrast to the searing, naked ferocity of Pettine and Carey.

If there was a flaw in Cuthbert's football résumé, it was that his two years as a West assistant coach constituted the sum total of his coaching experience. But to Carey and those who had come to expect perfection from the West program, there were broader concerns. Stone neither expected nor insisted that the next West coach replicate Pettine's and Carey's win-loss records; his charge to Cuthbert was "to grow young people in a successful program." With a wife and two young children at home, and with three math classes to teach daily, Cuthbert had to balance the commitments of his life and football in a way that Pettine and Carey didn't. The fact was, Cuthbert already had a full-time job, and it wasn't as a football coach.

The next day, the *Intelligencer* ran its news story about Carey's resignation across the top of its front page. Below that story was the page's centerpiece photograph. It showed an inside view of what had been Rudolph's Appalachian Trail Outfitters, a store that had sold outdoor clothing and camping gear and had been a fixture in Doylestown at the northeast corner of Main and Oakland streets since 1960. Now, it was three thousand square feet of jagged floor tiles, bare walls, and pregnant emptiness. While Carey had been answering questions at West, Jonathan Rudolph had told an *Intelligencer* reporter that his business was relocating. Chico's, the fashion chain that featured "snappy casual" clothing for women from ages forty to sixty, would be opening a boutique in March at the camping store's longtime location.

Yes, change kept coming to Doylestown.

Saturday, January 20, 2001

According to one report published in the aftermath, as many as twenty thousand protesters clogged the parade route along Pennsylvania Avenue, a pulsating mass of activists alive with anger over the inauguration of George W. Bush as the forty-third president of the United States.

For many of the protesters, the ceremony offered a suitable forum to expel their fury over what had been among the most contentious and controversial of the country's presidential campaigns. The previous two and a half months had been a political maelstrom: cable and television networks on election night projecting both Bush and Al Gore to win Florida's twenty-five electoral votes and, with those votes, the presidency; the introduction of the phrases *hanging chads* and *butterfly ballots* and the name Katherine Harris into the cultural lexicon; the thirty-six-day recount of the Florida popular vote that ended only with the intervention of the U.S. Supreme Court; the fact that the candidate who received half a million more popular votes than his opponent had lost the election. The protesters whose presence at the inauguration had been inspired by the circumstances of Bush's victory carried signs and placards that read *Bush Cheated* and *Hail to the Thief*. Others were unapologetic leftists, outraged that after eight years of the moderate, if scandal-plagued, Clinton administration, a conservative would assume the office of the presidency. They wore bandannas soaked in vinegar (to retard the effects of tear gas), shouted out insults, and threw bottles and tomatoes. Someone lobbed an egg at the presidential limousine. Seven thousand police officers were needed to keep the peace.

Only after his motorcade reached a secure zone near the White House did Bush step out of his limo and walk the final part of the parade route, through drizzle and darkening skies, to the steps of the

Capitol to take the oath of office. In October, during one of his campaign debates with Gore, Bush had dismissed the notion that "nation building" ought to be an aim of U.S. foreign policy or a responsibility of America's armed forces, and there was nothing in his first inaugural address to suggest that he had changed his position on the subject.

"We will build our defenses beyond challenge, lest weakness invite challenge," Bush said. "We will confront weapons of mass destruction, so that a new country is spared new horrors. The enemies of liberty and our country should make no mistake: America remains engaged in the world by history and by choice, shaping a balance of power that favors freedom. We will defend our allies and our interests. We will show purpose without arrogance. We will meet aggression and bad faith with resolve and strength. And to all nations, we will speak for the values that gave our nation birth."

Of the address's 1,584 words, only those 97—6 percent of the speech—dealt directly with foreign policy.

THIRTEEN

Decisions

Tuesday, September 11, 2001

In the apartment that housed him and his four roommates, Bryan Buckley woke at 8:30 A.M. to sweater weather—57 degrees and spiderwebbed clouds. He had a class just before noon and football practice later in the day. Amherst did not share the pure, perfect azure sky that broke over Manhattan that morning.

Bryan lived with Corey Potter and three other UMass football players, and they kept their apartment in the condition that one would expect five college football players to keep an apartment. When Bill and Connie Buckley visited their son, they would "wade through the beer cans," Bill recalled, while making their way from one room to the next. It was the consummate college abode, a home suited for those on the cusp of adulthood, living in the moment and giving only fleeting thoughts to the world outside themselves.

Off to an 0–2 start, the Minutemen were in need of a sharp, efficient workout. On Saturday, they had lost, 49–20, to Marshall University and its talented quarterback, Byron Leftwich, who had thrown for 331 yards and five touchdowns in the game. (The Jacksonville Jaguars would make Leftwich the seventh overall pick in the 2003 NFL draft.) Marshall had outscored UMass, 21–0, in the second half, hardly a heartening development, though Bryan had come away from the game with a modicum of satisfaction and encouragement. With the departure of Don Brown, the defensive coordinator who had recruited Bryan, to Northeastern, UMass head coach Mark Whipple had moved Bryan from linebacker to fullback, where Bryan was backing up a senior. During the game, Bryan had delivered a hellacious hit near the Massachusetts sideline, knocking out a Marshall player cold right in front of Whipple. Bryan hoped that the hit might earn him more playing time. He was eager to practice, to find out how much he had impressed his coach, or if he had impressed him at all.

He would not get that chance.

At 7:59 A.M., American Airlines Flight 11 had departed Boston's Logan International Airport on its designated route to Los Angeles. Sixteen minutes later, United Airlines Flight 175 also lifted off from Logan International for Los Angeles. One after the other, the planes passed over Amherst, only ninety-six miles west of Logan International. Had Bryan been standing in McGuirk Alumni Stadium, UMass's home field, at the right time, he might have seen Flight 11, which would not yet have reached its cruising altitude of 31,000 feet, whoosh through the clouds above him.

Flight 11 continued northwest to Albany, New York, then banked left and proceeded due south to New York City. Ninety-two people were aboard, among them the flight's captain, fifty-two-year-old John Ogonowski; first officer Thomas McGuinness, forty-two; nine flight attendants; and eighty-one passengers. Among those passengers were Abdulaziz al-Omari, Satam M. A. al-Suqami, Waleed M. al-Shehri, Wail M. al-Shehri, and Mohamed Atta.

Flight 175 took a different route to the same horrifying end that awaited Flight 11, staying on its western course before swerving south over northern New Jersey, making a U-turn, and heading north to Manhattan. The flight's fifty-six passengers included Fayez Rashid Ahmed Hassan al-Qadi Banihammad, Mohand al-Shehri, Ahmed al-Ghamdi, Hamza al-Ghamdi, and Marwan al-Shehhi, who considered himself a blood relative of Atta. The flight crew leaders were both from suburban Philadelphia. The first officer was thirty-eight-year-old Michael R. Horrocks, who was from Delaware County, where Connie Buckley was born and raised. The captain was fifty-one-year-old Victor J. Saracini, a Bucks County resident. Saracini, his wife, and his two children lived in Lower Makefield, less than twenty-five miles southeast of Doylestown.

Bryan poured himself a bowl of cereal, turned on the television, and sat down amid the mess of the apartment. Flight 11 had already knifed into the World Trade Center's North Tower at 8:46. Confused about what was happening, Bryan was watching the coverage of the first hijacking and crash when, at 9:03, Flight 175 slammed into the South Tower and disappeared into a billow of flame and black smoke.

Even apart from the stress and strain of his mother's breast cancer recurrence, Colby Umbrell found his first year at Johns Hopkins rougher than he had anticipated it would be. His courses in the fall had been pass/fail, per Hopkins's academic policy for all first-semester freshmen, and in passing all of them, he thought, *I can do this. It'll be easy.* But the spring semester had not been easy. He had pledged a sixty-man fraternity, Alpha Delta Phi, made up mostly of athletes: football players, baseball players, swimmers. It deepened some of his friendships—his teammate Ben Stopper, for instance, had pledged with him—allowed him to make new ones, and gave him another outlet for his sense of humor. As one of his pledging requirements, he strolled into one of Hopkins's campus libraries while wearing a suit and tie, unscrewed a mirror from the wall of one of the men's rooms, and walked back out the library front door with the mirror tucked under his arm. Neil Bardham, who lived in Colby's dormitory, had wondered how Colby could get in and out with the mirror, especially because every Hopkins student had to swipe his or her ID card at a security gate to enter the library, but Colby's explanation had made sense: The security guard probably thought, *Of course this guy in the suit and tie had a good reason to carry a mirror out of the library.*

"One hundred and ten percent confidence," Colby had said.

Such an approach had been fine for pilfering bathroom fixtures; it was not working as well for Colby in the classroom. His grade-point average had dipped well below 3.0 during the spring, and for the first time in his life, his academic struggles affected his self-esteem. Mark and Nancy had worried, when Colby picked Hopkins, that he had overreached, that he might be in over his head academically, but Colby knew that he could handle the rigors of Hopkins's curriculum. He just didn't want people thinking that he couldn't. His insecurity in this single area of his life led him, after his freshman year, to ask Nancy if he could get glasses. She didn't think that he needed them—Colby had always had perfect vision—and at first, he mumbled something about how they'd help him in big lecture halls. Soon, though, he confessed: "Everybody perceives me as this dumb jock. I thought that maybe, if I wore glasses, they wouldn't." (Colby did go to an eye doctor and bought himself prescription eyeglasses, but he lost them and never wore another pair.)

These would be happier times, Colby hoped. Nancy was in good health, so he was less anxious and better able to concentrate on football and his studies and to enjoy himself as he began his sophomore year. He was out of the dorms, residing now with his fraternity brothers at the Alpha Delta Phi chapter house. (The house was actually half of a large apartment building of dull red brick, with two dark, metal stairwells and a sizable community room on the first floor that, when cleared of furniture, made an ideal dance floor.) His sophomore football season was off to a good start. On Saturday, he and the rest of Hopkins's defensive line had held Washington and Lee University to a paltry twenty-seven rushing yards in twenty-four attempts in a 34–3 win—the sixty-first of Jim Margraff's coaching career, the most in Hopkins history. More, Colby had a clearer idea of what path he would take once he had graduated from college. Entering the Army would be a more cost-effective means of paying for law school. If he could gain acceptance to and complete the Army's Officer Candidate School, he could enter the Funded Legal Education Program (FLEP), in which the Army would cover three years of his tuition expense at a civilian law school.

That Colby would have to put in at least two years of active duty to be eligible for FLEP did not give him pause about pursuing his aims. His desire to serve in the armed forces had not waned, and what was transpiring that day on his fraternity house's TV screens, in New York City, and less than an hour south of Hopkins in Washington, D.C., only intensified that desire. "September 11 was definitely a turning point where Colby began to seriously think about his military aspirations," recalled Tom Deveney, a brother in Alpha Delta Phi and one of Colby's closest friends. This was a battle that Colby Umbrell knew, sooner or later, he would have to join.

At 9:45 A.M., American Airlines Flight 77 had crashed into the Pentagon, and in Baltimore, in Philadelphia, in every major city in America, rumors and fears spread that terrorists would carry out other attacks. Clark Hall, the new biomedical engineering building on Hopkins's Homewood campus, went into lockdown; still inside were American and Israeli researchers who had been attending an international symposium on biomedical science and engineering. Condoleezza Rice, President Bush's national security adviser, had been scheduled to deliver the Johns Hopkins School of Advanced International Studies Rostov Lecture on International Affairs that night in Washington. Rice's speech was, of course, canceled, as were all classes, rehearsals, and athletic events.

"I'm getting out of Baltimore," one of Colby's fraternity brothers said.

"Where are you going to run to?" Colby replied. "You can't run away from this. Where's the safe place?"

UMass's administrators also had canceled classes, but the football players straggled to the practice field that afternoon for a team meeting. A dozen or more players from the New York City area were on the team, and few, if any, of them had made contact with their families yet. The first person whom Bryan had spoken to was his friend Dave Armstrong, who was up in Ann Arbor, Michigan. Armstrong had called Bryan at 9:30 A.M., telling him that he couldn't reach anyone in Doylestown.

"I'm sure they're fine," Bryan had said, though he wasn't. Was anyone sure of anything now?

Whipple addressed the entire team, telling the players that their upcoming game against Richmond on Saturday, September 16, would likely be postponed. (Because McGuirk Alumni Field did not have lights, the Richmond game was to be UMass's only home night game of the season. But the portable light standards that were to have been shipped to Amherst for the game were instead rerouted to Ground Zero.) Whipple referenced the decision by former NFL commissioner Pete Rozelle to play the league's scheduled games on the weekend after President John F. Kennedy's assassination and the criticism that Rozelle received for the decision. In a contradiction only a single-minded football coach could appreciate, Whipple then suggested that the best way to clear everyone's head was to run some light passing drills. Jeremy Robinson, one of the team's captains, stood up. "You know, Coach," Robinson said, "on a day like today, I don't think we can practice football." Whipple immediately acquiesced, leading the players in a brief team prayer before sending them home.

Back at their apartment, Bryan and his roommates encircled the television, and the more Bryan watched of the coverage, the angrier he became, a primal patriotism now smoldering within him. He went into the bathroom and calmed himself down, staring at his reflection in the

mirror. He was twenty-one years old, still in search of a sense of purpose beyond whatever he accomplished between those white lines of a
football field. He had inflated his body to 245 pounds in an attempt to
armor himself against the violence of a more advanced level of football,
but to what end? He didn't like how he looked, how bloated he was.
How long could he expect to keep playing anyway? What was he going
to do with his communication degree? Host a talk show? Did he want to
become a caricature of that old Bruce Springsteen song, bouncing his
children on his knee, telling them about his glory days, about a life
whose most meaningful moments took place while he was still a teenager? He had never contemplated joining the military until those seconds when he stood in front of that mirror. Football had been his safe
place. Nothing was safe anymore.

He stepped back out of the bathroom. Without a game the following weekend, he could go to Doylestown to visit his family, get away
from football, and think about whether volunteering to wear a different
kind of uniform and plunge himself into the heart of harm's way was
something he really wanted to do.

Friday, September 14, 2001

Chris and Kim DiSciullo owned a townhouse in Perkasie, Pennsylvania,
and they had not seen their neighbor, Erich Maerz, for two days
now. Erich and his wife, Meg, lived two doors down from Chris and
Kim, and the couples had grown close. From his visits to his sister and
brother-in-law's home, Bryan, too, counted Erich as a friend. As he sat
with Kim and Chris in their backyard, discussing the terrorist attacks,
the sun starting to descend in the sky, the three of them worried about
Erich—not because they didn't know where he was, but because they
did know.

Erich's elder brother, Noell, had worked as a trader with Euro Bro-
kers, Inc., headquartered on the eighty-fourth floor of the World Trade
Center's South Tower, and he was in his office Tuesday morning, talking
with Erich on the phone, when Erich heard a boom in the background.

"A bomb or something has gone off," Noell had said before hanging up. "I've got to go." Only after calling home to tell Meg to turn on the television did Erich realize that the boom that he'd heard had been the impact of Flight 11's collision with the North Tower. He had called Noell back several times before finally getting through to him on his office phone at 9 A.M. The brothers said, "I love you," to each other. Their call had lasted a minute and a half. In another minute and a half, the clock read 9:03.

Until Wednesday night, Erich had dialed Noell's cell phone number over and over again, refusing to believe his big brother was gone. Noell was twenty-nine years old, a triathlete, a former quarterback at Hofstra University. Noell was strong. Noell was tough. Noell might have survived. Erich had to know. He went up to New York City on Wednesday night to look for him.

It was dark now, but from the backyard, Bryan, Chris, and Kim could see Erich's car pull up. "He looked like a wreck," Chris said, "like he hadn't slept in days." For forty-eight hours, Erich and his father, Ralph, had handed out and put up flyers with Noell's photograph on them, had gone from hospital to hospital searching for him. Nothing.

"If anyone's alive, my brother's alive," Erich said. "I can't give up on him because he wouldn't give up on me."

He hugged Kim and Chris. Bryan looked at Erich's face, tears streaking it like a tiger's stripes. This could have been anyone. This could have been Bryan weeping over the death of his older brother, Stephen. Here he was, helpless to relieve his friend's grief. Had he ever truly appreciated how charmed he'd been? His parents, Mike Pettine, Mike Stubljar, Don Brown—throughout Bryan's life, people had given him opportunities. People had done for him. He had done for himself. It was time, he decided, to do something for someone else.

Sunday, October 7, 2001

The American retaliation began at 12:30 Eastern Daylight Time. On President Bush's orders, the United States—with the force of fifteen land-based bombers, twenty-five strike aircraft, and fifty Tomahawk missiles from U.S. and British submarines and ships—attacked Taliban military installations and al-Qaeda training camps in Afghanistan.

Bush had first discussed with his top aides how to respond to the 9/11 attacks on September 15, during a two-day meeting at Camp David. Defense Secretary Donald Rumsfeld and his deputy, Paul Wolfowitz, had raised the question of confronting Iraq because Saddam Hussein had suggested in a letter to the American people that the events of September 11 were the United States' comeuppance for the destruction it had wrought in the Middle East. But in a private meeting with Bush as the meeting neared its end, Hugh Shelton, the chairman of the Joint Chiefs of Staff, reminded the president that there was no indication that Saddam and Iraq had been involved in the 9/11 plot.

"That's what I think," Bush said to Shelton. "We will get this guy but at a time and place of our choosing."

Indeed, in addressing the nation after ordering the strikes against the Taliban and al-Qaeda, Bush declared that the battle against terrorism was broader than Operation Enduring Freedom, the name of the Afghanistan campaign. "Every nation has a choice to make," Bush said. "In this conflict, there is no neutral ground. If any government sponsors the outlaws and killers of innocents, they have become outlaws and murderers themselves, and they take that lonely path at their own peril."

Iraq, already, was on the president's mind.

Tuesday, October 9, 2001
The vigil began at 6 P.M., as it would every Tuesday until America's armed forces stood down. A dozen or so people congregated in front of the Bucks County Courthouse, at the intersection of Main and Court streets in Doylestown, holding tall white signs that read *WAR IS NOT THE ANSWER* and *VIGIL FOR PEACE*. Standing with the small crowd of peaceful protesters was the eighty-one-year-old man who had gathered them there.

Larry Miller had come to central Bucks County in 1949 to replenish the plasma of one of Doylestown's lifebloods, its Quaker tradition and social activism. The Doylestown Friends Meeting had but four members when he arrived, but within five years, Miller's leadership had expanded the membership to nearly a hundred people. A conscientious objector during World War II, the former chairman of the Quakers' United Nations committee and the former president of central Bucks County's fair housing council, Miller was open and affectionate, a compulsive hugger and kisser of most anyone he met, and he peppered the editors of the *Intelligencer* with letters and essays against nuclear proliferation, war, and general disagreeableness.

"It is naïve to believe that, given the overwhelming support of Americans for the Bush administration's course of action, a radical change in foreign policy would now be possible," Miller would write in a December 9 letter to the *Intelligencer*. "Yet it is incumbent upon us to gain clarity on 'why they hate us' and to deal directly with the causes of terrorism."

Over the succeeding weeks, as few as eight people might take part in one of the vigils; sometimes, as many as thirty. Many, but not all, of the participants were Quakers. That the protesters had stationed themselves directly in front of the courthouse—because, Miller said, of the location's high visibility—likely did not endear them to those inclined to disagree with them. Along the eastern edge of the building's courtyard was a glossy gray marble wall: the Bucks County Vietnam Veterans Memorial. The protesters encountered a fair share of feedback from passersby and drivers negotiating the capillary streets of Doylestown—most of it in the forms of catcalls and honking car horns. But Larry Miller and the people who stood with him showed up in the center of town at 6 P.M. every Tuesday for their vigil, as reliably as a sunset.

Mark Whipple was as unaccustomed to losing football games as Bryan Buckley was. In his thirteen previous years as a college head coach at

New Haven College, Brown University, and UMass, Whipple had experienced only one sub-.500 season. His teams routinely set school and
league scoring records, his offensive expertise blooming during the late
1970s, when, as Brown's starting quarterback, he had spent his week-
day afternoons studying sixty-millimeter game films and had called his
own plays in the huddle during practices and games. He had a temper;
when angry, Whipple could scald a player with such vulgarities to cause
the kid to whimper (though playing for Mike Pettine had steeled Bryan,
Corey Potter, and Greg Ward to similar outbursts). While at UMass,
Whipple had received inquiries about jobs from a couple of respected
coaches, Mike Holmgren and Steve Mariucci, and it seemed only a matter of time before he made the considerable jump from being a Division
I-AA head coach to being an NFL assistant. But this season, 2001, had
been something out of a nightmare. Three years removed from a Division I-AA national championship in Whipple's first season as head
coach, two years removed from a conference championship, the Minutemen had lost their first five games and were 2–7 heading into their
final two games, each of which was at home. Whipple had brought in
a number of junior-college players in his initial recruiting classes and
wanted to develop more freshmen, more players who would be in the
program for a full four years. By funneling his recruiting time and resources toward that goal, he had left himself with a young roster in
2001, and he had anticipated before the season began that there might
be a decline in the team's win total. He had not anticipated 2–7.

Nor had Bryan. From both a team perspective and an individual
perspective, this had been the worst season of his career; there was
nothing comparable. Once they resumed practices after September
11, the Minutemen had begun preparing for their next game, at Delaware, and Bryan had still been optimistic that he might play more at
fullback. During an intrasquad scrimmage, though, a defensive lineman
had crumpled on Bryan's left leg. At first, Bryan thought his leg was
broken, but the injury had turned out to be a high ankle sprain. He had
worn a walking cast for two weeks, then had to fight his way back into

consideration for a place in the starting lineup. And the losses, one after another . . . His family and friends had come out en masse to watch him play at Villanova on October 27, and the Wildcats had throttled UMass, 47–13. To think he had been embarrassed in high school over games that his team had *won*.

More and more, Bryan's thoughts had been turning to the military. He had contacted an old West teammate, Joel Starzmann, who was in the Naval Academy, and asked Starzmann's advice about how best to go about becoming a midshipman. Starzmann had pointed out that if Bryan applied and was accepted to the academy, he would have to start his college career over again as a freshman. The better route for Bryan, Starzmann had said, would be to find a school with a strong Reserve Officers' Training Corps (ROTC) program. The school that he had suggested to Bryan was Villanova.

If there was any possibility left that Bryan might change his mind about the military, those final two games of the season, against Rhode Island and Richmond (which had been rescheduled for November 23), eliminated it. He made his first start for UMass in the Minutemen's 24–7 victory over Rhode Island. He neither carried the football nor caught a pass all day, but he had blocked well, and Whipple told him after the game, "You're going to be the starter."

Bryan's career as the number-one fullback for the University of Massachusetts Minutemen lasted exactly one more game. The following week, Richmond stormed out to a twenty-eight-point halftime lead on its way to drubbing UMass, 35–7. The Spiders sacked UMass quarterback Matt Guice six times; their defensive linemen seemed to be everywhere, and Bryan couldn't block any of them. More humiliating to Bryan than the final score or his own performance, however, was a comment that Whipple spat out during halftime.

"I should have left you guys when I had the opportunity," he said in the locker room.

Years later, Whipple said that he didn't remember making that specific statement, but he did acknowledge, "I would have said anything to motivate them. They did not want to be there. That game was one of the lowlights of my coaching career." For Bryan, the comment cemented his decision to leave UMass. As far as he was concerned, his coach had quit on him. *A true leader is someone you want to follow*, he thought, *not someone you need to follow*. He would transfer to Villanova. As hard as it would be, he would let the game go.

He waited awhile to tell his roommates, finally doing so on a Saturday afternoon, not long after the season had ended, as they sat around the bar at McMurphy's Uptown Tavern, their favorite hangout. Two of them, Ian Dyche and Luke Hobgood-Chittick, were surprised, but Corey Potter was not.

"I kind of had a feeling," Potter said to Bryan. "I've known you all my life. When you do something, you go a hundred percent, and you weren't really going into football a hundred percent. So I knew something was up.

"Hey, I'm proud of you."

He tried on multiple occasions to sit down with Whipple, to explain himself and his reasons for leaving the team. Whipple's secretary would tell him the same thing each time: *He'll get back to you.* But he never did, and Bryan instead told Keith Dudzinski, UMass's secondary and special-teams coach, that the direction of his internal drive had shifted. "He was torn," Dudzinski recalled. "He enjoyed playing football, but he saw a bigger cause out there, and he wanted to follow his heart with that." That was all Bryan wanted to say to the last football coach he would ever have. It was his single regret over leaving the University of Massachusetts, that he had never looked Mark Whipple in the eye and told him why he couldn't play football for him, or anyone else, anymore.

FOURTEEN

"End of an Aura"

May 2002

In the aftermath of September 11, politics, always one of Colby's keenest interests, had taken on a fresher importance to him. When he was home in Doylestown for one of Hopkins's semester breaks, he and his oldest friends engaged in the same current-affairs debates that had long been a fixture of their rapport with each other. Usually, Colby and his old teammate along Central Bucks East's offensive line, Steve Gonzalez, engaged in the most heated exchanges, as they had back in high school— Gonzo wielding rhetoric from the left, Colby from the right. These were salon meetings with much more beer and much less elegance, but during the discussions, Colby argued his positions with more gravity and urgency than he once had.

He did the same among his college friends. It was a common sight at the Alpha Delta Phi house: Colby stretched out on the couch like a marlin on a boat deck, the television flickering to the talking heads' back-and-forth battles on FOX News, CNN, or MSNBC. If one of the brothers lingered too long in the room, Colby would instigate a political argument with him, and there was no telling what topics the two of them might discuss, or how long they might discuss them. After a while, Ben Stopper and Tom Deveney, Colby's fraternity brothers, would often surrender out of sheer exhaustion and agree with him, fearing that if they didn't, the debate might never end. For regardless of the logic or soundness of his opponent's stance on a given issue, Colby was too stubborn, too sure of the soundness of his views, to concede a single point. "It wasn't so much a debate as it was him speaking his mind," Deveney recalled. "If you challenged him, there was no winning. He was always going to be victorious."

If the 9/11 attacks had acted as a stimulant to awaken a dormant feeling of patriotism within many U.S. citizens, they only reaffirmed Colby's deepest beliefs. He considered his country a city on a hill, in the phrase coined by the seventeenth-century Puritan leader John Winthrop and resurrected by President Ronald Reagan during his 1989 farewell address. As far as Colby was concerned, the destruction of the Twin Towers had been an audacious attempt to damage America's standing as a global symbol of freedom—a threat to his country's values, a threat to *his* values. It had rekindled in him the idealism that had once made the possibility of attending West Point his personal North Star. He talked with Deveney, when they were alone and it was quiet, about how much he had wanted to be at West Point, to be a U.S. Army officer, and how his knee injury had made his dream disappear.

What he was beginning to realize was that the same thing was happening to his football career. It was disappearing.

Hopkins had gone 6–3 in 2001, and given how many players would be returning for the '02 season, it was possible, even likely, that the Blue Jays would compete for the Centennial Conference championship. Their defense had not allowed a touchdown pass all season—Dayton had been the last Division III team to pull off the feat, in 1980—but Colby's role was strictly as a reserve now. Two of the linemen who started ahead of him, sophomore nose guard Paul Smith and junior defensive tackle Pat Boyle, were all-league-caliber players, and they weren't going anywhere. In the seven games he had played, Colby had registered only two tackles and half a quarterback sack, never regaining the step he had lost after tearing his ACL. Nevertheless, with the team's fortunes so promising for 2002, he would give football one more try. After Colby's three years of playing for the second-best team in his own school district, after another three years of waiting, the chance to win a championship was too enticing a lure for him to give up the game now.

Saturday, October 26, 2002

In the shallow space of War Memorial Field's bell tower, the losing locker room for ten of his eleven previous East-West games as a head coach, Larry Greene did something that he'd never done before. The Patriots were leading the Bucks at halftime, 14–7, and there seemed a hum in the tower, a palpable confidence among Greene's players that they would be the first East team to beat West since 1983, since before any of them were born, and Greene gave in to that confidence, too.

"It's been a long time, I know," he told his players, "but act like you've been there before."

It might have seemed no small measure of boldness for Greene to insinuate that victory was assured, particularly because his team led West—who had beaten East seventeen times and tied it once over the previous eighteen years—by just a touchdown and an extra point. But even though these Patriots were not among Greene's most accomplished teams—they were 2–6 entering the East-West game—this was not the same West program whose players and coaches had once regarded state championships and unbeaten seasons as their birthrights. Randy Cuthbert's was a respectable program . . . by any standard other than CB West's. In 2001, Cuthbert's first season as head coach, the Bucks had posted a 7–3 record, missing the district playoffs for the first time since the tournament's creation in 1992, and the beginning of the 2002 season had been ignominious, to say the least: two losses in which the Bucks had been outscored, 54–13. West had recovered to win six consecutive games before facing East, but nothing had better crystallized the difference between what the program had been under Mike Pettine and Mike Carey and what it was now under Cuthbert than a headline in the *Intelligencer* after West had fallen to 0–2: *END OF AN AURA*.

West's veneer of invincibility was gone, and if the population demographics of Central Bucks County were any indication, that veneer would never return. The school district had announced that it would open a new high school, Central Bucks High School South, in 2004. Since 1990, the populations of New Britain and Chalfont—boroughs that had sent their tenth-, eleventh-, and twelfth-graders to West—had increased by 27 percent and 43 percent, respectively. Over the same period, the number of students at East and West had risen 62 percent to more than 3,700. The community simply had grown too much; two high schools would no longer do. For a construction cost of $85 million, CB South would be equipped with state-of-the-art athletic facilities—including, much to the consternation of Greene, the Umbrells, and many other CB East supporters, a football stadium—and according to the school district's initial estimations, it would have the highest enrollment of the three schools. Not only would CB South have the deepest talent pool and the newest accoutrements, it would draw student-athletes from areas that traditionally had strengthened East's and West's football programs. Based on where each of them grew up, for instance, Dustin Picciotti, Bryan Scott, and Dave Armstrong would have attended CB South. So, in theory, would have Bryan Buckley, but Connie Buckley was quick to tell people: "We'd have moved to stay in West territory."

The region's relative urbanization, then, was bound to deal a blow to whatever hope Cuthbert had of approximating Pettine's success, and by holding a seven-point lead over West at halftime, Greene and the Patriots were providing a hint of what was to come: a leveling of the playing field between the two programs. East had performed so well in the first twenty-four minutes and Greene was so certain that his team would sustain its fine play that he allowed himself a small rationalization. *They're going to want to go crazy when we win, and I want them to carry themselves with class. I'd better say something to them now because I might not have another chance.*

So he said it: *Act like you've been there before.* The notion that he might jinx his own team did not cross his mind, and the second half never gave Greene cause to doubt himself. East scored two third-quarter touchdowns. Bill McDonnell, the Patriots' sophomore quarterback, completed nine of his eleven passes for 138 yards in the game. Senior tailback Brian Hogan ran for 100 yards. East outgained West, 310 total yards to 186, and forced three turnovers.

As the game clock dripped down to 0:00, the officials stopped play with six seconds left in regulation, with East on the verge of a 27–14 victory, and with the Patriots standing along their sideline and heeding their coach's request to celebrate with grace. But the people on East's side of the stadium couldn't help themselves. Because 6,911 days had passed since East had last beaten West, perhaps they were entitled to some premature rejoicing. Shirtless students, players' parents, and alumni poured out onto War Memorial Field, a stream of blue-and-red face paint. One of them swung from a goal post like an ape in a tree. Then they left the field, waited those six additional seconds, and charged back out again. Thirty minutes after the game had ended, after Doylestown Borough police had cleared everyone off the turf, several East players and rooters lingered on the perimeter of the darkened stadium, not wanting to go home just yet, leaning on their car horns and shrieking out of windows when they finally did drive away.

"If I was the principal," Larry Greene said, "I would have no school Monday."

His hands on his hips, Randy Cuthbert talked with a small cluster of reporters. Apart from ending the Bucks' nineteen-year unbeaten streak within the rivalry, the loss had ruined West's chances of winning its league title and reaching the district playoffs. "I'm disappointed in the way we played with what we had on the line," Cuthbert said, mindful that there would be other questions coming from other sources in central Bucks County. He heard those questions often whenever he happened to be walking around town or ducking into the Fountain House Starbucks for a coffee. It mattered not that the administrators who had promoted him did not regard his win-loss record as the definitive criterion on which they judged his effectiveness. People in the community wanted the old West program back. He wanted to make the program his own. Maybe it never would be.

December 2002

Here was what maddened Colby most: When he was healthy, when he was right, he could still contribute on a football field. But those occasions were rarer and rarer now, and he had to acknowledge that truth to himself. First, he had to acknowledge it to his coach.

Jim Margraff was not surprised that Colby was sitting in front of him, explaining why he had to leave the Johns Hopkins football program. "When you're at an academically elite school," Margraff said later, "guys leave for all different reasons. Junior and senior year, there's a lot of other things out there if football doesn't give you what you want." That was it, though: Football still gave Colby everything he wanted, when his body permitted him to accept the game's gifts. "He had a bull rush nobody could stop," Ben Stopper said. Circumstance could. What could have been the perfect cap to Colby's career was just another slog through a series of high ankle sprains. After thirty-two years without winning any sort of championship, the Blue Jays had won two in Colby's junior season. Their school-record nine victories had won them the Centennial Conference regular-season title, and by beating Frostburg State, 24–21, less than a week before Thanksgiving, they had won the more prestigious East Coast Athletic Conference Division III championship. Yet Colby had played in only two games all season, spending more time in the trainer's room than in his game uniform, never making a tackle or recovering a fumble or appearing in a box score. In effect, Colby Umbrell, Football Player, didn't exist anymore.

"He was one of the few guys—and I truly know this and believe this—who was an all-out guy," Margraff recalled, "and when he couldn't get at one hundred percent and give one hundred percent, it was time to look into something different."

There were other pursuits to which Colby would commit himself now, but nagging at him, as he left Margraff's office, was a feeling of unfulfillment. "I've never failed at something I wanted to do," he told his parents, and Mark and Nancy had to remind him that he hadn't failed, that the things he had come to value most—his education, his opportunity to become an Army officer—were still his to have.

Wednesday, March 19, 2003

The decision that would define George W. Bush's presidency was at hand. It had been more than a year since his 2002 State of the Union address and his use of the phrase "axis of evil" to characterize the triumvirate of Iraq, Iran, and North Korea. It had been more than a month since Secretary of State Colin Powell's presentation to the UN Security Council that, as Powell himself said, was intended to "demonstrate that Saddam Hussein and his regime have made no effort—no effort—to disarm as required by the international community." It had been two days since President Bush had issued his final ultimatum to Saddam: that unless Saddam and his two sons fled Iraq within forty-eight hours, the U.S.-led coalition would invade.

Now, during a meeting with Vice President Dick Cheney, Donald Rumsfeld, and Condoleezza Rice, Bush received a startling piece of information from George Tenet, the director of the Central Intelligence Agency. Saddam and his sons, according to CIA intelligence, were meeting in Dora Farms, a compound set amid a grove of palm trees on the western bank of the Tigris River. If Bush was willing to speed up the start of the invasion, he might take out Saddam immediately. If

Saddam wasn't bunkered at the compound and the attack failed, Bush would tip his hand that a ground invasion was about to begin.

Bush ordered the strikes. Two black F-117 stealth fighters fired four two-thousand-pound bunker-penetrating bombs, and Navy battle groups in the Persian Gulf unleashed 45 Tomahawk land attack missiles at the compound.

Saddam was not at Dora Farms.

"Fittingly," author Thomas Ricks wrote in his book *Fiasco: The American Military Adventure in Iraq,* "a war justified by false premises began on false information."

The next day, the ground war commenced, and a fighting force of less than five divisions embarked on its push to Baghdad. "It didn't take long," Ricks wrote, "for the Iraqi side to begin operating unconventionally." On March 22, a platoon sergeant in the U.S. Army's 3rd Infantry Division waved at a group of Iraqis from his tank, assuming that they would wave back at him. The Iraqis responded by firing AK-47s and launching grenades at the tank. The Army marked the incident as the first insurgent attack of the war, and over the next several years, the degree to which U.S. war planners had been insufficiently prepared for the insurgency in Iraq would become frighteningly clear.

August 2003

Marine Gunnery Sgt. Don Moeller's office was an aseptic room in John Barry Hall, a building unique not only among the majestic Gothic towers of Villanova University's campus but also in American history. Constructed in 1949 to house the university's Naval ROTC program, it was the first government edifice to have a cross carved into its front.

As a high school student in Lakewood, New Jersey, Moeller had met a retired Vietnam veteran and former Reconnaissance Marine who inspired him to enlist. After Moeller had become a Recon Marine and graduated from Airborne School, he had received a gift that he had treasured ever since: his mentor's pair of gold wings. Moeller had run the gamut of assignments during his sixteen years in the corps, serving overseas in Central America, South America, and briefly in Iraq during the first Gulf War, assisting the U.S. Border Patrol with counterdrug operations in the Southwest, toughening up recruits as a drill sergeant on Parris Island. Thirty-four years old, he was a solid, bald ball of muscle and tattoos, intimidating. It was not surprising that after knocking on Moeller's office door, the 240-pound former football player stammered ever so slightly at the sight of him.

"Gunny, I'm, a, I'm Midshipman Bryan Buckley. I want to be a Marine."

Bryan had been a student and a midshipman at Villanova for almost a year. His final semester at the University of Massachusetts, in the spring of 2002, had been a breeze. Without football, he could tease his roommates by saying, "See you guys later . . ." as they headed off to spring practice and he, in his words, "hung out with a cocktail in my hand." All the while, his father was helping him apply to Villanova and its NROTC program. Though Bryan had maintained a 3.2 grade-point average at UMass, he had scored a 920 on his SATs when he had taken them in high school, a score below Villanova's usual baseline for admission. In a meeting on Bryan's behalf with an admissions officer who, as it turned out, was an avid fly fisherman, Bill had noted that Bryan had been able to maintain an above-average GPA as a Division I athlete. When that line of argument didn't appear to persuade the officer, Bill had mentioned the hunting and fishing club to which he belonged. "Anytime you'd like to go up," he had told the admissions rep, "I'd be happy to take you." Bryan's acceptance letter from Villanova had appeared in Bill and Connie's mailbox not long after.

To get himself on track to finish the NROTC program by the time he graduated college, Bryan had spent eight weeks at the Naval Science Institute in Newport, Rhode Island, before he had ever set foot on Villanova's campus as a student. At the institute, he had earned eighteen semester hours of college credit in military science and received his first taste of armed-service indoctrination, learning how to march and going through physical training each morning. He had thought that he wanted to become a Navy pilot, spending part of the summer of 2003 flying P-3s at Whidbey Island in Washington State, but more and more, living the life of a Marine appealed to him. It seemed a greater challenge. He stood in Moeller's doorway and told him as much. Three semesters away from graduating from Villanova, he wanted to become an NROTC–Marine Option.

"I don't know if I can help you," Moeller said. "I don't know if we can make you a Marine Option within the year."

To transfer from the Navy to the Marines, Bryan would have to apply for a Marine Option–controlled scholarship, and assuming he completed the application material and mailed them off to Marine headquarters, there was no telling how long his application would sit at Quantico before the admissions board reviewed it. The time constraint wasn't the only potential problem, either. Bryan's SAT score of 920 wasn't going to help his chances—the Marines would want at least a score of 1,000 before granting him acceptance—and there was no fishing trip to dangle in front of an admissions counselor this time. He'd have to take the SATs again.

Undeterred, Bryan asked Moeller if he could train with Villanova's other Marine Option candidates. Impressed, Moeller said yes. *This guy wants it bad.* But he didn't yet know the depths of Bryan's desire, because during their conversation, Bryan hadn't mentioned that he wasn't merely a midshipman who wanted to be a Marine. He was also, as of that summer, a Central Bucks West football coach.

May 2004

As Colby Umbrell finished his senior year at Johns Hopkins and readied himself for the subsequent stage of his life, as a soldier, only his family and closest friends would have seen the same man before them.

Sure, he still possessed his high-and-tight blond haircut and his trademark grin—ear to ear, causing the block of bone that served as his chin to slide forward, revealing that sliver of space between his top front teeth—but most everything else about him was . . . smaller. Not long after his meeting with Jim Margraff, he had found something to replace football, all right: running. Knowing that he was entering the Army in June, knowing that at 240 pounds he might not be in the best shape (in the most literal sense of the word) to meet the physical demands of his upcoming military training, Colby used the most basic of methods to start trimming weight. He would find a treadmill on the second floor of Hopkins's Newton H. White, Jr. Athletic Center—directly above Margraff's office—and jog. When classes were in session and the weather permitted, he would run from Hopkins's campus to the Inner Harbor, a six-mile round trip, then do it again and again. During the summer of 2003, while he was home, he had turned Doylestown into his own personal quarter-mile track, adding a mile to his regimen every few days, galloping through the center of town so frequently that store owners and passersby, after a while, recognized him. He ate the same meal every day: boneless chicken breast with steamed rice and vegetables.

By October 12, when he ran the Chicago Marathon, he was 195 pounds.

Law school, and perhaps a track that led through the Judge Advocate General (JAG) Corps, had remained his long-term target, and he had used time that he once might have spent preparing himself for football season to broaden his life experience beyond the two settings that, for so long, had dominated his daily existence: the football field and the classroom. He had studied abroad in Florence during his final semester, a choice that had concerned his parents. Colby's GPA was 2.99 heading into that last term, and Mark and Nancy had urged him to keep in mind that in the minds of law-school admissions officers, the difference between a 2.99 and a 3.0 far exceeded one-tenth of one GPA point. But as a requirement for a semester spent under the Tuscan sun and amid the splendor of the Duomo and Piazza della Signoria, Colby had to take a course in art history, and to edge above a 3.0, he had to get an A in the course. He did. "It wasn't easy," Mark recalled. "But he said, 'If I have to get an A, I'll get an A.' That was Colby."

A junior-year internship with Congressman Jim Greenwood, a moderate-to-liberal Republican who represented Pennsylvania's Eighth District—Doylestown's district—had offered him firsthand exposure to the country's political culture. Greenwood chaired a subcommittee that oversaw energy and commerce industry practices, and Colby had conducted research for and attended meetings with the subcommittee. The insider's look at Washington, D.C., left him nonplussed. "All they care about is politics there," he said later. "You go out on the town and think you're cutting loose, and all they want to talk about is politics. I just like public service."

Basic training for the U.S. Army Officer Candidate School would begin at Fort Benning, Georgia, in late June or early July. Now having graduated with a degree in political science from one of the nation's most prestigious universities, Colby would be there, inspired by a measure of motivation apart from his longtime aspiration to serve his country. He was eager to quell the growing number of acquaintances of his and his parents' who wondered aloud why someone who had graduated with a degree in political science from one of the nation's most prestigious universities would volunteer to fight in a war, especially an ever more unpopular one. The questions stung Colby and his parents, and an excerpt from his OCS entrance essay had been a rebuttal to that attitude. It also was an indication of how important athletics in general—and football in particular—had been to his maturation into manhood.

"Many people measure their level of success in terms of individual accomplishment," Colby wrote. "I feel differently. I think that individual accomplishment is a personal way to view success, whereas greater successes will be achieved at levels above one's self. This is the concept of a team. Rather than terms of 'Look what I did,' more remarkable success is attainable through cooperation on one's team."

It was a rather remarkable thing, the way the game was still in him, the way it had shaped him.

* * *

On the day he had introduced Bryan Buckley to the 2003 CB West football team, Randy Cuthbert had given him the full banquet-speaker treatment, lauding Bryan as a leader to match any in West's legacy. In 1998, the year before Cuthbert came to West to coach and teach, he had watched Bryan play; they had met each other the following year, when Bryan returned for a pregame dinner with the players and coaches. Bryan, Cuthbert believed, was the type of player a team needed to have if it was to achieve anything: tough, unselfish, diligent. He had trusted that Bryan would offer the same qualities as an assistant coach.

Exactly when Bryan would have the time to put those qualities to use for West's current players had been an open question. Throughout the fall, his schedule had left him virtually no free time. Living at his parents' house in Doylestown, he would wake at 4:30 each morning and make the forty-five-minute drive to Villanova for the day's first physical-training session at six with the Marine Option candidates. Once he had finished PT and his day's classes, he would drive back to Doylestown, arriving at West in time, he hoped, for 3 P.M. practice. Often, when he didn't have time to change, he would wear his fatigues on the practice field. At night, after the West coaches' meetings had ended, he would head home to study before rising before dawn to do it all again the next day. His weekends had been almost as full. Friday nights were, obviously, when the Bucks played most of their games. On Saturdays, he would head to a nearby Sylvan Learning Center for the SAT prep course he was taking. And on Sundays, Bryan, presumably, would rest. (The work, from an academic standpoint, was worthwhile. Bryan upped his SAT score to 1050 and maintained a 3.86 GPA at Villanova.)

He had to rest sometime, because his physical training, at the hands of Gunnery Sgt. Don Moeller, was unlike anything he had been through before. Moeller put his Marine Options through combat conditioning: runs of three to five miles with forty to sixty pounds of utilities on their backs, rope climbs, calisthenics. At 240 pounds, "Buck was dying," Moeller recalled. "Dying." But it was another wrinkle of the training that had most pushed Bryan to his physical limits. Moeller had designed a grueling set of swimming exercises for his candidates, including as many as twenty laps in Villanova's fifty-meter pool with either survival strokes or fins. He might call out, "Crossovers," which meant that half the candidates would swim the entire fifty meters across the bottom of the pool while the other half would swim across the top. At all times, Moeller would keep four lifeguards on hand in case one of the candidates experienced shallow-water blackout or passed out, and when he first saw Bryan try to pull himself from one end of the pool to the other, Moeller had wondered whether one of those lifeguards might have to fish Bryan off the bottom.

Gradually, Bryan had trimmed off his football weight, and his and Moeller's relationship had deepened from student-teacher to friendship. Moeller had become and would remain a confidant, someone with whom Bryan, over time, could share his fears, his frustrations, and, during a formal dinner for Villanova's ROTC program, his joy over learning that the corps had officially accepted his transfer application. With just one semester of classes yet to finish at Villanova before he would graduate with a bachelor's degree in communication, Bryan would report to Marine Officer Candidate School at Quantico in July.

"We were standing there, two Coors Lights in our hands, and the Marine Officer instructor brings him over," Moeller recalled. "We're standing there with all the other Marine Options, and the major tells him, 'Congratulations. You made it.' It was like a weight off his shoulders. He was happy now."

For much of the previous fall, he had not been happy, mostly because of the state of an institution still so dear to him: CB West football. For the second straight season, the Bucks had won just six games, and coaching the team's defensive linemen and running backs, Bryan had returned to a program that he no longer recognized. Cuthbert's relaxed demeanor had replaced the in-your-face methods of Mike Pettine and Mike Carey, and the players and their parents seemed so . . . *sensitive*. Bryan would show up at practice, breathing fire as Pettine and

Carey once had, believing that if he couldn't turn a kid into a good football player, at least he could turn him into a man, and the kid's mother and father would complain to Bryan or to Cuthbert about how Bryan was treating the players. Cuthbert would call Bryan aside to talk to him, to tell him things were different now, but Bryan couldn't understand how anyone could coach in this environment. Where was the accountability? Where were the hard lessons that he had learned under Pettine? One night, on a Web site that covered Pennsylvania high school sports, he had found a thread on a message board about him. He was a "wacky Marine," according to the anonymous posters, who ran around the field yelling "c—" and "pussy" and who did very little actual coaching. He immediately logged in to the site and, using his real name, posted his own message: "I'm saying who I am. Come find me. I will gladly sit down with you if you have anything to say." The only person to contact him about the thread had been Pettine, who called Bryan from his vacation home in Florida to jab him: "I'm really enjoying your blogging."

In late October, as West was in the process of losing to East again, this time 17–10, Bryan had started screaming at a West player with such rage that one of the other coaches had to restrain him. He had been wrong, and he knew it, and he was ashamed of himself. It was difficult to coach, he would later admit, when part of you still wanted to play.

FIFTEEN

Training, in Bryan's Words

On July 7, 2004, Bryan Buckley reported to Quantico for Marine Officer Candidate School, the screening program through which the Marines select their officers.

From classroom instruction in combat tactics and Marine Corps history to pugil-stick battles and screaming platoon sergeants and obstacle courses set in steaming, noisome swamps, the demands of OCS can break even the most committed of candidates. Because he was a Marine Option in the Navy ROTC, Bryan would attempt to complete the course in only six weeks, rather than the customary ten. Yet as he drove down to Virginia that day, Bryan noticed that the back of his neck was stiff and sore and that the rest of his body, from his shoulders on down, was beginning to ache.

You park in a parking lot, and you're there for processing. You're just standing in line. They're giving you gear. They give you a number. They inform you you're no longer Bryan Buckley. You're no longer "me" or "I." You are this candidate, and you will be that until we tell you otherwise. Your identity's gone. Your head's shaved. And you're like, "OK, this is for real." I remember someone, standing in line, just passed out from the anxiety. Someone just dropped, and he was gone.

I felt instantly horrible when I was there. All this stuff's going on. My brain's just clouded with some sickness. I am just trying to get my bearings. We are sitting in this old plane hangar that has been converted into a classroom. There is no air-conditioning, and it is hot, and the Marine staff that is about to run you through the gauntlet that is OCS is just staring you down. They are in their Class "C" uniforms, their "Charlies." They all look like poster-child Marines. They stand at parade rest. Their upper bodies are shaped like Vs, their uniforms neatly pressed. Belts, shoes, and brass are polished, and their ribbon stacks are large. They all have a look on their faces that says "Do you think you have what it takes to be part of my gun club?" But they say nothing; the silence was eerie. You now realize that you are at Marine Officer Candidate School. Many have come before you, and a majority have failed. It was then I started to think to myself, "Do I have what it takes to be a leader of Marines?"

The battalion commander of Marine OCS walks in, and a Marine from the back yells, "Attention on deck!" All of the candidates pop out of their chairs and stand at attention. The battalion commander walks to the front of the classroom and introduces himself. He talks about the mission of OCS and says this is different from enlisted boot camp. OCS is not a place where they make Marines; it is a screening to see if you have what it takes to lead Marines. If you fail to meet their standards or, even worse, quit, you are done—no second chances. He tells a story about how he takes OCS a little more personally than others do. His son is an enlisted Marine, and ultimately, he is looking at men who may lead his son into combat. He then introduces his staff, and as soon as he says, "Staff," boom, it's on. The pickup day has begun, and it is live and in color. It sounded like an explosion went off. Those guys who five minutes earlier were standing in front of us like stoic statues have now become insane pit-bulls. They were all over us. We're flying out doors, gear everywhere. They're flipping stuff, emptying our packs in front of us. They're saying, "Find this pencil right now. . . . 3-2-1, time's up." You're still getting to your pile, and they're yelling at you. You've definitely been introduced to the "fog of war," something that you just need to accept, or you will never make it through OCS. It was controlled chaos. You're definitely at the point of friction.

You wake up in the morning, and you don't know if you're going to make it to the end of the day. The attrition rate is high. At night, you would return to the squad bay, exhausted and wanting nothing more than to call it a day and go to sleep. But the day was long from over. At a moment of pause, you could look around and see [that] the racks that once had potential Marine officers sleeping in them were gone. The candidates had either quit (or "DOR'd," meaning "dropped on request") or had not met the standards. To say the least, it was tough. We started with more than 300 people, and we ended up in the high one hundreds graduating. It was a lot of testing and a lot of physical work and not much time to sleep.

The one thing I didn't like about OCS was it was very individualized. There wasn't a team atmosphere there. It was almost like you didn't trust the people behind you. You're definitely thinking, "Why do I want to do this?" I remember they challenged me. I was highlighted in the beginning because I could not do the weapon-drill thing. We'd spend all our nights doing drills, and that's not why I got in the Marine Corps. I could care less about twirling a weapon around. However, that was one of the first things we did, and I got highlighted because they knew I didn't like it.

While training before OCS, I would usually run three miles in mid-19 minutes. At OCS, I was running three miles in 22 minutes, and it hurt. I thought, "What's going on here?" My nose was bleeding. I couldn't eat. I couldn't swallow. They sent me to the doctor. They did tests. I was clean. However, every time we would run or do anything physical, my nose would start to bleed. I had to hide that this was happening to me because I did not want them to drop me for medical reasons. I had my goal in mind; I was going to complete OCS come hell or high water. I just had to tell myself to stop feeling sorry for myself and acting like a pussy, to push through the pain and discomfort.

In the first week of training, the staff made me the candidate first-sergeant. I was under the microscope. If I did well, things would improve for me. If I failed, I was all but finished in the Marine Corps. While holding this billet, I had to take accountability for the company. I had to make sure I knew where people were and what was going on, and I was being mirrored by another first-sergeant. The first-sergeant is a senior enlisted guy who is one rank away from being a sergeant major, the highest rank an enlisted Marine can attain. I did well. He gave me a favorable on my evaluation, which basically meant, "You're going to make it." Guys who are evaluated unfavorably are really highlighted. They start getting kicked out.

Even though I did well on my evaluation, OCS was far from over, and whatever illness I had, had worsened. I was hacking up blood and crud. Mentally, I was drained from fighting both the illness and all of the curve balls the OCS staff would throw at me. I didn't want to quit. I was more scared about not making it than about my body breaking. I could accept if I fell down and keeled over because at least I put everything out there. But I was worried. I had never failed anything in my life, and the doubts in my head were growing: Do I have the mental toughness to push through this?

It was then that I received a letter from Coach Mike Pettine. In the letter, he described to me what type of player I was at CB West. He said that I had a no-quit attitude, and no matter how much crap the Marine staff threw at me, I would take great joy in throwing it back at them—something, he said, I took great pride in doing to him at CB West. He told me that, at the end of the day, he knew that I would be the last one standing. That letter could not have come at a better time. It was the shot of adrenaline that I desperately needed.

Soon after the letter from Coach Pettine, we began pugil-stick fighting. You are put into a pit with other candidates. Each of you has padded sticks, and you fight it out. I did pretty well. My aggressive, football nature just came out. I was head-butting guys with no helmet on. The platoon picked me as one of the top fighters, and I had to fight other candidates from other platoons during the pugil-stick competition. That was a turning point. Things started going better for me with the staff and the guys in the platoon. Things started to become easier. I made it through all of the small-unit leadership exercises, the endurance course and, of course, the "Quigley," the infamous obstacle course in which you are running in swamps and streams, going under water through a cement pipe with all of your gear, mud oozing all over your body. None of that mattered. Nothing mattered to me but mission accomplishment. I knew at that point I was going to make it. I had what it took to be a Marine Officer.

After graduating from OCS, Bryan returned both to Villanova, for his final semester, and to Randy Cuthbert's coaching staff, for his second and final season as a West football coach.

I went back to Villanova. I couldn't eat, and I knew something was wrong. I was just running, and I didn't have the stamina I usually have and couldn't get it. My nose would start bleeding, and you'd have to hide it. I couldn't keep up with the Marine Options. That's when Gunny Moeller was like, "What's wrong with you?" "I have no idea, but I'm beat." I was getting embarrassed. I couldn't do anything. Here I am. I just got done [with] Officer Candidate School. I've been cleared to become a Marine officer. And I can't do anything. It was killing me. As much as I tried, I'd run 10 yards and break out in a sweat. It was very frustrating.

West had a scrimmage up in the Lehigh Valley. I was shivering and cold out there, and the temperature that night was in the mid-80s. The entire weekend, I was cold. I had a 103-degree temperature. On Sunday night, my parents were like, "Enough's enough. You're going to the *hospital." After various examinations and blood tests at Doylestown Hospital, the doctors told me that I had mononucleosis and pneumonia. They asked me what I had been doing, and I told them that I just completed Marine OCS. I felt horrible during OCS, but the medical staff in Quantico had said that I just had a cold. The Doylestown doctors told me that it actually takes six weeks before mono will show up in a blood test, the exact amount of time I spent at OCS. I developed pneumonia because my body was so weak and I was basically living in swamps down at OCS. The x-rays showed [that] one of my lungs was crudded up with mucus. When I described to the doctors what I went through at OCS, they looked at me, stunned. Then, they said, "Oh, by the way, your liver is pretty much shot right now, so don't drink any booze." They were about a day late and a dollar short on that one. It had become a ritual for my friends and me: Whenever I come home to Doylestown, we all go out and have a good time. My liver was messed up from the mono, the virus. My body was beat up. We were at Doylestown Hospital all night long.*

Basically, I couldn't work out for a month, just to let my body recover. My liver was messed up. I was at 'Nova just helping guys out by giving them pointers, just being out there with them. But then, I got cleared, and two or three weeks later, I was back where I was before, beating guys in runs. It was a pretty quick turnaround. I healed up and just went back to finishing up at Villanova and coaching at West. It was a good gut check. Everyone needs one now and again.

Some people at Villanova were good people. I'm definitely a blue-collar guy, and it was definitely a white-collar school. You'd go to parties, and people would be sitting around, talking about philosophy, saying, "We're getting drunk. This is wild." This was nothing. I was used to seeing kegs thrown through windows and mayhem while I was at UMass. It was different people. It was fine. I didn't really hang out with the Villanova crowd too much. The Marine Options were all good guys; I really enjoyed training with them and hanging out with them. I could relate to them, but overall, the guy I was closest with was probably Gunny Moeller.

CB West underwent a small renaissance in the 2004 season, going 9–1 in the regular season before losing to Neshaminy, 38–34, in the first round of the district playoffs. After the season, Randy Cuthbert resigned as West's head coach, and speculation persisted in the Central Bucks community that the pressure of succeeding Mike Pettine and Mike Carey had become too much for him to bear. Cuthbert, however, said years later that he had hoped to become the head coach at Central Bucks South when it opened in the fall of 2004, and when those plans fell through, he decided it was time to leave West.

Whatever the reason, his coaching career at West was over, as was Bryan's.

Randy was a great guy. I enjoyed being around him. There was talent there. That was a good team. We gave Neshaminy a run for its money. I changed more as a coach. CB West was not the same as it was when I was playing there. As a player, we definitely had the mentality of team first, individual second. It was our world, just the players and the coaches. Parents got involved by working in their booster club and by cheering us on. They never dared to interfere with game plans or personnel. That was a different story when I was a coach. A majority of the parents thought that they had all the answers and that all of their kids should be starting. They were not bashful about it, either. A lot of unnecessary headaches came from that mentality, and Randy had to be the one to absorb the gut punches. I really respect him for how he conducted himself. He protected his coaches and players. Randy exudes the word "professional." I could not stand how things had changed; however, to be an effective leader, you have to learn to adapt to your players, push the right buttons. It was a growing-up experience.

I always tried to impart to people that you just don't rise to the occasion. I don't believe in that. Michael Jordan didn't do what he did just because his name was Michael Jordan. He worked his ass off to be what he was. What you have going into something is what you have. Some people just thought you put on that jersey and became Superman, and that's not the case. The teams I played for at West trained our asses off. It was how we prepared for a game that made the difference. Most of the players I coached did not understand that. Only a handful of the guys I coached would have played on the teams I was part of.

In a ceremony on December 17, 2004, Bryan received his commission as a 2nd lieutenant in the U.S. Marine Corps.

It was in the trophy room of John Barry Hall, a carpeted area where our TVs were. There was a buffet. It was just me and another guy getting our commissions. He went into the Navy. You put on your dress blues for the first time. You raise your right hand, take the oath, and at that point, you're officially a Marine. You're in for four years. You sign your contract. You are finally a part of the gun club. It was a good feeling. A lot of family and friends were there. Mike Pettine, Leo Carey, Jim Benstead, Brian Spratt, Corey Potter, Ed Hillman, Matt Volitis—a lot of people were there. Coach Pettine was proud. My parents were proud. I just remember how happy they all were.

I stuck around 'Nova a while afterward to help out. Then the slot for SERE school came up, and Gunny Moeller told me, "You're going."

Moeller's two words were Bryan's welcome to the furtive world of elite military training, to the thin line between immunizing a warrior to torture and shattering him, body and soul. SERE is the acronym for Survival, Evasion, Resistance, Escape, the program that teaches military personnel—particularly those at "high risk," such as Navy SEALs and Recon Marines—how to evade capture and how to withstand the worst agonies that an enemy can inflict. Bryan's SERE experience lasted two and a half weeks, from mid-February to early March 2005, at Brunswick Naval Air Station in Brunswick, Maine.

It's kind of a "secret school," so everyone's like, "Wow, you went to SERE school." Eyebrows go up.

The first week is a lot of classroom time. They talk to you, show you POW stories, show you how to survive out in the wilderness. The second week, you're taken up to the hill, and you do a couple of field exercises. Guys are showing you that you can eat this type of bark and here's how you make a snare and here's how you make a sleeping area in the snow by using pine needles. You build a fire. You stay warm. Basically, it is like "Survivor," no big deal. Then one morning, you wake up, and they're like, "All right, your plane just crashed. You need to get to this grid corner now. You're in hostile territory." You're moving. It's an Eastern European kind of place. You hear people driving around in their vehicles, screaming for the Americans to come out. People are chasing you. They're all over the place. It's like an intense manhunt game, I guess.

You live out in the elements in Maine, and wintertime in Maine is crazy. You live and eat off the land; you don't have any food with you. People are coming after you. Ultimately, they capture you and put you in a POW camp. They go through the different types of interrogations, and you learn how to defeat them.

SERE was a Cold War creation, an attempt to understand and counteract the premeditated mistreatment of American soldiers during the Korean War. Its intention was to expose U.S. troops to similarly strenuous interrogation methods—in controlled, cautious environments—so that, should they become prisoners of an enemy who did not heed Geneva Convention standards and international law, they would be mentally and emotionally equipped to resist the abuse. The military officials who conduct the school psychologically manipulate each student, according to conclusions reached by the Senate Armed Services Committee in 2008, through various brutal techniques, including "stress positions, forced nudity, use of fear, sleep deprivation and, until recently, the waterboard." Food is withheld, and "much of SERE's fearsome reputation was based on this starvation," wrote former Marine captain Nathaniel Fick in his 2005 book *One Bullet Away: The Making of a Marine Officer.* "It slowly degraded our decision making, putting us in a more vulnerable state of mind."

Since the publication of Fick's book, the SERE program has come under intense controversy and scrutiny. Published reports and the Armed Service Committee's formal inquiry have revealed that U.S. government officials used many of these same techniques on detainees in U.S. custody.

I can't go into details because I have signed a statement that says I will not speak about the course. I will say that even if the student was confused or did not really know what was going on, it was a very professionally run course and was very controlled. No one got hurt.

They debrief you, and that ends the entire thing. Oh, boy, I was pretty skinny. I had a beard and had lost close to 15 pounds. I went in there 190 and came out at 175. You're weak from what your body has been through. You're greasy and shaggy. They tell you that your body has experienced a lot of stress, more than you realize.

Once he had regained his strength, Bryan reported back to Quantico to fulfill a requirement of every Marine lieutenant: matriculation through The Basic School (TBS), a six-month grind that provides the underpinning for Marine leadership. Across the street from TBS headquarters was his next stop, the Infantry Officer Course (IOC) building, where he would spend another ten weeks. Together, TBS and IOC would ply

Bryan with enough knowledge of and expertise in marksmanship, artillery, advanced tactics, and the tangible and intangible skills essential in combat that, after finishing IOC in December, he would be ready to command his own platoon.

The good thing about TBS is, even though you are a 2nd lieutenant at the time, you're treated like a 3rd lieutenant, which doesn't exist. We joke about that. They want you to live like an enlisted Marine so you know exactly how they live. So you're in the barracks. The goal is that everyone, male and female, could be a provisional rifle platoon commander. It's kind of tough, but you're growing up a little bit. Not much free time for yourself. Everything is very regimented, but they've got very good instructors there. Captains are instructing you. You do basic fire maneuvers, fire support, controlling air, logistics—the whole plethora of what you need to do as a platoon commander. They always humble you. You'd be out field-daying the parking lot, picking weeds out of the ground, to make sure you know what your Marines are going to go through. The course does a very good job with that. You have to earn respect. You're still kind of in that baby stage as a Marine lieutenant. You're not going to leave that place until you're ready in six months. It is not uncommon for a lieutenant to be recycled and repeat the course. The Marine Corps will not advance anyone if he is not ready.

After you graduate from basic school, you go on to your military occupation specialty school. Marines will not go out to get a platoon for at least nine months if you're in the infantry. You're very knowledgeable in what you need to know. You learn how to become a Marine officer. The only thing that you lack is experience, but at IOC, they do the best they can to teach you in "the fog of war." The staff wants to prepare you in everything from tactics to death, something every infantry officer will experience during this time of "The Long War."

The thing about IOC is, it's not very well known, but a lot of it is modeled after the U.S. Army Ranger course. They try to take the best of all the schools they have and put it into that because it is the premier infantry fighting course. We learn a lot. You're getting taught by some really stellar captains who are all war vets and war heroes. You come out with a great knowledge base from it. The instructors warn you that when you check in to your platoon, the Marines are going to look at you like, "Who's this new lieutenant? Does he know anything?" They don't know the paths we came from. You will start training, and you know what it's going to take to gain their respect. You wait for that one moment where you do something and look good. It does not matter if you're the fastest or strongest in your platoon, but you had better be the toughest. The course is a great time. You're using every Marine asset that's out there. That's the way they train us—a lot of physical training, a lot of fighting, the whole mentality of going through that stuff.

They would send us to the trauma center at the Washington Hospital, just to watch people die, so we'd get used to it. On Friday and Saturday nights, the course students go over there and watch people pass away. I only went one night. When I was driving down to the trauma center from Quantico, I got lost. I was trying to figure out the streets there, and I saw this one guy on a moped, and he had dreadlocks. When I got to the hospital, there were eight of us there. It was a slow night at first. They showed us some videos of a guy who tried to kill himself but ended up blowing his face off with a shotgun. He also had HIV. I thought, "If that happens, I'm not dealing with that mess." While we were there, they said, "OK, we've got a motorcycle victim coming in, major head trauma." They bring him in, and it's him, the guy with the dreadlocks. I said, "You've got to be kidding me. I saw him two hours ago." His hip was all out of place, and he had massive head injuries. He was bad, and they're like, "He's not going to make it. We can't do anything else for him." We sat and watched him die. It looked peaceful. He was just lying there. There wasn't any struggle or hacking up or anything. He just went limp. That was it. He gave a last breath, and then he was gone.

You're going to go into battle. When you're out there on the battlefield, you're going to see it, and you've got to be numb to it. People are *going to die. If the commander turns around and starts to get nervous, it's just going to cause more dead bodies. You cannot be the guy who freezes when he sees one of his Marines down because you'll get more Marines killed. You need to focus on the enemy and destroy the enemy. It's the best thing you can do for yourself and the Marines. It has to be mission first.*

SIXTEEN

Training, in Colby's Words

Colby Umbrell had his mind buried in a book when he began basic training at U.S. Army Officer Candidate School at Fort Benning, Georgia, in late June 2004. He was reading *Band of Brothers*, Stephen Ambrose's recounting of the heroic exploits of Easy Company, the airborne light infantry unit that parachuted into Normandy on D-Day and later took Hitler's Eagle's Nest at Berchtesgaden. Easy's story was, for Colby, an inspiration.

He tried to write regularly to his parents, brothers, and sister during his fifteen months at Fort Benning, where he completed OCS, the fourteen-week Infantry Officer Basic Course, his sixty-one days of Ranger School, and his three weeks in Airborne School. But maintaining regular correspondence became more difficult as his training intensified. He handwrote sixteen letters during basic training and OCS, then another three during Ranger School. They reveal him to be a man confident, from the instant he became a soldier, that he would do his duty and do it well.

Dear Family,

Today is the 5th of July. I'm still in preprocessing, getting equipment and shots and signing things. It's regimental, just like Basic; we have formations five or six times a day, have to maintain our barracks. We got yelled at (actually, I never do), so it's like Basic will be, but with little exercise. My back used to hurt a lot from standing at attention and parade rest all of the time, but it has gotten strong and feels good now. Most people really can't wait to start Basic, even though it will be hard, because we're tired of dealing with all of the discipline and regiment for no particular reason; at least when it sucks at Basic, we will be accomplishing things.

Here's some info you might like to know. Basic probably starts this Friday and lasts nine weeks. OCS starts a few days after (I don't have the exact date at the moment), and I may have a chance to leave the base between the two camps. I will almost never have phone privileges in Basic. Toward the end of OCS, I will. . . .

My squad is a mishmashed group. Other squads consist entirely or almost entirely of people who have the same military occupational specialty (MOS). Mine is a squad of people with random MOSs. There are five or six guys in my squad. I like them because they are some of the more motivated people around the place. A couple of them need to calm down a bit, though; sometimes they act like the other[s] should treat them like officers already and talk and brag about being in OCS all day long. They'll learn, though. I try not to talk about it unless I am asked because I don't think my squad should think of me on a separate plane from themselves. That probably has a lot to do with why they respect me a lot and listen to me when I ask the squad to do things. Anyway, when those couple of OCS guys come around, I think they will make good leaders because they are dedicated. My marathon training is going to pay off big time. There are very few people who are in my physical shape, and I expect to be a major standout in our physical test tomorrow.

The best thing that happens every day is Roll Call. It's my favorite thing, and here's why. We stand out in this field with about 10 other squads (with an average of maybe 35 people per squad). We stand at parade rest perfectly still and quiet while the drill sergeants have each squad sound off each person's name, one by one. Our squad, 823 Charlie-Oscar, has a gentleman whose last name happens to be "Dick." So you hear each person call their line number and name at the top of their lungs. "Zero Nine Smith, One Zero Jones . . . ONE THREE DICK!!!" Every single time, everyone laughs, and it never gets old. Even the drill sergeants can't help but laugh. So the NCOs (non-commissioned officers, fancy term for sergeants) pick on poor 1-2-3 Dick every morning. He told me that he has military in his family, and they all told him to get ready for this.

I'm going to go now. I'm halfway done reading "Band of Brothers." Mom, you might want to get a copy if you want to know why I want to be in the Army.

Love,
Colby

P.S. We have literally no access to the news at all. Could you collect and send the most important news stories from the newspaper/Internet/ whatever, especially in relation to politics and Iraq? I know Saddam was indicted and saw a picture but know nothing of what's going on. I'm also interested in the presidential race.

11 July 04

Hi everyone,

It's Sunday, and it's sort of like a day off. They aren't strict with us today; there's no exercise so far. It's 6:00 p.m. Lights out at 9:00 (except for me. I'm usually working for one person or another at nighttime for a while).

Basic is awesome. It's very, very challenging. There's always some-body watching and critiquing and YELLING at us. We do tons of hard exercise as punishment, which is called "smoking." Yesterday, it was so bad that I got close to muscle failure by dinnertime, and I consider myself to be the most physically capable soldier in my training platoon (63 people), so it was really hard. I think I will be exercising with the "A" group, which according to some drill instructors is hell on earth. I like things like that, you know. I was picked to do this job called "House Mouse" for the platoon, which is a bitch. I basically do all of these an-noying chores, like making lists, organizing patrols for nighttime (fire-guard), things like that.

The good thing is that the drill sergeants interact directly with me, sometimes like a liaison to the other training soldiers. The other good thing is that the soldiers always come to me to ask questions and get help, so I am clearly in a leadership position around here. The bad part is that it's a real headache . . . to deal with everybody needing my help literally all day long. The really ironic thing is that above in this letter, where I wrote "[. . .]," that was me running off to help somebody yelling for the House Mouse. The drill sergeants are extra critical of the OCs, which is understandable, to be expected, and welcomed. So far, so good.

It's funny. When you train, you have to begin and end every state-ment you make with "drill sergeant" (if you're talking to a drill sergeant). "Drill Sgt, yes, Drill Sgt," "Drill Sgt, I need to pee, Drill Sgt." Sometimes when I'm back working in their office, they will actually have a normal conversation with me, but it's silly because to have a conversation, I have to say the phrase "Drill Sgt" like a hundred times. I actually found myself saying to one of them in the office yesterday, "Drill Sgt, yes, that does suck very much, Drill Sgt." He laughed.

Sometimes when the platoon gets smoked by the Sgts. for somebody messing up, the guys get mad at each other. I think that they should not get mad at each other because the drill sergeants will do it one way or another; they're just picking people out to have an excuse to do it. But you can't get mad at the drill sergeants either, because that is what they have to do, and that is what we need to improve ourselves. I think that they are fair. Hopefully more people will understand how it works and become a more cohesive team. I think our platoon is pretty good already, though. We get along really well. There's a lot of different types of people here.

I just looked at my military ID from when my head was shaved. I look like a Marine.

Love,
Colby

14 July 04

Hi,

I've decided to write letters over a day or two, so they'll seem like journal entries. That way, I can write in little bits whenever I get a chance. Right now, it's nighttime Wednesday, and it's the end of week one. Our platoon is getting better. Our kids are less childish and learning some discipline. It's taking a load off of some of the OCs' backs because we're not under the same pressure to keep them in control. . . .

We worked on marching a lot today, which is great because I've been saying how much work we need on that particular skill. Tomorrow morning, we will start hand-to-hand combat. I can't wait. It'll be fun, but there's one funny thing. A lot of the guys around here think I'm this big tough kid. They don't know that I've never had to fight before. I hope I do well so I can keep my tough reputation.

I'm not writing in coherent paragraphs; sorry. Oh, I'm pissed. My mile run was 15 seconds off in the "A" group for exercise. The "A" group has barely anybody in it, and I destroyed all the kids in "B" group practice the other day. I'm just going to practice with "A" group without telling anybody. I bet they won't care. If anything, the drill sergeants will be glad I'm being ambitious. I'm still really happy to be here. I still like it. I can't wait for it to get more challenging.

Love,
Colby

16 July 04

Hi,

Today I messed up a task for the first time, but it wasn't my fault. We got our M-16s, and I had to create these check-out inventory cards. The corporal in charge gave me bogus directions on how to create them, and when they were handed in incorrectly, my drill sergeants weren't happy. But I had to suck it up and take the heat because there would be hell to pay if I blamed the corporal. Such is life. I remedied the problem a lot more quickly than they expected, though. When push came to shove, I think they weren't too upset.

Yesterday, we did this teamwork confidence course, the kind you always see on TV where they give you a tough task and a few weird supplies and you have to get your team from point A to point B. We did awesome, beat the other team 5 events to 1. That was the most fun thing so far. Everyone had a great time.

Today, we worked with our guns, disassembling them and doing marching moves (drill and cadence, or DNC). I'm not very good with mine yet. I need practice time, but a lot of nights, I don't even get enough time for a shower because I work so much for the platoon. Hopefully, I'll find time for improvement. Next week we have camping and also the gas chamber. Some say the gas chamber is the worst part of camp and that it feels like you're going to die when you remove the gas mask. Exciting. It's lights out, but I don't care. I'm going to go take a shower now.

Love,
Colby

22 July 04

Hi,

I've been very busy for a few days. We just came back from an over-night camping trip. I had to organize the nightwatch, which surprisingly went flawlessly. I'm in charge of the firewatch all night here in the bar-racks, and almost nightly someone has to wake me up to solve a prob-lem, so I thought for sure that the camping nightwatch would be five times worse. It was fine, though. I got a jolt in the heart last night. A lot of the guys in the platoon have been telling me that they expected me to be appointed platoon guide (which is the best position around here), but last night a drill sergeant hinted that it would be this other OCS guy. He'd be okay at the job, but I think I am the most-respected and relied-upon private (technically, specialist) in the platoon. I think they like him because he's a bit more well-spoken than myself. He'd be good, though, and I like him. I think the platoon will still look to me for leadership even if I don't get that position. I'm just bummed. I've been on call basically 24 hours a day with this House Mouse job, and I have about twice the responsibility of any other person here. I run pretty much everything in this platoon, and it's hard, and I don't get free time, and I work so hard. Such is life. I'll get by.

Love,
Colby

23 July 04

Hi everyone,

Today was the most famous day of boot camp, the gas chamber. I'll tell you what, it wasn't as bad as people say it is. Basically, they stick you in a closed room and spray hot sauce all over the damn place. It's actu-ally tear gas, but it feels like hot sauce in your eyes, mouth, and nose, *and it burns in your lungs. I did well. Didn't cough until I got back out in the oxygen because I didn't want to inhale more tear gas than I had to.*

My battle buddy is Ray Tuberville. I call him Tuber. He's the best guy to have as a battle buddy because he is proficient with weapons and used to do this program called "Explorers," which is like ROTC. He can help me with things that I'm not good at. He's also a well-liked guy with a good head on his shoulders. He's from southern Michigan. He helps me out with my work when it piles up. His MOS is as a fuel truck driver, which in the Army is extremely dangerous. He's just out of high school.

A funny anecdote: Our platoon's name was "the Cobras." It has since been changed, on account of bad behavior, to "Grub Worms," "Care Bears," and now we are the "Cupcakes." It's really funny hearing 63 of us sounding off in tough-guy voices, "CUPCAKES, HOOAH!"

I am getting better with my rifle. I haven't fired it yet but have become familiar with how it works and how to assemble it. I can also drill with it much better (like at the beginning of "A Few Good Men," but I suck much more).

I never told you, but on the first day, when we arrived, all the recruits were outside with our baggage, meeting the drill sergeants for the first time, and they were yelling at us and trying to scare us (it didn't work on me, if you did exactly what they told you to do, they'd leave you alone). One kid peed his pants, and there was a huge puddle. His drill sergeant has been calling him "Peebody."

Lights out. Goodnight. I still like it here.

Love,
Colby

P.S. Send more good news articles.

24 July 04

Hi,

Today was a really good day. A lot of people have been telling me that they want me to be platoon guide. On second thought, the job doesn't seem as locked on the other guy as I thought.

This morning was a PT test, 1 minute of push-ups, 1 minute of sit-ups, 1 mile run. I had the best push-ups in the platoon with 58, and one of the drill sergeants brought me out in front of 2 platoons to make an example of me. In the entire company (4 platoons, about 240 privates), one person beat me by 4. He was also about 140 pounds. Also, a drill sergeant who didn't know me saw me eating doughnuts at breakfast. He grabbed me and goes, "You're a little big, Private, to be eating doughnuts. How fast was your mile this morning?" I told him 6:28; he was really surprised and told me to continue eating, and he walked away.

Love,
Colby

Hi everyone,

I'm really depressed. One of our drill sergeants, in a rare sympathetic moment, pulled me aside to let me know that they are going with the other guy as Platoon Guide. They wanted me to know before they announced it in a few days, probably so it wouldn't come as a shock. Like I said before, I think he is a good choice, but I have worked unbelievably hard, way harder than anybody else, including him, for the platoon. I have to wonder if they didn't select me because of the mere fact that the platoon would fall to hell if I wasn't House Mouse (nobody else knows how to handle all of the management work that I need to do). It sucks because he gets to do all of the Ra-Ra-Sis-Boom-Ba fun leader stuff, and I'll be stuck running the show with all the shitty work that people don't feel like dealing with. I know that the entire platoon expects me to be Platoon Guide because every day so many people tell me that it's only a matter of time. . . .

I know that he'll do fine. It's just that I deserve it a lot more. It's exactly like at the football banquet at East when I was overlooked as captain (though the coaches eventually were practically forced to reconsider by minicamp). I suppose I will have to deal with it the same way as then: Keep doing everything the way I do things and make sure not to let this setback bring me down. . . .

I actually like him a lot and expect him to do well. I'm just unbelievably frustrated. I'll be better tomorrow.

Love,
Colby

Dear family,

Well, all has not been lost. The drill sergeants made me assistant platoon guide. More or less, me and the Platoon Guide are in charge, but he gets to call cadence and be out front a little more than I do. . . .

We're practicing with our M-16 rifles, and we'll use live rounds next week. Tomorrow is the first official PT test, and I expect it to be awesome. By the end of boot camp, I am hoping to score a perfect on the PT. That would be three 100% scores, a 300. It would be 75 push-ups in two minutes, 80 sit-ups in two minutes, and a 13-minute 2-mile run. Tomorrow, I should get about 280 points which would earn me a PT badge for my class A uniform. Tomorrow, I will have more time to write.

I love you all.

Colby

31 July 04

Hey,

Today was interesting. For that PT test, something went wrong, and I only got 60 push-ups where I expected over 70. But my sit-ups were a startling 75. And (drum roll) a 12:52 2-mile run. I couldn't believe it. My drill sergeant was yelling, "That's my House Mouse!" to the other DSs when I was headed to the finish line. I beat just about the whole company except for a few skinny kids. . . .

We went to a country concert and had a blast. Rhett Atkins, Chad Brock and Darrel Singletary were all performing. My battle buddy, Tuberville, tells me that they're really famous. They were doing some kind of Army tour. All of the trainees were invited. I drank 4 Cokes and had a candy bar and pizza. I totally have forgotten how I missed that stuff. Now I wish I hadn't eaten it because I'm thinking about it.

Love,
Colby

8 Aug 04

The more I think about it, the more I want to go to Ranger School. I think that I have what it takes to survive that torture. That would only happen for me if I was assigned to combat arms after OCS (I would say the chances of that are extremely high, given the demand for combat arms at the moment and my particular areas of talent).

We are now on week 5 of 9. I believe I have a few days off between Basic and OCS. With that time, I was thinking of relaxing at a hotel in Atlanta and catching some movies or something along those lines. A few of the other OCs are thinking along those lines and might stay with me. We'll see. I'm gonna sneak a little Sunday morning nap in. ZZZZ.

Love,
Colby

11 Aug 04

Dear family,

It's been a few days since I've had a chance to write. We've been extra busy, and a lot has happened. The reason that I've been busy is that we've been doing Basic Rifle Movement (BRM). I started with high marks but deteriorated. Last night, I practiced aiming after lights out in the barracks and was better on the firing range as a result. I still have a ways to go before I'm anything special with that rifle. I have to qualify with it on Friday, not a problem. . . .

A few days ago, we were eating chow in the field. When we do that, we have a food truck come by, and the trainees run the chow line, handing out food. So I'm going through the line, and the trainees are putting food on my plate as I walk along: my salad, my potatoes, an apple, some beefaroni, and a slice of cake. I put my tray out to get some gravy, and after it was too late, I realized that it wasn't a private giving out cake but a drill sergeant. With a big shitty grin, he poured gravy on my salad, apple and all over my cake, completely passing up my potatoes and beefaroni. It turned out he had been amusing himself in that fashion for about 10 minutes because all of the privates that I'd eaten with had those gross gravy cakes. Ha! What a jerk! Sometimes Basic is just like pledging a frat, where they just mess with us for giggles. . . .

I keep having to march the platoon around (part of being Assistant Platoon Guide). I am not very comfortable with it yet and usually make mistakes. I don't get near the amount of practice as the PG (as APG, I fill in on marches when he can't be there). I'm not too bad, though. The guys always wind up where they need to do. I do small things wrong like stand in the wrong spot outside the formation, or do cadence a little sloppy. Nothing serious goes wrong.

PT testing is again on Saturday. I may be close to that perfect score. Cross your fingers.

Love,
Colby

16 Aug 04

Dear family,

Our new drill sergeant is good. He calls me "Tiny." I'm a little bummed because today we did pugil-sticks, which is fighting with those Q-tip-looking things from "American Gladiators." I lost a fight against another platoon. Later, when the DS, the PG, and myself were driving together in a van, he mentioned how our platoon was awesome in pugil-sticks. I mentioned that I had "gotten my ass kicked." He agreed, said he was disappointed, and said he expected me to be the best one there. I was a little upset about the performance, but oh well.

Something awesome happened at pugil-sticks, though. The entire company was having matches, pitting guys from each of the 4 platoons against each other. One of our guys (4th platoon) was fighting a guy from 3rd platoon and was winning. Suddenly, one of the 3rd platoon spectators ran out and cracked our guy in the back of the head. I took off after the kid, jumped straight at him Superman style, cracked him hard with the pugil-stick, and proceeded to absolutely pummel the hell out of the kid. Half of my platoon followed a few steps behind me, and a huge brawl broke out. The DSs broke it up and pretended to be mad, but they really weren't. Perfect example of teamwork and having your platoon's back. The guy from my platoon thanked me. . . .

Still happy to be here. Thanks for always sending letters and news articles.

Love,
Colby

25 Sept 04

Hi everybody,

It's been some time since I've caught some time to write. Tomorrow, I will have been at OCS for two weeks! It's going pretty well, and as always, my motivation is still high. I think I'll start out by explaining a day at OCS:

0430–0530ish → Wake up for Physical Training or a road march. PT is either hand-to-hand combatives or some pretty heavy running. When we run, I am in "A" group (the best one) and I like being road guard because it's extra hard. Road Guard involves a lot of sprinting from back to front of formation to stop traffic. Road marches involve carrying about 40 lb ruck sacks and M-16s 5+ miles. They are boring. I road guard them sometimes, too, which is similar to the runs, but you're sprinting with all that weight.

0730ish → Chow. Eating is the most stressful thing. We have about 4 minutes to eat in silence with our eyes on the trays. We have to memorize tons of information daily that the TACs (teach assess counsel, they are like drill sergeants but some are officers) will quiz us on and give us a hard time about. There is a complicated and precise manner in which we travel about the chow hall and serve food to each other.

0830ish → Classes or trips to the field to train. Classes are boring. Training is usually fun.

1200 → Chow. Same as breakfast procedure.

1230 → Classes or field.

1800ish → Dinner Chow. Same as other chow, except includes Operations Order (Opord) retrieval. This is something everybody hates . . . I love it. We have these things called PARK points that we want to have a lot of. When you mess up a procedure, such as saluting an officer improperly or whatever the TACs want, they take points away, ESPECIALLY during Opord retrieval. The whole platoon line up next to where the TACs eat and move over to the table with precise facing movements, then, to the ranking officer, sound off. "Captain McCal-

lister (or whoever), sir, Basic Officer Candidate Umbrell requests per-mission to enter the forbidden zone (the area where they eat) to retrieve the Bravo Company daily operation order!" If you mess that up, even by a word such as "the," they tear into you, yelling, taking PARK points, whatever. If you get that far, they start quizzing you on memorization and stuff, which is more ammo for hollering and PARK points. When they are happy with performance, they let the person take the Opord, and the platoon gets to leave. It usually takes 6–10 tries, so the platoon takes turns rotating who has to stand at the front of the line. I am in the first 3 people every day, just for fun. It bugs the TACs, too! Last night, the TACs took me hostage so my platoon had to request me and the Opord.

1900 → Study barracks.

2130ish → Lights out procedure. This cracks me up. We all line up outside our rooms at attention while the TACs inspect us, our rooms, and have us do exercises and sing the alma mater and Army song. The following procedure cracks me up. We receive the command, "Prepare to mount!" We respond, "Prepare to mount!" We run next to the bunks, prepare our sheets quickly, then stand at attention. They command, "Mount!" We respond, "Mounting!" We jump into bed, pull sheets to armpits, and lie stiff at position of attention. We then get, "Prepare to sleep!" followed by "Sleep!" at which time we are ordered to close our eyes and instantly fall asleep. Maybe it's not that funny, but I laugh at it every night.

Wow, I've written a lot. Okay, here's the important stuff. I'd say I am a 99% chance of getting branched infantry, which I really want. Being infantry is pretty much the most honored branch, even though it is thought of as jarheads. That would entail IOBC (Infantry Officer Basic Course) and Ranger School. I would, at one time or another, probably go to airborne school and possibly air assault (ropes hanging from helicopters) and pathfinder school (how to get around the woods, to be reeeeeal vague). Also means, and be ready, that I am very likely to be deployed to Iraq or Afghanistan. FYI, there is huge talk in the Army about planning war in IRAN. You hear officers mention it all the time. . . .

I just got called to a conference. It's official, I will become an infantryman! Paperwork starts tomorrow. . . . When I'm home for Christmas (hopefully. It's likely), I'll be a lieutenant. Awesome.

Just thought of something. Eventually, my absentee ballot will be sent to the home address because I did not know the OCS address a month ago when I sent for it. When it comes in, forward it to me.

I've written so much. I'm going to call it quits. I love you all.

Love,
Colby

> *And it's hi hi hey*
> *The Army's on its way*
> *Count off the cadence loud and strong!*
> *♪ For wherever we go,*
> *You will always know*
> *That the Army goes rolling along!*
> *♪*

11 Oct 04

Dear family,

I apologize for not having an opportunity to write for some time, but I have been extremely busy, trust me. . . . We're in week 5, which is great because at the end of week six we transition to intermediate phase, which will make life easier. . . . I signed the request for my branch, which is expected to be approved in early November. Pending that, I will have IOBC starting January 2nd. . . .

Everything goes well here on my end. They are hard on us. Up until yesterday I had myself convinced that the TAC officer in charge of us

*thought of me as a knuckle-head, but it turns out he respects me; he
told my platoon that when I wasn't around because (you'll get a kick
out of this one) I've been turning over the candy that I get in the mail
as contraband and it shows integrity. HA!! You're going to have to stop
sending candy. I'm not allowed to eat it, but thank you anyway. I just
finished Land Navigation, which many people think is the hardest part
of OCS. They give you a map of about 100 sq miles and tell you to go
find these little poles hidden miles out in the woods. Then you have to
do it again in the middle of the night. We camped there for 5 nights and
practiced day and night before the test. It tore many people's feet to
mincemeat, but mine held up. . . .*

*Last night, we watched "We Were Soldiers." The movie was awe-
some (except for some cheesy montages). A lot of scenes were filmed at
places that I walk through every day here at Ft. Benning. It's cool to
watch war movies now because I understand what is happening so
much better.*

Love,
Colby

*P.S. Something annoying about the Army, I never hear my first name
anymore.*

14 Oct 04

Dear family,

*I was a squad leader last week and was counseled by my TAC (as we
all are). I failed on leadership, but several people had; it's not a big
deal. There was excellent insight on the areas where I require improvement, so I will improve them and pass next time. It didn't come as a
surprise to me, and I realized something. I have been on cruise control
since I've been here. I haven't had any physically demanding challenges,*

and I've sailed through all the tests, passing them all with limited study-
ing. I think I was simply complacent during my leadership evaluation
period. Since then, I've been a lot more alert and enthused. I'm more
confident. I suppose that is the point of the evaluation. Next week, we
go back to the field, which I like. Time goes quickly out there because
we get practical training. . . .

That's all I have. I love you all.

Love,
Colby

In May 2005, Colby entered Ranger School, a madman's amalgam
of obstacle courses, mud pools, wall climbing, and near starvation. The
school had a graduation rate of less than 56 percent from 1991 to
2001, and considering the costs of completing the course, it's no wonder why.

Ranger School consists of three phases: the Benning Phase, which
assesses the physical condition and endurance of each student; the
Mountain Phase, which takes place at Camp Merrill in the North Georgia mountains; and the Florida Phase, in which the prospective Rangers
master air and water operations on beaches near Florida's Eglin Air
Force Base. Through those phases, a Ranger student consumes no more
than 2,200 calories a day—the average soldier takes in as many as
3,200—to power (insufficiently) his nineteen to twenty hours of daily
training. It is routine for a student, by graduation, to have lost twenty
to thirty pounds of body weight, and it may take him as long as a year
to recover fully from the exhaustion and emaciation. Should Colby
endure the ordeal and graduate, he would be "an elite soldier," according to the Ranger Creed, "who arrives at the cutting edge of battle by
land, seas, or air," part of a select force equipped to carry out infiltration, ambushes, and other small-unit tactics—the finest fighting men in
the world.

Dear family,

It's the end of Day 4 at Mountain Phase at Ranger School. . . . So far, this phase has been very easy. We have trained in mountain climbing, knot tying, and very little else. We eat well and sleep well. That will change soon. This week is sort of a recovery week before training gets hard core. This is known to be the most physically difficult phase. Patrol missions are now at a platoon-sized level instead of squads. Patrols are over 10 km each and move through mountains. Sleep and food will become limited, if not non-existent. They say that our bodies will begin burning muscle for energy, which will make our sweat smell like ammonia. Wow.

Tomorrow, we are headed to Mt. Yonah to put our rock-climbing training to use. It's an hour drive from here. Today, we were learning to build a suspension-traverse (which is a zip-line), which we will use at Yonah. So the zip-line is at the top of a hill, goes down across a creek, and ends at the other side of the creek, tied off to a tree. Rangers are supposed to tie into a pulley, go down the zip-line, which is attached to a rope so they can be slowly lowered. And a brake at the end stops them so they can safely dismount on the other side. The first Ranger gets on this zip-line that he buil[t], and as he's lowered down, the slack on the line causes his butt to drag in the dirt and the stream, so it was kind of a failure. So our retarded instructor decides that if we just let go of the rope and let the next Ranger free-fall down the zip-line, the momentum would prevent him from dragging his butt. It was my friend Tim Ball. Tim travels down the line very fast. Tim hits a rock on the far side of the river and does a 360. Now backwards, he gets soaked in the creek. Then the brake at the far end fails, and Tim rams butt-first into a tree. He didn't get hurt. It was so funny. It was like a Wile E. Coyote cartoon.

I don't expect to have opportunities to write for 2–3 weeks, but I will be able to receive and read mail.

I love you all,
Colby

Dear family,

It's now halfway through our field exercise here in Mountain Phase. We get a one-day refit, where we come back to the barracks, sleep, get some good food. Otherwise, we have been working in the field without coming in for 4 days straight (right now I am at the refit). Wow, has this field exercise been outrageous. We sleep 30–60 minutes per day, eat 1 or two meals, and simply plan missions, rock march and execute missions in the mountains all day long. The national park that we train in is called TVD (Tennessee Valley Divide). It's part of the Appalachian Trail. It is gorgeous but very difficult terrain. When we walk and march, we are occasionally surprised by a clearing with a view or a huge waterfall. It's nice, and I wouldn't mind visiting sometime when I am not training; it's a public park, after all.

So far, I've been evaluated once on a mission as a platoon leader. I had to plan, establish and perform an ambush. The planning and establishment went pretty well, but my execution was crappy. Good learning points. They don't tell you if you pass patrols or not until the last day, so I don't know if I'm a "go" or not. That instructor had great things to say about me, including that I have "really great leadership potential," which is that particular RI's (Ranger instructor) main criteria for grading. . . .

It's funny what the sleep and food deprivation does to you. I just fell asleep writing those 3 items. Last night, I was standing on a patr

Okay, it's now one day after I fell asleep writing that stuff up there. To continue, we were standing in a patrol base in the woods. It's pitch dark, literally no moon illumination, and my night-vision goggles were broken. I hadn't eaten in 24 hours and hadn't slept in 48. I had this hallucination that Haggar the Horrible (from the comic strip) walked into our base and was talking to our squad leader. I was so messed up that I didn't even find this to be unusual.

I got some intel on the patrol that I led and whether or not it was a go. 11 people have been graded as PLs (I was one of them). Only 3 PLs passed. I know almost as a matter of fact that 5 of them were no-gos (if you haven't figured this out, pass/fail is go/no-go in the Army). That makes me a 50% chance of a go, and I have suspicions that two of the other patrols didn't pass. Either way, I still have one or two more chances to pass, and they would be squad leader positions (easier than PL). I'm planning on finishing this school on time. It's a real pain in the ass.

I may have the opportunity to write one more letter at the beginning of Florida Phase, but no phone until the very last few days. Additionally, I won't know if I pass Ranger School until one of the very last days. I'll let you know the very second that I can that I finished on time. Just realize that it could be at the last minute. I'm doing very well, though, and fully expect to go straight through.

Anyway, I need to get moving. We get some good sleep tonight, then go back out for 5 more days of hell-on-earth, no-sleep, no-eating mountain training.

Love,
Colby

P.S. I'm skinny as hell. I have nice-looking abs.
(written 10 Jun 05–11 Jun 05)

Dear family,

Day 2, Florida Phase. . . . We'll go to the field for our 10-day field problem on Thursday. Getting some rest and food to heal our bodies up before the 10-day. It's boring.

After talking with RIs and recycled students, I've determined that this phase will be a piece of cake. Only 5% of students here recycle. Unless something screwy were to happen, I will graduate on time. Count on it. I will work hard to guarantee this. . . .

I think I have developed an ear infection. As the day has gone on, I have lost hearing in my left ear, and it has begun to hurt. I'll go to sick call in the morning for meds, get this knocked out.

I've been giving a lot of thought to buying a motorcycle when I finish this course. . . . I could get a half-decent Harley to ride for the remainder of the summer, and I could ride in the spring and summer in Alaska. I think it'd be awesome.

Speaking of Alaska, I've talked to people who are driving/have driven there. If I drive there from Ft. Benning, it'll take a week +/– to do the drive, but the Army reimburses for mileage, gas, and gives more money on top of that. Plus, I could visit a few places on the way that I've never been. Might be a whole lot of fun, who knows. I'll give it more thought. . . .

Love,
Colby

Two weeks after Ranger School's end, Colby would begin Airborne School. He knew that after about twenty days of leave, his first assignment would send him to Fort Richardson, Alaska, sometime in either late September or early October.

Mark and Nancy Umbrell flew down to Fort Benning for Colby's graduation from Ranger School. As they do before every graduation ceremony, the Rangers Training Brigade, using ropes and special rigging, rappelled to the ground from helicopters hovering overhead, then presented "Rangers in Action," a sixty-minute demonstration of, among other skills, hand-to-hand combat and knife fighting.

As Nancy watched the Rangers perform, an unsettling thought flickered in her mind: Her son could now kill a man, if he had to.

SEVENTEEN

Sand and Snow

January 2006–July 2006

Bryan Buckley never liked to leave Doylestown. If there was a drawback to his career and calling as a Marine, it was the impermanence of his living situation. Six weeks at Quantico. Two weeks in a frozen forest in Maine. Another nine months at Quantico. Each time he visited his hometown after the latest stage of his training, it was harder for him to go. He and Dave Armstrong and Brian Spratt and Ed Hillman and Matt Volitis would ricochet around the bars of Doylestown, and his sisters' families would come over to Bill and Connie's house for what the Buckleys called "Sunday Fundays," complete with a barbecue, with lengthy debates about the state of Philadelphia and New York pro sports, and with seven of Bill and Connie's grandchildren scurrying about the house and backyard. (Bryan's older brother, Stephen, and his wife and two children had moved to Houston in early 2005.) Bryan still had thoughts that, once he had retired from the Marines, he would return to Doylestown, find a job, raise a family, and coach peewee football with Armstrong. He always assumed, when he had those thoughts, that there would be time for those things.

But Bryan owned a home now, and it wasn't in Doylestown. Before Christmas 2005, he had bought his house in Jacksonville, North Carolina, knowing that he would be assigned, as a platoon commander, to a company out of Camp Lejeune. Once New Year's Day came and went, Bryan drove back down to Jacksonville for company training. In Lejeune's officers' club, he was informed that he would lead 4th Platoon in Fox Company of the 2nd Battalion, 8th Marine Regiment, and he shook the hand of his company commander, Capt. James Mingus.

Mingus was thirty-six, a former drill instructor, a Charlotte native whose voice was flavored with the slightest of Southern drawls. "He looked like a grizzly bear," said Dan Clark, a towheaded twenty-one-year-old sergeant in the platoon. Like many Marines, Mingus was a habitual tobacco chewer, his lower lip always bulging with a clump of the nicotine-laden plant, and when he spoke or listened to one of his men, the repeated need to expel a stream of brown juice was the only matter that distracted him. "He would sit down, stop what he was doing, and look at you," Clark said. "Most people who are really important, if they're really busy and you tell them something, they'll walk away and won't even look at you. He might spit once in a while, but he would give you every fucking bit of attention."

Fourth Platoon was originally supposed to have been a weapons platoon, managing the heaviest of the company's mortars, machine guns, rockets, missiles, artillery, and aviation assets. But a month and a half into Fox Company's training, Mingus decided that he didn't need a traditional weapons platoon. Defeating the insurgency in Iraq did not depend on heavy artillery; the insurgents weren't using tanks, after all. It depended on infiltration and intelligence, on Marines and soldiers acting and reacting swiftly and decisively and fanning out to engage the enemy. Mingus made 4th a regular platoon. "We could cover more ground that way," he said later. What he knew about Bryan made the decision easier. Mingus had heard and read reports about Bryan's strong performance during the Infantry Officer Course, and he said later that he wanted someone to "grab the platoon by the scruff of the neck, a bull lieutenant." Bryan, he believed, could be the bull.

Fox Company had started its training in the woods and marshes around Lejeune, practicing combat operations and raids—a warm-up for its thirty days at the Marine Air Ground Combat Center at Twentynine Palms, California. The monthlong exercise, known as Mojave Viper, was broken into two parts. In the first, Marines negotiated live-fire ranges—firing their rifles, shooting mortars, calling in air support, simulating attacks—so they would grow accustomed to carrying out those responsibilities in real battle. In the second, paid actors played the roles of Iraqis in fake cities, where platoons and companies established areas of operations and conducted assaults on insurgents—soundstages for war. Since September 2005, the center, which occupied more than nine hundred square miles in the Mojave Desert, had become a mandatory and essential proving ground for any Marine unit preparing to deploy to Iraq, its weather conditions a replica of what the men would face in the Middle East. Each platoon lived in its own Quonset hut, cots on a sandy floor under a thin roof. Temperatures in the desert could climb to 130 degrees Fahrenheit, and wind gusts picked up sand by the tablespoon and threw it into the Marines' eyes and mouths. The sand was not the only source of irritation at Twentynine Palms. During a briefing after Fox Company arrived, Clark was dumbfounded as military officials said that the Marines had to mind the endangered species on the center's property, the desert tortoise in particular. *Yeah, don't mess with the turtles*, Clark thought. *We're getting ready to go thousands of miles away, where we're going to try not to get shot or blown up, but God forbid we mess with the turtles. They're national fucking property.*

Clark was among the men whom Bryan most trusted. From the moment Bryan had reported to Lejeune, his platoon sergeant, who will be called Gunnery Sgt. Paul Rosenbach, had seemed unsure of himself, indecisive, while Clark appeared to have his finger on the pulse of the platoon, to read the men's concerns and collective mood. Moreover, he relished the manner in which Bryan demanded that his platoon work harder than the rest of the company. "Some of the other platoons would be sleeping," Bryan said later. "We'd be moving. I was going to push them and push them, just so they wouldn't be able to bitch at each other. They'd just bitch about me." But early in the company's stint at Twentynine Palms, Bryan's leadership strategy didn't seem so sound. When it came time for 4th Platoon to conduct an attack on one of the center's smaller fire ranges—three enemy bunkers stood between the platoon and its raid target—the men's movements were sloppy, out of sync. They would have been self-made sitting ducks. Looking on, Mingus and Lt. Col. Kenneth DeTreux, the battalion commander, lowered their heads in disgust. In the first true test of its capacity to perform under the strain and friction of a firefight, 4th Platoon had failed.

Bryan was livid. For the next two days, he had the platoon perform "buddy rushes," a drill in which each Marine sprinted several yards, dropped to the sand to fire at the enemy, then popped back up to sprint again. He held physical-training sessions on fifteen minutes' notice, running the platoon until men started ducking behind sand dunes to puke. He didn't consider it punishment. He considered it training. Back to basics. Back to fundamentals. He wasn't punishing them. He was *coaching* them, as he had been coached. The following week, when the men of 4th Platoon led a company-wide attack exercise on a larger range, moving up on a rock face to establish a fire position to allow the other units to advance, they did it flawlessly. "That was one of my proudest moments," Bryan would say later. "The company finally realized how good these guys were."

One problem remained, though, and the second half of Mojave Viper manifested it. Rosenbach was becoming a liability. To get a gauge of where Rosenbach stood, Bryan had him plan a raid on one of the faux Iraq buildings, a U-shaped structure. As Rosenbach briefed the men on the raid, Bryan couldn't believe what he heard. Rosenbach planned to have two forces wrap around the outside of the U and come together at the break in the loop; the Marines would end up shooting at each other. The raid was a near disaster, and afterward, Clark met with Bryan and confessed to the men's lack of confidence in Rosenbach. More and more, Bryan viewed Clark as an adviser and confidant, and though the men could start "noticing the drama," as Clark put it, and could pick up on the tension between the two official leaders of the platoon, Bryan at least had an alternative. By the midpoint of Fox Company's deployment, in fact, he would approach Mingus and request permission to replace Rosenbach with Clark, which Mingus granted. But for the time being, Dan Clark provided only some much-needed peace of mind as Bryan went on leave in late June.

Back in Doylestown, he had a month to marry two conflicting aims: to enjoy himself, and to prepare for the possibility that he might not return from Iraq. His family threw that two-hundred-person party for him on July 1, and away from the kitchen full of food and the four beer-pong tables in the driveway and the fireworks that his friend Ed Hillman was setting off, Bryan made sure to get a moment alone with Mike Pettine. He had prepared that special envelope with his last wishes for his sister and brother-in-law. He had written his eulogy, just in case, and he wanted Pettine to deliver it, but now was not the time to tell him that. "You'll be getting some papers," he told Pettine, "and I'll want you to do something." That was all he would say.

He was due to drive down to North Carolina, for the final days of preparation before his deployment, on Sunday, July 23. There were loose ends to be tied first. He called Dave Armstrong to say good-bye. *I'm giving something to Chris*, Bryan said. *If something happens to me, you'll get a phone call from him or Kim.* On Saturday the 22nd, he went to Kim and Chris's house for a double birthday party for their two youngest children, two-year-old Domenic and one-year-old Olivia. The Buckleys had moved Sunday Funday to Saturday. It wasn't nearly as much fun. Bryan pulled Chris aside, handed him the envelope, instructed him not to open it unless . . . His sisters, Kim and Moey, couldn't look at him for too long, and when the party ended, he couldn't talk to them as he slipped into his car. He had to get back to Bill and Connie's house to pack. He turned the ignition and put his left hand to the window, and Kim and Moey stood outside, their faces wet, and watched him drive away, not knowing if they'd ever see their baby brother again.

October 2005–October 2006

So officious, so unwavering in his adherence to the doctrine of his training, the new lieutenant toted around his U.S. Army Ranger Handbook like he was Charles Schulz's Linus and the book was a blue blanket.

Sgt. Amal Agalawatta had been through this before, had broken in young lieutenants, shown them the way things really worked among the men of an Army infantry battalion. Agalawatta was thirty-one, six years older than his new platoon leader, 1st Lt. Colby Umbrell, and early in their relationship, he could only shake his head whenever he saw Colby try to apply what he'd learned to living, breathing soldiers. There was a natural glitch in the transition from the theoretical scenarios that the Army had set up in those leadership courses to the reality of commanding.

"When they send us someone out of OCS, there's a mindset," Agalawatta said years later. "He's been to Ranger School. He's been to OCS. He's been to IOBC and all that stuff. I'm not saying he didn't know a lot of stuff, but he thinks he knows everything. You have to realize that there are some things they teach you that we have to unteach, basically. He was like, 'I've been to school. I know what's going on.' The thing is, it's not like that."

Some of the men of Charlie Company, 1st Battalion, 501st Parachute Infantry Regiment, 4th Brigade Combat Team (Airborne), 25th Infantry Division had been deployed once already, either to Iraq or Afghanistan, before they had been assigned to Fort Richardson. Agalawatta was one such man, and from his experience, he knew that Colby's treasured Ranger Handbook was merely a terrific template, a guide— that on a battlefield, nothing went according to anyone's plan. Some of the other men were barely men, years younger than Colby. So when Colby told them that he had run the Chicago Marathon and then had run another in Rome (during his semester in Florence) and wanted to set up a marathon team at Richardson, fifteen of those pups were all for it . . . until the day of the race arrived, and only three of them competed. "They just didn't want to spend their weekends running," Agalawatta said. "They wanted to get drunk and party. It's what young Army guys do." That was most assuredly not in the Ranger Handbook, and Agalawatta finally advised Colby, "Sir, you've got to put this thing away. You can't get upset at them. They're just kids, you know?"

Born in London to Sri Lankan parents and raised in New York City, an imposing presence at six feet four and close to 250 pounds, Agalawatta was admittedly a bit jaded after serving ten months in Afghanistan in 2003–2004, but not so much that he couldn't connect with Colby. After a while, there were few at Fort Richardson who couldn't. In a meeting on his first day at Richardson, Colby met Capt. Doug Smith and was reunited with Capt. John Lafferty; he had gone through IOBC with Lafferty. Lafferty and Smith eventually were pushed over to the 509th, the sister regiment of the 501st, but because they were neighbors with Colby, their apartments adjacent in the same complex, they became fast friends. Smith, who had worked in a grain elevator in his hometown of Armada, Michigan (population 1,573), before starting college and enlisting in the ROTC at age twenty-four, had never come across someone as stubborn or opinionated as Colby. The man could turn a discussion about what to have for dinner into an hourlong forensics competition, only to settle on Quarter Pounders from McDonald's. On Sundays during football season, the three of them would head to Steve's Sports Bar in Anchorage at 9 A.M. so that Colby could don an old leather football helmet and watch the Philadelphia Eagles on TV. And a prank war that he initiated with some of the men in the battalion culminated on a morning when Colby walked into his office and—in his desk drawers, on his computer screen, on his cell phone screen, everywhere—found photos of David Hasselhoff.

Early on, Colby sought out one of Charlie Company's other platoon leaders, 1st Lt. Kevin McDaniel, and peppered him with questions. Though McDaniel believed that most of the soldiers in the battalion thought of Colby as just a football jock, through the curiosity of those questions he could see Colby's intellectualism, could see the Johns Hopkins graduate beneath the giddy jester. After purchasing a Kona mountain bike for himself, Colby joined McDaniel and Matt Didier, Charlie Company's executive officer, on a weekend trip to traverse the mountains near Richardson. The trips had become old hat for McDaniel and Didier, and they wondered if Colby would be able to keep up with them along the steep, undulating terrain. He did more than stay with them. *We were coming down the mountain fast and were rounding a wide, narrow turn in the woods,* McDaniel wrote in a letter, *when a giant moose appeared in the middle of the trail ahead of us. We locked up the brakes and nearly skidded into it. Backing up, we noticed that it was a momma moose, and her calf was in the woodline to our right. Getting between a momma moose and her calf is a very dangerous situation. Feeling brave, I suggested that we ride around both moose on the left side of the trail (there was only about four feet of room to squeeze by her). The voice of reason, Colby suggested we go back to the last intersection and take a different route, and we did. He probably saved me from getting stomped to death.*

The fun, the jokes, and the encounters with the local wildlife lightened Colby's days in Alaska, giving him little time to dwell on the danger awaiting him and his men. Come the fall, 1st Battalion was scheduled to spend twelve months at Forward Operating Base Iskandariyah in Musayyib, a Shiite-majority city thirty-five miles south of Baghdad, located in a region of Iraq that had come to be known as the "Triangle of Death." Bordered to the southwest by the Euphrates River and running between Baghdad and Al Hillah, characterized by a combustible mixture of a Sunni minority and a Shiite majority, the triangle's land was among the most treacherous in Iraq. Anthony Shadid, the Pulitzer Prize–winning reporter for the *Washington Post*, in November

2004 described the area as "a swath of territory where residents say insurgents have imposed draconian Islamic law, offered bounties for the killings of police, National Guardsmen, Shiite pilgrims and foreigners, and carried out summary executions in the street." Over the successive months, American forces and Iraqi citizens remained just as vulnerable, if not more so. On July 16, 2005, a suicide bomber walked into Musayyib's town square at 8:30 P.M. and—with a blazing-hot day cooling, with hundreds of people shopping and dining, with a tanker carrying cooking gas passing by—detonated a device attached to his belt. Dozens of buildings burned and crumbled into charred pieces. At least one hundred people were killed.

"Preparation for the deployment was pretty fast and furious," recalled Smith, whose regiment wouldn't be stationed far from Musayyib.

Colby, Agalawatta, and the battalion's other platoon leaders, platoon sergeants, and squad leaders went to the Northern Warfare Training Center at Fort Wainwright, at Fairbanks, for the Cold Weather Leaders Course—twelve days of helicopter jumping, skiing, and survival in temperatures that plummet to 60 below. When the men first jumped down through the plumes of snowy wind and landed on that unremitting white canvas, they couldn't discharge their weapons because of the paralyzing cold. Helicopters had to pick them up so they could complete their exercise in a slightly warmer area. To assist in another unit's training, 1st Battalion then spent February at Fort Irwin in California's Mojave Desert, with half the battalion acting as the Iraqi Army and the other half as insurgents. On August 4, the entire 4th Brigade traveled to the Joint Readiness Training Center at Fort Polk, Louisiana, for a month of rehearsal missions and role-playing to prepare for the people and problems they would encounter in Iraq—but not before Colby had to deal with some upheaval in his platoon. Weeks earlier, Colby's newest squad leader had celebrated his birthday by renting a party bus to drive himself and his friends around for the night. One of the partygoers, a drunk private, sneaked off, jumped in his car, and sped away, sideswiping two other cars. Though he had nothing to do with the private's drunk driving, the squad leader, as Colby put it, "got relieved of his job." Colby learned of the situation on the morning of August 2, two days before the brigade's departure. That afternoon, a platoon sergeant in the battalion was relieved of duty for ordering his squad to skip physical training, then lying to his commander about it. Colby's platoon sergeant moved over to fill that spot. "So today I lost a squad leader and a platoon sergeant," Colby wrote in an e-mail to his parents. "Pretty wild. But I still think my platoon is going to get by just fine on leadership."

First Battalion deployed to Camp Iskandariyah on Thursday, October 5, 2006, the day passing in the Umbrells' home much as any other had during Colby's time away from Doylestown. To Mark and, in particular, to Nancy, Colby might as well have been in Iraq already. Alaska . . . Iraq . . . how much difference in distance was there? "I told him to make sure, even if he had to e-mail, to let me know he was okay, but I can't explain it," Nancy said later. "I never really worried about him. I mean, I worried about him like any parent would. I just kept saying, 'I know he's coming home.' I just knew he was coming home."

Brandon Heath did not have a similar mantra to ease his worry over his friend. He, Steve Gonzalez, and Mark Reilly still lived in the central Bucks area, but the other half of Colby's circle of boyhood friends had scattered to various parts of the country. Steve Kreider worked as a sales representative for Medicis Pharmaceutical Company in Raleigh, North Carolina. Dan Tamaroff was an attorney in San Antonio. Rich Weber was a graduate student at the University of Chicago. All of them had returned to Doylestown in July, though, to spend a weekend together before Colby left, and Brandon clung to Colby's monthly phone calls from Alaska and, later, from Iraq to keep himself from worrying. They had been hanging out, just the two of them, at Kildare's, a bar in West Chester, Pennsylvania, when Colby, amid the din of the crowded pub, first told him that he was going to Iraq.

"Don't worry," Colby had said. "I'm not going to die."

EIGHTEEN

Fallujah

He arrived to the thunder of mortar and artillery fire, disquieting booms in the distance that resounded near Camp Fallujah and originated from no source that he could see. On his first day in Iraq, Bryan Buckley lay on a bed in a tin-can trailer and wondered where the people shooting at him and his Marines were, and when they would stop.

The Marines of Fox Company spent their first few days in Iraq at Camp Fallujah before moving to their command post, Outpost Viking, an old Iraqi farmhouse fifteen miles northwest of Fallujah. The house's main building served as the company's command operations center, the briefing room, and the sleeping quarters for Fox's leadership. The rest of the men slept in a storage area that the Marines had renovated into barracks. There was running water, but it was always warm. The base's electrical power shut down and fired back up for no particular reason. All the while, mortar explosions rang in the men's ears, as they had at Camp Fallujah. Some of the sand berms that surrounded the base reached eighty feet in height, ideal for obscuring insurgents and their intentions. It was an open question how long the attacks would continue, because from the moment that the Marines of Fox Company had landed in Kuwait, another problem had presented itself. Capt. James Mingus, the company commander, had to figure out a way to keep his men upright. For three weeks, Mingus couldn't send a squad or a platoon on a patrol, couldn't deter insurgents from their indirect bombing of the base, without having a Marine drop to the sand from heat exhaustion. "A guy goes down from heat, you can't just put him in the shade and leave him alone," Mingus said. The situation could hardly be considered surprising, given that summer temperatures in Fallujah routinely reached 125 degrees Fahrenheit and, depending on the nature of his mission, a Marine might wear and carry upwards of ninety-five pounds of gear and body armor. The foot patrols were murderous treks, anyway—hours in the oppressive sun, the dry wind blowing into the men's nostrils and hardening their snot into sandy clumps, garbage and chicken coops at their feet, the air perfumed by piles of sheep manure and by diesel fuel from overturned trucks. But what most frustrated Bryan, who as a former football player knew from experience the value of a good swig of Gatorade, was that he and the men had nothing but water to drink for their first two weeks in Iraq—no vitamins, no nutrients, nothing to replenish electrolytes. As Mingus lobbied his superiors for a better supply of fluids, Bryan started his Marines in 4th Platoon e-mailing their parents, family, and friends, asking them to send over bottles of nutrient-rich energy drinks.

Only when Fox's men were acclimatized and accustomed to their surroundings could Mingus decide what to do about the hail of mortars toward the base. Fallujah was a primary nest for al-Qaeda in Iraq and for other foreign fighters whom Saddam Hussein had allowed to stream into the country before the coalition's invasion. Though their leader, Abu Musab al-Zarqawi, had died in June when two F-16 jets bombed the building in which he was hiding, these insurgents still held control of Fallujah and the areas around it. Fox Company's command post was near the city of Saqlawiyah, and among the berms and canals encircling the post, the insurgents could hide almost anywhere, unless someone rooted them out and into the open.

* * *

It had become the dirtiest four-letter word in the war: IEDs. It stood for improvised explosive devices—jury-rigged bombs that could be remotely detonated. After coalition forces had failed to dispose of all of the 650,000 to 1 million tons of ammunition and explosives that they had seized during the Iraq invasion, insurgents stole a sizable portion of the munitions and began building bombs themselves. Often made from a 122-millimeter or 155-millimeter artillery shell stuffed with explosives, an IED was capable of destroying a Marine amphibious assault vehicle (AAV) or a Humvee truck, used by both the Marines and the U.S. Army. By burying the IED in the ground or in a wall, by hiding it under a trash bag or can, by monitoring from afar and triggering the device with a remote signal—a cell phone or an electric garage-door opener, for instance—insurgents could seize a tactical and psychological advantage over U.S. troops. The number of IED attacks had reached 100 per month by the fall of 2003, and for an American soldier or Marine, there was no such thing as a routine patrol anymore, including the one Bryan Buckley was leading at 4 A.M. on Wednesday, August 23.

He was in the front passenger seat inside one of five Humvees that were rumbling down a canal road near Saqlawiyah, shadowing a security foot patrol. In front of the Humvees were several members of Bryan's platoon, and along the rims of the canal road were pump houses, generators, and small buildings made of clay and brick. The goal of the men patrolling on foot was to get a feel for how people lived and interacted in the area. If they were lucky, they might see a suspicious-looking wire or scramble the signal of a detonating device. "On the patrols, it's like, 'Yeah, let's go out and die'," said Cpl. Stephen Turpin, a member of 4th Platoon. "The guys who would go in front of the convoy, we would rationalize: 'It's better us two go than the whole platoon.'" Luck would indeed have to be involved if any Fox Marines were to spot an IED, for none of the men was entirely sure what to look for. The company had sustained only one IED attack so far, during a foot patrol that included Platoon Sgt. Paul Rosenbach and one of Bryan's squad leaders, Jeremy Graham, a tall, beefy corporal. The bomb had been buried in the wall of a pump house, and though the detonation had bloodied Graham's nose and reverberated in his head like a cymbal's gong, it had never knocked him off his feet. A short firefight had then ensued, and Graham had been shot in the chest. His ballistic plate had protected him, but the bullet had shattered his M4 rifle and left him with an ugly blue welt. Once they had returned to the base and realized that Graham was all right, the men had laughed off the incident, cracking jokes at Graham's expense because he had been dumb enough to get his weapon destroyed. Dark humor and laughter were often the only ways that the Marines could deal with the danger of their missions, and during mounted patrols in their Humvees, they sometimes broke into song, maybe Britney Spears's "Toxic" or an obscure ditty from the 1980s, just to stave off the stress.

Bryan wiped off the screen of his guidance computer, then glanced out his window. A flash filled it. Everything seemed to slow down. *Oh, shit. I'm dead.* He hunched down and pulled up his legs; maybe he could cover himself from any shrapnel. Inside the vehicle, Graham tried to yell, "IED!" Instead, he yelped, "I-yaaaaahhh . . ." It sounded like a woman's scream.

An IED had exploded near Bryan's Humvee. Simultaneously, a second bomb fired next to the vehicle behind Bryan's. He fumbled for his radio, trying to get the men in the vehicles to "roger up," to signal they were okay. Remarkably, beyond a nosebleed or perhaps a slight concussion, none of the men on the patrol was seriously injured. Graham was perhaps the most fortunate. A hunk of shrapnel had glanced off the Eye Pro goggles he was wearing. The Humvees' windshields were cracked.

The Marines searched the area for any sign of insurgents. Nothing. Underneath a dead bush, Bryan and Graham found another IED—a 155-millimeter shell filled with C-4 explosives. They dropped the bush, and Marines sprinted in all directions. Nothing.

Bryan radioed in an explosive ordnance disposal unit, then radioed Mingus back at the base.

"Here's the deal," Bryan said. "We're setting up a cordon. I've got jammers out. No worries."

"Why don't you guys come back?" Mingus said, relieved to hear the smooth assurance in Bryan's voice.

"Nah, we're all good. We're going to finish what we're doing so they can see that. Even though they tried to blow us up, we're not going to walk away."

Once Bryan and his platoon had returned to the command post, Mingus had them detail for the entire company what had happened on the canal road and how they had been able to avert disaster. Strangely enough, the IED incident relaxed the men. Roadside bombs were a fact of life in Fallujah, and Fox had survived its first two. "You could see the calming effect it had," Mingus recalled. "It wasn't that bad, and the company learned that IEDs are preventable and that you had to trust that you weren't going to get blown to smithereens every time."

Mingus began assembling what he termed "warrior councils," meetings with the company officers to share ideas and suggestions—a fairly unconventional measure in Marine culture—and Bryan sought to apply the same principles to his command of 4th Platoon. Even before he had met Mingus or even joined the Marines, he had a model for this philosophy: Mike Pettine. Particularly during his senior year at Central Bucks West, Bryan had picked up on the way Pettine, as alpha male as a male could be, still solicited advice and insight from his assistant coaches. There was never a doubt that Pettine was in charge, but he maintained a Knights of the Round Table atmosphere among his staff, trusting them. So Bryan called Sgt. Jeremy Graham "Graham," and he called Sgt. Dean Lucier, another of his squad leaders, "Loosh," and his new platoon sergeant, Dan Clark, was always "Clarkie."

"If you tried to do that in normal situations without saying, 'Cpl. Graham, Sergeant Lucier,' it wouldn't work," Clark said later. "There would be a breakdown in the system. There would be such a lackadaisical attitude in the platoon that stuff would stop working. It just does not work. But we had a unique situation where we could do that, and when it came time for focus time—like, this is the game, this is 'Friday Night Lights' here—it was all good."

It worked because when Bryan had "coached" his men after their sloppy firing range performance at Twentynine Palms, he ran the three-mile pack runs and pumped out the push-ups with them. When the enlisted men had to heave sandbags on the roofs of their sleeping quarters to fortify them against mortar attacks, Bryan heaved them, too. He was, in the platoon's parlance, a "dude among dudes."

As September 11 approached, Bryan wrote a letter to Erich Maerz. It had been five years since Erich's brother Noell had been killed in the World Trade Center attacks. Since Brian saw Erich, slumped and despondent, return from Manhattan after searching for Noell for two days. Since Bryan first contemplated entering the military.

Dear Erich,

On 9/11 we all lost people who were important to us, and we all lost our sense of invincibility. It saddens me to write and think about that day. It also makes me sad to think about how many Americans have forgotten about that day. It was the darkest day in our history, but it is a day we must never forget. . . .

I have been over in Iraq now dealing with these Islamic fanatics. The news has this thing all wrong. The enemy is a bunch of cowards. I have been shot at, had mortars hit around me, and I have been hit by an IED. The enemy is a bad shot and runs at our sight. They are afraid of us. I guess they are not big on the idea of Marines slinging lead at them. But, we are doing things now to make sure they have nowhere to run. It is amazing to see these Marines who I serve with act the way

*they do. No matter what happens to them, they just keep on going. No
matter how crazy the mission or how dangerous, they just go.*

Wednesday, September 13, 2006

In Fox Company's command operations center, Bryan had his feet up
and a magazine in his lap, the communication radio buzzing in the
background. Fox Company's 1st and 3rd Platoons were on patrols
eight to ten miles away, tracking a member of al-Qaeda that Fox's
Marines knew as Hamid Romano.

Romano, Mingus said, was a nickname that in Arabic meant "hand
grenade." The man had earned the moniker. According to intelligence
reports, Romano was a coordinator of terrorist activity, responsible for beheadings, IED attacks, and mortar attacks in the region near
Fallujah—a "high-value individual." Mingus had accompanied 3rd
Platoon, which was acting on intelligence that suggested Romano was
in a house east of Fox's base, closer to Fallujah. But neither 3rd Platoon
nor 1st Platoon had found him. That wasn't unusual. Two other
Marine battalions had previously searched for Romano and had failed
to find him.

Bryan was in charge of the quick-reaction force for the mission; if
either platoon needed more support, he and as many men as he could
scrape together would provide it. As it turned out, he would have to
provide more than support. Lt. Charles Nash, the company's executive
officer, handed him a fresh intel folder on Romano from the battalion
commanders, complete with a photograph and a new location for where
Romano might be. "This one," Nash said, "sounds pretty legit."

Outside the ops center, Marines wandered around the camp. Some
of them were getting haircuts. Some were half-dressed. It was coming
up on 7 P.M. The sun would soon set. Bryan gathered the first twelve
men he could find and was gone. One of them had a half-finished haircut and was covered in his shavings.

As Bryan rode in a Humvee away from the base, Sgt. Dean Lucier
in the gunner's turret, the 2–8's operations officer came on the radio

and directed Bryan to a location near Romano's house. There, Bryan's men were to rendezvous with a section of amphibious assault vehicles. *Hmmm. They're loading me up for a reason.*

When the four Humvees and three AAVs reached their meeting point, Bryan spread out a map of the house's neighborhood across the hood of his vehicle.

"This is where we are. . . . There is where we need to go. . . . And this is how we're going to set it up. I will lead in. AAV guys, wherever these people are, I need you to surround the house. To be honest, wield your guns and make us look bigger than we are. If they pull their weapons, it's on. That's it. Any questions?"

No one said a word. Bryan paused and glanced up. *I'm planning a raid to go after some al-Qaeda guys,* he thought. *I can't believe I'm fucking doing this. If people could see me now* . . . Above, the sun was pink as a melon and full in a purple sky.

The Humvees and AAVs rolled toward the two-story house, and what the Marines saw stunned them: 130 people, men and women and children, wearing white cloaks and head wraps, most of them sitting in white plastic chairs, the sort that one would buy at Wal-Mart. They had arranged the chairs into a giant horseshoe on the house's front lawn. Women were walking in and out of the kitchen. Children were darting about, playing, doing what children do. It reminded Bryan of the wedding scene in *The Godfather.* In actuality, they were raiding a funeral.

"Sir," Lucier said to Bryan, "are we going to shoot?"

"I hope not. This is going to be insane if we have to get into a fight here."

The vehicles rumbled onto the lawn and parked in the center of the horseshoe. Lucier aimed his M240 machine gun but did not fire. No one did. After securing the area, directing the AAVs and Humvees into position to block any escape, Bryan took a six-man team to a house thirty meters down the road, to make certain no one could surprise them. The house was empty.

Bryan and his team returned. Out on the lawn, the patrol had divided the partygoers by gender, and Bryan began questioning the men one at a time, demanding to see each man's identification. He approached one who had a plump face. Bryan knew Romano had a heavyset build.

"Give me your ID."

The plump man said he didn't have it.

"Give me your ID."

The plump man handed it over. Bryan compared it to the photo in the intel dossier.

It was exactly the same photograph.

Bryan said the man's name out loud. Romano flinched, the half-second of confirmation. Bryan grabbed him and threw him to the ground. He searched him, zip-tied his hands behind his back, blind-folded him.

"He started yelling at me," Bryan said later, "and I yelled back. I did what I had to do to make sure he knew I was in charge. He started to get upset. He started weeping. I held him up and basically showed everyone: 'Here's your man, crying.'"

Bryan radioed Mingus as the other Marines shot spotlights and signal flares to make their position clear. Third and 1st Platoons soon arrived. So, too, did translators and intel officials from the battalion until some sixty Marines were there, including Lt. Col. Ken DeTreux, the battalion commander and a Philadelphia-area native. In all, Fox captured seventy-one insurgents, thirteen of whom shared Romano's designation as "high-value individuals."

"Good job, Buck—I feel like Andy Reid, coming in to celebrate with his team," DeTreux said, slapping Bryan's back and referencing Reid, the head coach of the Philadelphia Eagles. "Go get some sleep."

It was 8 A.M. before Bryan and his men returned to Fox's command post. A breakfast of premade eggs awaited them. Bryan had just lain down on his bunk when a rocket landed near the base. He poked his head out his room, saw that the base was still standing, and went back to sleep.

Two days later, Bryan wrote a letter to his parents describing the Romano capture. He closed the letter this way:

I do not have much time to write. Make sure everyone back home knows about what we did. Call Gunny Moeller up and let him know . . . let him know that his pupil has done a good thing. Tell everyone I am fine and how proud I am of the guys in my platoon; they are awesome.

   This was a big win, but there is still more for us to do; that is why I have to go. I will write you soon. Tell everyone "hello."

Love,
Bryan

Thursday, September 28, 2006

Everyone knew what went on there. Marines referred to it as "Ahmad's Garage," a complex of chop shops and truck stops and storefronts near the railroad tracks that ran along the northern edge of Fallujah. It was an insurgent stronghold, an IED factory, a symbol of the U.S. military's inability to stabilize the unstable.

   Ahmad's Garage had been the responsibility of 2–8's Gulf Company. But a few months earlier, after one of Gulf's platoon patrols had established a base in one of the complex's buildings, insurgents drove a dump truck into the building and blew up the patrol's base, causing multiple Marine casualties and compelling Gulf Company to give up trying to quell the goings-on there. DeTreux turned jurisdiction of the complex over to Fox.

Based on Bryan's handling of the September 13 raid, Mingus now knew implicitly that he possessed the sort of platoon commander who could bring to bear the more aggressive tactics that he wanted to implement. Mingus spoke often of wanting his men to be "hard targets," to be the rock in the middle of a stream of insurgents and terrorists. He sent 4th Platoon to the garage complex on a combat patrol. Bryan commanded the mission. Seventeen men from the platoon went with him, among them twenty-one-year-old Cpl. Blake Johnson, who had a fondness for Harley-Davidson motorcycles.

They moved in, some in Humvees and some on foot, sweeping a dirt median for IEDs, and the bullet cracked from the rooftops almost immediately. A sniper. Bryan was around the block when he heard the shot. Johnson had been one of the men on foot in front of the Humvees. Now, he was prone on the ground, the life leaking out of him.

Bryan and the platoon corpsman ran over to Johnson, dragging him behind a Humvee. The bullet had penetrated his back. There was no exit wound, and no telling whether Johnson's vital organs or spinal column had been damaged.

"You've got to give me a time frame," Bryan shouted to the corpsman. He needed to know how much time he had to get the platoon out of there before it was too late to save Johnson.

The rest of the platoon, meanwhile, was now facing AK-47 fire from a house to the east. On Bryan's order, the entire platoon responded by unloading a barrage of .50-caliber rounds at the house until the fire ceased. It bought the men enough time to reorganize and disengage.

Johnson had a half hour. Not a minute more. Fourth Platoon retreated to Camp Fallujah, where doctors could treat Johnson.

That afternoon at five o'clock, Mingus and Bryan led a larger patrol back to the complex. The platoon cordoned off the house to the east. There were bullet holes and dried blood on the walls—Bryan and his men had presumed that they had dropped a couple of insurgents there—but no bodies. The only man in the firefight Bryan knew for certain had been hit was one of his own. Bryan wished it had been himself.

October 2006

The mortar showers had subsided for three weeks—Mingus speculated that the insurgency had needed time to recover from Hamid Romano's capture—before starting again, and sitting back and waiting for them to stop was the height of wishful thinking. The sources of the attacks varied, but most of them seemed to originate from an area ten miles north of the command post. One suggestion that came out of the "warrior councils" Mingus immediately implemented: The men built fake security cameras, birdhouses with lenses and electrical cords, and mounted them on the camp's fence. If the insurgents thought that they might be caught on camera firing mortars or setting up IEDs, it might give them pause.

Mingus liked it. Now, he wanted something more direct. He pulled aside Bryan and Joe Luevano, 3rd Platoon's sergeant and a man with a mindset similar to Bryan's. Luevano and Bryan had become friends at Lejeune and Twentynine Palms, and Mingus now gave them a special assignment. They were to cull the seven to nine best men from their respective platoons and create a quasi-recon patrol to the north of the base. They were to conduct surveillance and, if necessary, take action.

It was out there, halfway through his tour, that he trained his rifle on one individual, just one, for the first time. He was eyeing a road in a desert area. He and eight other men had burrowed themselves into a hole in the sand and lived there for days, subsisting on bite-size Snickers bars and strips of beef jerky. No one could see them. To his immediate right was Graham, gripping a machine gun. There was a group of insurgents planting IEDs and caching weapons. Bryan was four hundred yards away, a good shot, and he glimpsed one of the men through his optic. The Marines had positioned themselves to surprise the insurgents, and Bryan would initiate the ambush by firing first.

This guy has no idea that I'm about to shoot him.

The Marines waited on Bryan, in silence, until he heard Graham whisper, "Sir?"

His trigger clicked. Out there, he could see a puff of red mist. Graham's machine gun cracked and cracked. One Marine fired a pair of rockets toward the insurgents. Bryan's world was metallic pops and streaking sounds and what he could see through his optic. He radioed Mingus, requesting a quick-reaction force to extract the men. "At that point," Bryan said later, "the jig is up. Everyone knows you're there."

He could still see the red mist where he had felled the insurgent. He had decided to shoot a man, to wound him. He did not feel anything. In three and a half months, he would be going home.

The Marines rose from the hole and, with the help of the quick-reaction force, took the wounded insurgents to the base infirmary. After eight days, the mortar volleys, at last, stopped.

Thursday, February 15, 2007

Like most of the other Marines who were also heading home, Bryan passed his final few days at Camp Fallujah smoking cigars and swapping stories. He was relieved that his deployment was ending, but his emotions were more complex than mere thankfulness that he had survived seven months in such an unstable, hazardous area of the world. President Bush had recently announced the implementation of the "surge," the increase in troops and reevaluation in tactics that, Bush promised, would turn the war's tide, and Bryan couldn't help but believe that there was more that he and 4th Platoon could have done to make the surge unnecessary. It would be strange to return to peace, to not have to think about whom he was chasing and why he was chasing them and what might happen to him in the pursuit, to be able to let his guard down and let his mind go and just *relax*. He felt guilty that there were other Marines who wouldn't be able to do that. At some level, he didn't want to leave Iraq. He wanted to stay. He was accustomed to war.

There was an unspoken acknowledgment among the men that they were confronting the same conflict within themselves. Once in a while, Bryan might express his feelings (in as much as Marines "express feelings") to Joe Luevano, who would respond with a nod and a "Yeah, I hear ya." Bryan was certain that Mingus, who was contemplating retiring from the Marines, shared the same ambivalence. There were instances when Mingus was discussing tactics with one of his men that he would stop himself, chuckle, and say, "Man, I'm gonna miss this," and by "this," Mingus meant all of it—the thinking, the planning, the scheming, the exhilaration that swept over him in the heat of a mission and that swept over Bryan, too. Mingus could see it, sense it. Unsolicited, he asked Bryan one day, "You want to go to Recon, don't you?"

"You know I do," Bryan said. Recons were the intelligence collectors of the corps, the artful dodgers, silent hunters who conducted special operations. It was customary for a Marine to serve two tours before the corps allowed him to go through the Recon screening process—long-distance swims, thirteen-foot-high platform pool jumps, pack runs, and review-board interviews. But Mingus was a Force Recon man himself, and Camp Lejeune was home to the 2nd Reconnaissance Battalion, 2nd Marine Division; once Bryan worked himself back into shape, Mingus could shake a few hands and wink often enough at the right people to get Bryan before the screening board not long after his return from Fallujah. And there was the dichotomy. Even while Bryan was on his way his home, he was planning his way back.

If there was one aspect of the deployment over which Bryan and Mingus and Luevano had no regret at all, it was this: The company had not sustained a single fatality. Every Marine in Fox Company who had left Camp Lejeune in late July would return to Camp Lejeune. Waiting in Kuwait for the company's flight to Liechtenstein, Bryan collapsed into one of the reclining chairs that the USO provided for troops.

He was exhausted. The stress left him, as if he had been wrapped in a damp, heavy blanket that someone had peeled off him. He fell asleep.

In Liechtenstein, he drank his first beer in seven months, a nice German lager. After three of them, he was "the happiest man on earth." Before the company's next flight lifted off the tarmac, Bryan took the microphone from a flight attendant and delivered the "Welcome aboard" brief to the passengers. En route to Cherry Point, the plane passed over Maine, and the pilot announced that the Marines aboard had just entered American airspace. Bryan would never forget how the men of Fox Company roared, or the small spasm of guilt that he felt when he roared with them.

The atmosphere at Camp Lejeune was that of a gigantic block party—the day beautiful, hamburgers and hot dogs grilling, a pavilion erected where parents and grandparents could rest their feet while they awaited the arrival of the Marines of the 2–8. Via cell phone text messages and word of mouth, updates on the Marines' journey home spread through the crowd. *They just landed at Cherry Point! They're off the plane! They're on the buses!* It seemed to Bill Buckley that everyone there held an American flag. He held his video camera. Connie Buckley stood next to him, vibrating like a tuning fork from her nervous eagerness at seeing her son. Kim DiSciullo, Bryan's eldest sister, kept an eye on her two eldest sons, seven-year-old Christopher and five-year-old Dylan. The boys wanted to greet their Uncle Bryan when he got off the bus.

Among the five of them, no one was more relieved that Bryan was coming home than Connie. She had been, Kim said, "a hot mess" throughout Bryan's tour, fearing the worst with every phone call, every television or Internet report that mentioned casualties in Iraq. "Charlie Gibson and I became good friends," Connie said later, referring to the anchor of ABC's nightly news program. One night, ABC reported that several Marines had been killed, but the network could not release their names because their families had not yet been notified of the deaths. Bill and Connie looked at each other. Twenty minutes later, Connie's boss called, asking if she had heard from Bryan lately. A few minutes after that, the phone rang again. It was Mike Pettine.

"How's everything going?" Pettine said, tiptoeing around his real reason for calling. "Uhhh . . . have you heard from Bryan?"

"No," Connie said. "And we're worried, too."

Connie stayed awake the entire night, certain that the doorbell would ring. Of course, it never did.

For Kim, the torture was more incremental. When Bryan had told his family, in 2001, that he wanted to give up football and join the military, Kim at first was neither proud nor surprised. She was *angry*. "My thought was, 'You have so much going for you. You're so smart. You have this possible football career. If not, you're so colorful. I'm sure something's going to come your way,'" she recalled. "Somebody else's brother can do this. Somebody else's son can do this. But then, on the flip side, your job is to support him, and you get over your anger." While Bryan was in Fallujah, Kim checked the Marine Corps's website with an addict's compulsion, reading letters that had been posted on the site by Marines serving in Iraq, scanning casualty releases from the Department of Defense for the only name she would recognize. She knew very well that if anything were to happen to Bryan, she would find out before it had been posted on the site. But she couldn't stop herself. That damn envelope that Bryan had given her and her husband, Chris, was tucked away in their strongbox, and there were so many names in those releases. . . .

When the buses pulled up, the crowd started to move as one toward Lejeune's main gate. Bill hopped up on a table near a building to get a better shot with his video camera, but the screen suddenly went black. He didn't know why. Within five minutes, he didn't care. There was Bryan, stepping down off one of the buses, crouching down to say hello to his nephews. "All right, guys," he said to them. "Drop and give me twenty." And they did. Bryan then introduced his family to Lance Cpl. Blake Johnson, leaning on a cane, who had come home before the rest of the company, who the week before had ridden a Harley for the first time since he had been shot in the back in September.

They drove back to Bryan's house. He called the rest of his family and friends. Connie and Bill thought that Bryan might want to sleep after his trip, but no, he wanted to go out to dinner, have some drinks, enjoy himself.

"It was all," Bill said later, "pretty exciting."

Bill and Kim went upstairs to get cleaned up and changed. Bryan stayed downstairs, talking with Connie in the kitchen. His mind wandered. The men who had been wounded in Fallujah had been there at Lejeune to greet the rest of the 2–8. To see them . . . to see Blake Johnson limping over on that cane . . . to see his family waiting for him . . .

"You start thinking about things that happened," Bryan would say later. "You start thinking about some of the tough times. It starts to hit you because, over there, you're not thinking about that stuff. Here, you can't really express yourself and talk to people about what you've done because nobody really understands. And when they try to talk about what you've done, they don't really know. You kind of feel like you don't have much in common with them anymore, which is weird. It's almost like you have more in common with your enemy than you do with your loved ones at home.

"That's when you start noticing, 'I'm different.'"

Bryan stopped talking. Without warning, he approached his mother, laid his head on her shoulder, put both of his arms around her, and hugged her.

Still training his Marine Option midshipmen at Villanova University, Gunnery Sgt. Don Moeller had been sending the occasional e-mail to the Marine he now considered the brother he never had. Moeller knew Bryan needed to focus on his job at hand during his time in Fallujah, and he didn't want to "clutter his mind with any bullcrap."

Bryan was back in the States now, though; after flying to California to visit his friend Corey Potter for a week, he would be driving up from Jacksonville to Doylestown to spend twenty days at his parents' house. Through their e-mails, Bryan had told Moeller about his desire to go to Airborne School and to become a Recon Marine. Moeller asked Bryan if he wouldn't mind speaking to one of his ROTC classes at Villanova, to tell Moeller's future Marines what combat missions were really like, how their training really would prepare them to perform in the most difficult of moments. He knew Buck. Buck would be light. Buck would be funny. Buck would give the students a sense of the war.

Buck was none of those things. For the hourlong class, he was straightforward, detached, almost placid.

"Are you all right?" Moeller asked him when the class ended.

"Yeah," Bryan said. "I just don't feel the same."

On the day after he had returned from Fallujah, Bryan had run an errand to K-Mart, and a white bag blew across the parking lot. His mind raced: *What's this bag doing here? That bag shouldn't be here. What's in the bag? What's under it?* When he entered a crowded restaurant, the first thing he did was locate the nearest exit. When he drove underneath an overpass or bridge, he swerved his car. He was driving along Route 24 in Jacksonville one afternoon when the driver in front of him started pulling over to the side of the highway. Bryan followed him, stopping right behind him. The driver shot him a look, and Bryan merged back into traffic.

In Fallujah, a bag might hide an IED. A crowded place was a potentially dangerous place. A driver might pull over his vehicle to plant a bomb.

He had not left Iraq behind.

"You could see it in the look on his face," Moeller recalled. "He was climbing the walls. Over there, there's never enough time. There's always action, always work to be done."

Moeller did what he could to re-create some of that action for Bryan. He invited him to train with Villanova's Marine Options. He set up a mini–mixed martial arts camp for him, swam him in the pool, ran him on the track, opened the weight room for him, tried to burn away Bryan's antsy energy by pounding his body with physical training. It didn't work. The look was still there.

Then Moeller tried something else. For a lot of Marines, Moeller believed, pulling the trigger in battle wasn't difficult. It was merely a matter of doing what they needed to do to defend other Marines. He viewed combat operations in the same manner a professional football player viewed the Super Bowl. A football player practiced and practiced and played and played for the chance to participate in one game, just as a Marine trained and trained to do one thing. That was the part that many civilians never grasped. Did they think that twenty-first-century Marines didn't want to be in places such as Fallujah and Baghdad? Of course they wanted to be there. They *volunteered*. It was like the Super Bowl. *Everyone wanted to go*. And once you went, how could you wean yourself off the rush?

"I knew what I was going through," Bryan said later. "Your body has been through a tremendous amount of stress. Mentally, you've aged. You talk it through. You accept it. Then, you have to be a man about it and move on.

"The only guy I could talk to was Gunny Moeller—because he's a Marine. Around everyone else, I was kind of quiet. I look at it like this, and this is a corny analogy but it makes sense: There are wolves and sheepdogs. The wolf was the enemy, and we were the sheepdogs. We both have fangs. We're both made to kill. The difference is that the sheepdog protects the flock whereas the wolves try to get through the gates and kill the flock. Sometimes, that sheepdog has to do some nasty things to those wolves. No one wants to know about it, but they want to know they're protected. That's the life we have to live."

So Moeller took Bryan to a pistol range in New Jersey. And for those few hours, with steel in his hands and a target in his sights, Bryan was the most relaxed he had been since coming home.

Bryan had been back in Doylestown for a while when his friends and family threw a welcome-home party for him at the New Britain Inn, and everyone who could be there was there: Bill and Connie; Kim and Chris; Moey and her husband, John; Erich and Meg Maerz; Dave Armstrong; Brian Spratt; Ed Hillman; Matt Volitis; Bryan's aunts and uncles; Jim Benstead; Mike and Leo Carey; Mike Pettine. They were there to celebrate, and they passed around full pitchers of beer as music blared inside the bar. And it was familiar, because it was hard to forget why people who lived in and around Doylestown, who were part of the football dynasty that Mike Pettine had built, used to celebrate at the New Britain Inn years ago.

Of all the players he had coached at Central Bucks West, of all the players he admired for what they had accomplished while they were in the program and once they had left it, Pettine couldn't put any of them above Bryan Buckley. He still cringed at the thought that he might have had to stand before a congregation at Our Lady of Mount Carmel Catholic Church in Doylestown and read the eulogy that Bryan had written before departing for Fallujah. He has never seen the speech. No one except Bryan has. "I don't know how I'd get through something like that," Pettine said, "with what I know about Buck and how I love him."

In time, Bryan's friends would say that his experiences in Iraq had not changed him, that he was the same "party guy," as Matt Volitis called him, he always had been. He never offered much detail to them about what he had seen or done there, and he did not say very much now, either, until Don Moeller entered the NBI. "Brother," Moeller said, and he did not even look at anyone else. He shook Bryan's hand, and the two of them sat together at a table, talking to each other the rest of the night.

It was late now, and most everyone had left the party, and the two Marines were still drinking beer and talking about Bryan's time in Fallujah and about his aspirations to go to Airborne School and join Recon. Finally, Moeller said, "I want to give you something," and he reached into his pocket and handed Bryan his gold wings.

"I want you to have these."

"Oh, man," Bryan Buckley said. "I can't believe this." And he looked down at the floor. Whatever he was feeling, he kept inside with so many of his thoughts and memories of his life as a U.S. Marine, stored away in places far from the light of day, in a strongbox and in his dreams.

NINETEEN

Musayyib

November 2006–January 2007

The four smokestacks of the Musayyib power-generating plant, set at the center of the American military's Forward Operating Base Iskandariyah, resembled great fingers from a behemoth's hand, reaching to grasp the sky. Only one of them functioned efficiently enough to spout an acrid cone of dark fumes, but that single stack was enough to have some of the men of 1st Battalion, 501st Parachute Infantry Regiment wondering whether their lungs would soon blacken and collapse. This was where they lived and worked. This was where 1st Lt. Colby Umbrell lived and worked. If he had concerns about the conditions, he kept them to himself.

Colby and 1st Battalion had spent a month in Kuwait, where they went through their final preparations before settling in at FOB Iskan, located on a bank of the Euphrates River. The battalion had arrived in Iraq with one company, D, serving as its antitank company, but as part of those preparations, 1st's leaders reshuffled the platoons to balance the battalion's antitank capabilities throughout its four companies. When the music stopped, Colby and his platoon were no longer in C

Company. He now led the thirty-four men of 2nd Platoon, Delaware Company, under the command of Capt. Eric Lawless. As Marine Capt. James Mingus had concluded with 2–8's Fox Company, having one heavy-artillery unit in a company or battalion did not fit the style of war that the military was fighting in Iraq. Even the power plant's presence at FOB Iskan was an example of how unorthodox and difficult the military's mission in Iraq had become. The plant, designed by the Soviets years before, was a technological jalopy of rusting turbine fans and tunnel-sized piping. It delivered just a third of the electrical power it was built to produce. Yet when coalition forces landed in Musayyib in 2003, the city's residents anticipated that the Americans would repair the equipment and have the plant running at full efficiency in less than three months. The soldiers still hadn't fixed the plant by September 2006, which only heightened the tension between the troops and the people they were supposed to be helping.

"I got the sense that they were not happy with us," Sgt. Amal Agalawatta recalled. "They didn't smile. In Afghanistan, when you went on a convoy, everyone got out of the way. In Musayyib, people just kept walking down the street. You weren't sure who was on your side and who was not."

Colby, for his part, wanted to alleviate some of that uneasiness, and he believed the best way to do it was to counterbalance the ugly necessities of the war—the patrols and the raids on Iraqi houses that might harbor "the bad guys," as he always called them—by reaching out to the country's children. The idea came to him midway through November, when his parents held a Saturday party to collect food, toiletries, DVDs, and other items for Colby's unit. Mark and Nancy soon shipped over more than thirty-five care packages containing candy, shaving cream, toothpaste, lip balm, granola bars, and movies, and on his patrols into the more urbanized areas of southern Iraq, Colby thought he could do something similar for the schoolchildren there who lacked the most basic of supplies: pencils and paper.

This was not an idea with which his commanding officer was enamored. Lawless was, in some respects, exactly what Colby wasn't: soft-spoken, always serious. He did chuckle to himself whenever he saw Colby sitting at his office desk at the base, wearing that leather football helmet of his as he fiddled on his laptop, reading his orders or drawing up a platoon schedule. And because Lawless had obtained a law degree from Seattle University, he was happy to advise Colby on how best to expedite the processes of applying to schools and taking the LSATs. But Lawless was not in his first deployment to Iraq, as Colby was. He did not see Musayyib as a place fresh with possibility, as Colby did. Lawless had commanded Charlie Company, 1st Battalion, 161st Infantry, during a yearlong deployment in Baghdad that started in April 2004. Back then, "people were happy to see us," he recalled. "There weren't that many attacks against us."

The situation was different now. On December 20, 1st Battalion sustained its first combat fatality when an IED detonation detached a power line—turning it, according to one description, into a "lethal whip"—and the line electrocuted a soldier. One of the explosion's survivors lost his legs below the knee and his penis. The following month, ten miles south of Musayyib in Karbala, a group of insurgents, disguised as American soldiers, infiltrated a city council meeting, killed one U.S. soldier, and kidnapped four others. The attacks were increasing in frequency and audacity, and Lawless couldn't find much value in handing out No. 2 pencils to the sons and daughters of those who might try to kill him and his men. But Colby could.

From the end of November to the first week of January, Colby sent six e-mails to his mother's account, most of which dealt with his finances, the Eagles, and the holidays. By then, he had figured out how he would collect the school supplies for his outreach project. He e-mailed Ann Kuntzmann, his guidance counselor at Lenape Middle School and the adviser of the school's chapter of the National Honor Society, and asked for her help. Perhaps the NHS students and their parents would be willing to contribute what they could. Kuntzmann gladly agreed, and Colby promised to speak to the students himself when he came home on leave at the end of March.

Tue, 28 Nov 2006 10:35:35

Hi,

I just finished another patrol cycle. This one was a little more stressful than the last, but my platoon and I have done a great job. Yesterday we were tapped to take the brigade commander on a tour of two towns. . . . This is now the third patrol I've had to take colonels on. Most platoons never have to take somebody that high in the chain of command at all, but as coincidence would have it, they always, by chance, request my company during my patrol cycles. It's been good, though, because we've had high compliments on the quality of the patrols. . . .

I spend whatever spare time I have practicing LSATs and learning about law school. . . . I think Temple is an unbeatable deal. It's a very well respected school that's ranked formidably. In state it's only $14,000. No other school I've researched comes close to that affordability. Plus, it's in Philly, which would be a place I'd prefer to practice. . . .

love,
Colby

Tue, 12 Dec 2006 11:39:21

Merry Christmas everybody,

I'm still doing pretty well over here in Iraq. Patrols keep us very busy, so time moves quickly. It's hard to believe that almost a quarter of this deployment is already over. In a few months I will have midtour leave, which I look forward to. . . .

I'm sure people are interested in what the situation is really like over here. This is how it is: What you see on the news is usually true, but it's only a small part of what's going on. There are bad attacks from time to time, and probably nationwide, anti-coalition forces produce 1 or 2 successful attacks per day. However, we usually manage to foil their attacks. So far, my company has been attacked 3 times by roadside bombs. Two of them blew up (two patrols I was on), the other was found before it detonated. No damage has been done to vehicles or personnel. . . .

You will hear on the news that Iraqis want us to leave, but they don't. You wouldn't believe the stories that I have heard from the locals about what Saddam had done to them. Some of them had been in hiding while their entire families were executed. 95% of the people we come in contact with are eternally grateful for what we do.

Local and national governments as well as Iraqi police and armed forces are slowly growing in competence. They have suffered for a long time under an oppressive regime that nobody could trust, so naturally adjusting to democracy and having faith in a new system takes more than a few years. Therefore, troop withdraws are a bad idea. They need us to be here to train their government and forces. I spend less time on patrols searching for bad guys and more time at meetings with politicians and local leaders, teaching them to help themselves rather than begging us for money and supplies.

Please DO NOT support the "graceful exit" strategy in Washington. It undermines everything we have worked on here. I know that people miss their soldiers, but the "graceful exit" strategy will pull the rug out from everything we have done so far, and will destroy this country.

I need to give the computer up now, Merry Christmas!

Colby

Sun, 24 Dec 2006 18:49:36

hi.

I'm a little tired and irritated. I just came back from a patrol that was supposed to last 12 hours but wound up lasting almost 48. . . .

   Merry Christmas! Maybe I'll get a chance to call tomorrow night. If not, it's probably because everyone will try to use the phones that day. . . .

colby

Sun, 07 Jan 2007 08:28:14

My platoon had a big milestone. We caught two terrorists, and at least one of the two is going to jail big-time. The other, they need to determine how involved he has been in attacks (I'm not certain myself). A good operation, though. We snuck in in the night and brought them out of their homes. Tried fake IDs on us, and some slicky-boy moves like that, but we figured them out. It was fun. . . .

colby

March 2007

There were moments, Eric Lawless had to admit, when Colby's idealism, his near naïveté, paid dividends. One day, a prisoner at the Musayyib jail began to jabber about a hidden stash of homemade explosives and wanted to make a deal with U.S. soldiers: If they would let him out of jail, he would show them where the explosives were.

   "I never believed anything an Iraqi told me because I'd talked to so many and very seldom would anything true come out of their mouths," Lawless recalled. "One thing about Colby, I wouldn't say he was gullible, but if you told him stuff, he believed it. He always believed the Iraqis, all the time."

After requesting use of a bomb-sniffing German shepherd, Colby and his platoon, directed by the prisoner, drove out to a large plot of sandy soil. Despite the detainee's insistence that the cache was under the shepherd's paws and the soldiers' feet, the dog smelled nothing, electing instead to prance around the dirt. But the prisoner kept insisting, so Colby ordered the platoon to start digging. Deep below ground level, they uncovered twenty-five hundred-pound bags of explosives.

Back at the base, Colby cursed and complained about the German shepherd. What was the point of using a bomb-sniffing dog if the dog couldn't sniff out any bombs? In front of Lawless and several other soldiers, he reenacted the puzzled dog's movements during the weapons search, stopping once his entire audience had burst into laughter.

The cache was a good find, and it occurred around the same time that Musayyib's courthouse reopened after a three-month renovation project. Together, Iraqis had worked with 1st Battalion's soldiers to complete two security buildings on the courthouse grounds and install a new water system, latrines, furniture, and an electric generator. These were two encouraging events at the beginning of what would become a precarious three-month stretch for the battalion. In Musayyib, coalition forces had begun focusing their search-and-capture efforts on members of Jayish al-Mahdi, a militia formed from the followers of the infamous Shiite leader Sheik Muqtada al-Sadr. "This small minority of young men perceived its own political and religious ambitions crushed by coalition commanders," counterterrorism expert Malcolm W. Nance wrote in his book *The Terrorists of Iraq: Inside the Strategy and Tactics of the Iraq Insurgency.* "They believed the Bush administration intended to occupy Iraq and place its own leaders in positions of power." In turn, Jayish al-Mahdi had retaliated with a cycle of IED attacks on U.S. forces along and around Route Caroline, a logistical supply road that Army convoys often used. Worse, these IEDs were often of a specific, deadlier type: the explosively formed penetrator, or EFP.

On May 15, 2004—a month after poor Shiites in southern Iraq began openly attacking coalition forces—the first confirmed EFP appeared in Basra. According to U.S. intelligence, CD-ROMs that provided instructions on how to build EFPs soon circulated among insurgent groups. The device fired a dense, molten copper disk into a passing vehicle, and because no radio waves were involved, the passive infrared trigger used to detonate an EFP could not be jammed. By July 2005, U.S. forces were finding a more advanced version of the device, one that meshed the passive infrared trigger with electronic, radio-controlled circuitry. Now, by emitting a simple radio signal, an insurgent could choose exactly when he wanted to attack, and exactly whom.

One measure that U.S. forces took to defend themselves against EFPs was the invention of the Rhino 1, a mechanism in which a toaster-shaped ammunition can, attached to a ten-foot pole in front of a Humvee, detected and destroyed an EFP before it could fire at the vehicle. But not every Army Humvee was equipped with a Rhino 1, and insurgents already had started to design an EFP that could defeat a Rhino 1, and the number of IED and EFP attacks was increasing throughout Iraq and, more specifically, in the Musayyib area. From July 2003 through April 2007, there had been 1,354 U.S. military fatalities by IED, an average of 29.4 a month. In March 2007, there were fifty-four, and the IED death toll would peak at ninety just two months later. There were six in Musayyib during a twelve-day period in March, and their primary targets were patrols using Route Caroline to return to FOB Iskan. To those concerned for Colby Umbrell's safety, there could have been no better time for him to take two weeks of leave.

April 2007

He had slept too much. It was a luxury neither the men in his platoon nor the people who loved him most could afford, and it was Colby Umbrell's greatest regret after his two weeks of leave ended on Wednesday, April 11—after he had boarded a plane bound for Baghdad and had an opportunity to e-mail his parents. Of his more than two weeks in the States, he had spent four nights in Las Vegas with friends, playing poker and ogling spangled dancing girls, and the rest in Doylestown at his parents' house, staying out late with his neighborhood buddies at the various bars in town, sleeping off his nightly revelry until early each afternoon. He did find time to visit Lenape Middle School, as he had promised Ann Kuntzmann, wowing about thirty National Honor Society students as he showed them photographs of Iraq's dingy, two-room schoolhouses and told them that, yes, he had indeed seen a dead body or two.

But Colby's longtime friend Steve Kreider could sense his distraction during their Vegas vacation: "He kind of felt guilty about being home. He felt he should have been back out there." Throughout their years growing up together, even while he was playing linebacker at Division III Muhlenberg College and Colby was weighing whether to struggle through his setbacks at Johns Hopkins, Kreider always had connected Colby's desire to join the military to his affection for football. In Kreider's mind, the two were inextricably linked for Colby, part of a continuum in his friend's life, in a way they weren't for himself.

"To be an Army Ranger and a college football player are two totally different things," Kreider would say later, "and there are a lot of people, like me, who could be a college football player but not an Airborne Ranger. But it's the same kind of drive, desire, commitment, discipline, and structure of lifestyle that you're used to in football that can transition over into a military career. Only a few can do what he ended up doing, and that's what was so special about it.

"He chose to be an Army Ranger. It's the toughest of the tough."

Still, the trip had been cleansing, necessary, for Colby. There was much on his mind. The Army had recently extended his deployment, which meant he was due to return home again in January 2008. (The bright side was that once he had been in Iraq for a year, he would earn a bonus of $1,000 for every month thereafter.) He was anxious to begin the application process for the JAG Corps, and he didn't know whether his deployment might put him up against a deadline or even make it impossible for him to apply at all. Moreover, he had heard rumors that the Army was considering shortening the soldiers' periods of leave and lengthening their deployments. If that turned out to be true, he wrote in an April 13 e-mail, "I may have to call it quits. . . . I do not want to spend my entire career deployed."

He also didn't want to spend his entire career in the Baghdad airport, but as he typed away on his laptop, it was starting to look that way. There was a shortage of available aircraft at the airport; he'd have to wait for transport back to FOB Iskan. Boredom had set in. "I want to get back to my job," he wrote. "I really need something to do."

His parents already had something to do: bail out of their basement. A record rainfall of more than five inches doused Doylestown on April 15 and 16. Mark and Nancy knew their son was stuck in Baghdad, and they didn't know how long he'd be there, but it did them no good to worry, and besides, the rainwater was rising.

Once the basement was dry again, Nancy typed a quick e-mail message to Colby, asking offhandedly, "Are you back yet?" By then, he was. The next day, April 18, Colby Umbrell sent what would be his final correspondence from Iraq to his family.

"It's actually not bad to be back," he said in the message. "No more news to report. I'll call you in the next few days."

Colby never did tell his parents of an incident that they might have considered newsworthy, perhaps because it would have been too unsettling for them. Lt. Col. Robert Balcavage, the battalion commander, who had previously accompanied Colby on one of his patrols, rode in Lawless's Humvee to a meeting of the Musayyib city council late in the month. After the two-hour meeting had concluded, Balcavage climbed back into the Humvee. As he closed the door, a bullet struck the vehicle's bulletproof glass. A sniper had tried to take out the man in charge.

"Everything," Lawless said later, "was going to shit."

Sunday, April 29, 2007

Travis Manion had been the rare Doylestown high school student who did not attend either Central Bucks West or Central Bucks East. He was an athlete, though, wrestling and playing varsity football at La Salle College High School, a Catholic school in Wyndmoor, Pennsylvania, just outside Philadelphia. He entered the Naval Academy, graduated in 2004, and rose to become a Reconnaissance Marine, serving with the 1st Recon Battalion, 1st Marine Division, in Fallujah.

It was there, while Manion was conducting a combined Iraqi-Marine patrol, that in the midst of an insurgent attack, a sniper's bullet passed above Manion's armor plate and struck him in the heart.

Manion was the third Doylestown resident to have been killed in combat in either Afghanistan or Iraq. First Friday Doylestown, a non-profit organization that sponsored a monthly street fair in town, planned to hold a vigil in honor of Manion. The crowd in Doylestown on Friday, May 4, figured to be bigger than usual.

On Sunday afternoon, Colby called his sister, Casey, catching her on her cell phone as she drove near her Savannah, Georgia, home. He wanted to know how things were going with her and her boyfriend, Michael Nonemaker. They talked for forty-five minutes. It was the only time Colby Umbrell ever called his little sister from Iraq.

Monday, April 30, 2007

At Lenape Middle School, a student asked Ann Kuntzmann if the man from Doylestown who had been killed in Iraq was the same man who had just talked to the National Honor Society. *No*, Kuntzmann said. *It wasn't.*

Wednesday, May 2, 2007

Nancy Umbrell walked through the front door around eleven in the morning after running some errands. She noticed a 199—the phone exchange for Iraq—on the house phone's caller ID. No one had left a message. She assumed it was Colby, but she wasn't certain. When he called and no one picked up, he usually left a "Sorry I missed you" sort of message, just so his mother could hear his voice. This time, nothing.

Maybe, she thought, *this is the only time of day he can call me.* A friend had once told her, "You can't wait at home every time you think Colby's going to call." Her response: "Watch me."

She decided to make sure she was home the next day, in case he called back.

Later that night, Lawless passed Colby as the two of them walked through camp. Colby was on his way to bed. He had to rise early the following morning. He was taking out half of 2nd Platoon to conduct an overwatch, a patrol of several nearby convoy roads, among them June, Jennifer, Cleveland, Michelle, Jackson, and Caroline.

"Make sure you're extra careful," Lawless told him.

"Thanks for your concern," Colby said. "I will be."

Lawless went one way. Colby, the other.

Thursday, May 3, 2007

Their mission that morning was supposed to last eight hours, and Amal Agalawatta, one of 2nd Platoon's squad leaders, wasn't supposed to be part of it. He was scheduled to go on leave that day, but the night before, his name had been posted on the patrol pass. He would be riding in Colby's Humvee. Someone had made a mistake, and there was nothing that Agalawatta could do about it. He barely slept that night, awaking before the sun came up, calling his wife, Rebecca, to tell her that he wouldn't be leaving just yet. He was loading his gear into the Humvee when Colby approached him.

"What are you doing here?" Colby asked him. "You're going on leave, aren't you?"

"Yeah, but I'm going on the mission."

No, he wasn't. Colby made a phone call and took Agalawatta off the patrol. Pfc. Servando Koschny replaced him. Agalawatta wasn't scheduled to depart the base until the evening, so he went back to his room—"a two-man can," he described it—to take a nap.

"I didn't feel very comfortable when they left me back," he recalled. "You're on pins and needles because all my guys went out that day, and I'm supposed to be their team leader. But there's a reason. The way it works is, prior to leaving, you get forty-eight hours off. But we were so short-staffed. A lot of guys had gone on leave. We were pulling twelve-hour shifts, guys getting burned out. It was so hot."

After Colby, at 5:30 A.M., briefed them on the mission, seventeen soldiers from 2nd Platoon moved out of FOB Iskan in four Humvees. Each soldier wore a standard Army combat uniform of muted green and sand-colored camouflage; sixteen pounds of interceptor body armor with plates covering his front, back, and sides; a neck yoke; throat and groin protectors; protective goggles and gloves; a headset for ear protection; and an advanced combat helmet that weighed between three and three and a half pounds. Each of the Humvees wielded either an M240B or an M2 .50-caliber machine gun.

Two of the four patrol vehicles were fitted with Rhino 1s. Colby's vehicle was not.

Colby rode in the front passenger seat of the second vehicle. Spec. William Swails was driving. Seated behind him and Colby were two soldiers, Koschny and Pfc. Anthony Pardella, and an Iraqi interpreter named Jawod Kadhim Nasear. The men of the platoon called him "Nick." Sgt. Frank Aguilar, the platoon medic, was a passenger in the fourth Humvee, as was Sgt. First Class John Zaremba, the platoon sergeant. Raised on a farm in Owensboro, Kentucky, Zaremba had joined 2nd Platoon just before deployment. He did not know Colby well, but he appreciated his sense of humor and physical strength. Once, he saw Colby pick up one of the squad leaders and start squatting him, as if the squad leader were a barbell. What every man in 2nd Platoon, Delaware Company, did know well were the dangers of Musayyib. Every soldier at FOB Iskan knew them, and other soldiers did, too. Musayyib had a reputation. Sgt. Bryan Druce, a twenty-seven-year-old native of Salt

Lake City and a squad leader in Colby's platoon, often would speak to troops serving in other parts of Iraq, and they would give him grave looks and tell him, *We don't want to go through your area.* He rode in one of the two vehicles behind Colby's.

His nose as wide and flat as an unsuccessful boxer's, Druce had tried to join the Army ten years earlier, to get away from what he called "bad influences, bad friends and stuff." He finally enlisted when he was twenty. By then, he had a wife, Holley. At the time, he thought that he would get his four years in, get out, and go to college, but he liked Army life, liked the discipline that he now had and once lacked, and he often teased Colby for the "college words" that he would use when briefing his squad leaders. In turn, Colby countered with his endless array of corny one-liners. ("A proton walks into a bar and tells the bartender, 'Give me seven shots of whiskey!' The bartender says, 'Are you sure?' And the proton says, 'I'm positive'!") For a few moments, in his laughter over Colby Umbrell's dumb jokes, Bryan Druce could envision the end of his days in the desert, away from Holley, and the violence and evil seemed more distant.

Amid the death, though, there were pockets of life. Because Musayyib rests on the eastern and western banks of the Euphrates, it has higher humidity than most regions in Iraq. Trees, grass, and other vegetation flourish. Whenever he would talk to Holley, his friends, or anyone else back home, Druce would tell them the same thing: *People picture the entire country as a desolate desert, but you would be surprised how green that part of Iraq really is.*

The Humvees headed east along Route June, then turned right onto Cleveland before heading south on Jennifer. Two more turns—left on Michelle, right on Caroline—put them at their mission site. At 7:12 A.M., the patrol split into two groups and began searching Caroline for anything suspicious. The first vehicle spotted a green bag on the left side of the road, but a sweep of the twenty-five-meter area around the trucks confirmed that the bag was not an IED. The patrol continued along Caroline until the road dead-ended into Jackson. After repositioning each vehicle, the men watched Caroline for an hour and twenty-two minutes. They saw nothing out of the ordinary.

At 8:52 A.M., after only three hours of patrolling the convoy roads, the soldiers heard Colby's voice coming over the radio: "There ain't nothing going on out here. Let's roll." Druce knew Colby didn't cut corners, and from his Humvee, Druce couldn't see anything going on outside, either. The message in Colby's words was implicit: *Let's go back inside and chill out.* The other men hooted and cheered, happy the overwatch was ending early. They started heading back the way they had come. The four Humvees trundled along Route Caroline at an average speed of twenty-five miles per hour, fifty meters of space separating one from the next, as they approached the T-shaped intersection at Route Michelle. One by one, the Humvees made deliberate left turns from Caroline onto Michelle.

The last vehicle was completing its turn when, peering out their windows, the soldiers in the third and fourth vehicles saw the explosion before they heard it. Black smoke, then sound. They never saw an insurgent in the shadows, watching the patrol, waiting until the second Humvee rolled right to the spot on the right side of Route Michelle where he had buried a twenty-pound, multi-array EFP. The bomb actually was three EFPs—two large steel EFPs and one small copper one—that had been merged into one devastating package. The patrol troops never saw the insurgent, never caught him, but he had to have been somewhere in the vicinity, so that he could use some sort of remote device—a cell phone, most likely—to activate and detonate the bomb.

Druce got on the radio to find out if the first truck had been hit. No, came the answer. Druce figured the bomb had gone off between the first two vehicles.

Colby's call sign was Delaware 26. Druce radioed the second Humvee.

"Two-Six," Druce said. "Is everybody okay?"

There was no answer.

The blast impact had thrust Pardella straight up, out of the gunner's turret, and down on his back. He screamed. He saw yellow smoke and had trouble breathing. Thinking it was a chlorine gas attack, he started to reach for his promask before realizing there was no poison in the air. He stood up, took a deep breath, and climbed down from the truck to look for casualties.

From the driver's seat, Swails could hear Pardella screaming. *Okay*, Swails thought. *I know he's alive.* Shrapnel had lacerated the fingers on his right hand and cut his right cheek. Smoke filled the truck. The monitor of the vehicle's guidance computer was lying on Swails's lap. He turned around and looked at Koschny, who gave him a thumbs-up sign.

He reached across the passenger's seat for Colby. He couldn't feel anything. He kept reaching. The first thing he touched was the door.

The fourth truck, where Aguilar, the platoon medic, was riding, pulled up alongside Colby's vehicle. Druce, having climbed out of his Humvee, swept the area to make sure no other IEDs were nearby. When Druce returned to his vehicle, Zaremba was waiting for him.

Zaremba had contacted Swails on the radio. Swails initially had said that he, Pardella, Koschny, and the interpreter were okay, but that Colby was injured and unresponsive. Then Swails called back to tell Zaremba that Colby was dead. When Druce finished the sweep, Zaremba broke the terrible news to him. "It kind of hit me like a ton of bricks," Druce would say later. "I didn't want to believe it."

He, Zaremba, and Aguilar hustled over to Colby's vehicle. The other four occupants were already outside. Pardella was still somewhat shaken up. Koschny seemed disoriented. An Iraqi citizen had been riding his bike nearby, and the explosion blew shrapnel into his leg and knocked him to the ground. He eventually got up and walked into town. The interpreter was sitting on the side of the road, covered in blood.

Druce and Zaremba tried to pry open the Humvee's front door. It was jammed shut. Most of the windows had cracked into spider-web patterns, making it difficult to see anything inside. There was a hole, the size and shape of a baseball, in the passenger-side door to the rear of the window.

Finally, they opened the back door. Druce stuck his head inside. He could see Colby in the front passenger seat. His body had sustained the brunt of the bomb, muting its impact on the other passengers. His sheer size had probably saved the other men's lives.

Zaremba, Druce, and Aguilar pulled Colby out of the vehicle. Then they opened a body bag.

It took Capt. Eric Lawless ten minutes to arrive at the site. He had been only a thousand meters away, in a meeting with the Musayyib City Council, when he heard the explosion. He and Zaremba arranged for an "Angel Flight" helicopter to pick up Colby's body and take it back to FOB Iskan.

Sgt. Amal Agalawatta woke from his nap to the news of Colby's death. "I felt so bad," he said later. "I was so angry about not going on this mission. I was just angry, angry, angry all night long."

He threw on his sneakers, gathered eight men, and told them to get in uniform. They would be the detail to escort Colby from the ambulance. There would be a ceremony at the base.

The car pulled up to the Umbrells' house at 10 A.M., and two men in military uniforms got out. Nancy heard them shut the car doors, watched them walk up the driveway, pass in front of the living room windows, and knock on the door. She let them in. She knew what they were going to say.

"Are you Colby Umbrell's mother?"

"Yes."

Mark and a crew from his contracting company, Middle Bucks Mechanical, were working at a house on Sugar Bottom Road, less than two miles away. "I cannot talk to you," Nancy said, "until I talk to my husband." She fumbled for the phone.

She invited the men to sit down. She tried to ignore them, but they told her anyway, the words swirling together in her mind. *Son . . . IED . . . dead . . . condolences.* She was numb. Her son was gone. None of it—the pain, the grief, the reality, or the ramifications—was seeping in yet. She asked the two men if they had served in Iraq. They had. She thanked them. When Mark arrived at the house, he broke down. Nancy began making phone calls, her voice flat and rote as she uttered the same words again and again before hanging up: "Don't ask me any questions. I can't talk about it now."

Steve Kreider, a sales representative for the Medicis Pharmaceutical Co., had just finished a business meeting at the Hilton Hotel near Chicago's O'Hare Airport when his cell phone buzzed. He looked down at the phone to check the number of the incoming call. It was from Mark Reilly, one of his and Colby's friends. Kreider didn't take the call. Reilly sent him a text message: *YOU NEED TO CALL ME.* Kreider was walking through the hotel when Reilly told him what had happened. Then he called Brandon Heath, who already had been called by Steve Gonzalez.

In San Antonio, Dan Tamaroff had his cell phone off all day at the law office where he worked. When he finally turned it on that night, he had twenty voice-mail messages from twenty people. He listened to the first one, from his father, and lost his breath. He listened to four more before he couldn't take it anymore. He erased the other fifteen messages without checking them.

Outside her open office door, Ann Kuntzmann could hear her secretary say, "Nancy Umbrell's on the phone." The secretary didn't say why Nancy had called, and Kuntzmann couldn't think of a reason.

*   *   *

Larry Greene had finished teaching his special-education classes for the day and was sitting alone in his Central Bucks East classroom at 1:45 P.M. Joseph Jennelle, East's principal, knocked on the door and said, "Larry, I have some bad news."

Over his previous eighteen years of coaching high school football, Greene had confronted tragedy before—kids killed in car crashes, cancer stealing some too soon, ex-players who had gone on to college and productive lives and still died before he did. The chronology of it hurt the worst. *I should go before they go*, Greene would say to himself at each funeral. He was saying it now, at his desk, as he remembered Colby Umbrell.

He composed himself, then continued the phone chain that Nancy had begun, calling the sports department of the *Intelligencer* and reaching Ed Kracz. Hired by the paper in 1996, Kracz had been the *Intelligencer*'s high school football columnist during the years that Colby had played for Greene. The affable Kracz was built like a former lineman himself, stout and round. He had a deft writing touch and knew how to draw interesting anecdotes out of interview subjects, often by telling them about how he doted on his wife, Linda, and their three children. As he and Greene talked, Kracz hunched over the keyboard of his computer, his office phone pressed to his right ear, and transcribed Greene's words in choppy fragments. "Just a great, great kid, a great, great leader . . . Kid whose motor was always running a hundred and twenty miles an hour and would do anything you asked . . . Just a tragedy . . . It slaps you right in the face. It's different if a guy ten years older than you passes, you can say, sure he had a good life. I'm sure Colby had a great life, it's just tragic in these situations to think what could have been for him."

After finishing his interview with Greene, Kracz hustled over to the desk of Christina Kristofic, the paper's news-side beat reporter for central Bucks County. Because the *Intelligencer* was headquartered in Doylestown and the town's residents regarded it as their hometown paper—even if it did cover the region around Doylestown, too—Kristofic's position was not unimportant. During Colby's tour in Iraq, Kristofic had been Mark and Nancy Umbrell's primary media contact. Whenever Colby was handing out school supplies to Iraqi children, Mark and Nancy called Kristofic to let her know, and the relationship made for a few easy, fifteen-inch stories for Kristofic during otherwise mundane days of borough council meetings and discussions before the zoning board.

Kracz and Kristofic quickly decided how they would attack the story: Kracz would track down as many of Colby's teammates and coaches at CB East as he could. Kristofic would do the heavy lifting. She would drive to the Umbrells' home and interview Mark, Nancy, and whoever else might be there. The strategy made perfect sense. Mark and Nancy knew Kristofic, trusted her. Though she was only in her midtwenties, her intelligence and calm demeanor conveyed a maturity beyond her age. As it turned out, she was the first reporter to get in touch with Mark and Nancy.

"I'd like to come out and talk to you," she said to Nancy over the telephone.

"We're not sure if we're ready," Nancy said. "Can you come tomorrow?"

Kristofic agreed, but deep down, she knew that she would be back on the phone with Nancy or Mark soon. Colby Umbrell's death was a significant story for the *Intelligencer*, and there was no chance that Kristofic's editors would let her write the story without knocking on the Umbrells' door. At 3:45, she called back, trying to be as empathetic as she could, given her deadline constraints.

"I'm really sorry," she told Nancy, "but the article's going to run whether you talk to me or not."

Her hand cupped over the phone's mouthpiece, Nancy relayed Kristofic's words to Mark. They agreed: The prospect of having someone else report or comment on Colby's death was unacceptable.

"Well," Nancy told Kristofic, "come over here now."

Kristofic jumped into her car, turned left out of the newsroom parking lot, drove three blocks, and made a right onto Main Street. She drove past the Bucks County Courthouse on her left, where she saw people sitting and standing in the courtyard, smoking cigarettes in the sun. She drove through the center of town—the Fountain House Starbucks on her right, The Gap on her left, all around her the shops and bars that had been as familiar to Colby Umbrell as the rooms of his parents' house.

When Nancy Umbrell answered the door, the first thing Kristofic noticed was what she was wearing: a light-blue men's button-down, one that was too big for her. Mark was weeping. The three of them went into the living room. Wearing that baggy shirt, Nancy Umbrell slumped onto the couch and looked like she might drown in blue. *My God*, Kristofic thought, *she can barely stand up*.

When she learned of Colby's death, Dana Cumberbatch, his classmate at Lenape Middle School, called her closest male friend.

"Did you hear about Colby?" she asked Bryan Buckley.

He had not. He had neither seen nor talked to Colby Umbrell in almost eight years.

"He was in the Army?" Bryan said. "Jeez. I had no idea."

They were quiet for a while.

"Bryan, you can't go back. You *can't* go back."

"Dana, this is what we do."

That night, Sgt. Frank Aguilar sat down over a sheet of looseleaf paper, gripped a black pen, and, in crisp, cursive hand, began writing a letter to Mark and Nancy.

I was the medic on site. I know the hurt and pain I feel is nothing compared to yours. I just hope whatever memories you have of Lt. Umbrell were great and happy ones. I am honored that I had the chance to meet and serve next to him in what is going on out here. Guys back here are just thinking of the good times they had with him. We talk about what happened and wish it could be [rewound] so that we could change what [happened] but the Lord let it happen for a reason. This is my second deployment, and one thing I ask the man upstairs is why are the good guys the ones being taken from us? But the answer is never [there]. Guess He wants me to figure them out on my own. Huh? But there's one thing I do know . . . that he left us to a better and safer place . . .

In time, Bryan Druce would write a letter of his own to Mark and Nancy. In time. For the few hours that passed from the moment Colby was killed until the platoon returned to the base, Druce had had no time to put pen to paper or to weep for his friend. He buried his emotions and completed his mission, as he had been taught a leader should. But at 1:07 P.M. Musayyib time, when the "Hero Flight" helicopter that had been dispatched to pick up Colby's remains landed, Druce could no longer contain himself. Tears streaking his face, he and Agalawatta and Lawless and Aguilar stood ramrod straight with the rest of Delaware Company, 120 men lined up facing the helicopter. They were all still standing at attention at 2:19 P.M., near the groves of trees and the green grass and the river waters, saluting 1st Lt. Colby Umbrell, U.S. Army Airborne Ranger, the toughest of the tough, as the chopper lifted off to carry him home.

TWENTY

Remembrances

Friday, October 19, 2007

The closed closet doors in Colby Umbrell's old bedroom hid his dress blues from sight, one of the small measures his parents had taken to keep from falling apart. *Anything can be a trigger*, Mark and Nancy Umbrell would tell people. *Anything can make you lose it.* So although some memorabilia were easily visible in the room—Colby's diploma from Johns Hopkins University and a photograph of his headstone—it was as if his parents understood how much they could take.

If Nancy didn't touch the two corkboards covered with photos of Colby, if she left them on the floor near the bed, maybe she wouldn't start flipping through them and start thinking about Colby and cry.

If they hung his dress blues in the closet, and if the closet doors stayed shut, then they wouldn't have to remember that part of Colby's death that cut them so deeply.

According to the Army's official report on Colby's death, the IED that killed him caused such severe injuries that it had rendered his body "not viewable." That meant his casket had remained closed at the funeral service at Our Lady of Mount Carmel Catholic Church in Doylestown on Monday, May 14, and at his burial in Arlington National Cemetery on Friday, May 18. "That hurt—not only that he was dead, but that we couldn't see him," Mark said. "Those are the kinds of things you don't want to think about."

At the foot of Colby's bed, folded into a rectangle, was a "quilt of valor," a blanket with a broad American flag sewn on it. It was a gift from the Bucks County Veterans of Foreign Wars. When she first got the quilt, Nancy draped it over the bed. But after a while, she couldn't stand to walk past the room. So she drew another sanity-saving conclusion: If she folded up the quilt, the bed wouldn't look like Colby's casket, draped in the flag.

Mark and Nancy kept busy, trying to live as they would have if Colby were off at college or stationed in Alaska—somewhere, anywhere, safe. Mark drove his pickup truck from job to job. Nancy took art classes at Bucks County Community College. Yet each anticipated the smallest thing that might bring Colby to mind, that might ignite the stabbing in their stomachs.

"The first class was . . ." Nancy said. ". . . But there was one girl in there who knew, and she'd been to Colby's viewing. And I called her before I went and said, 'I'm going to see you there, and I want to come up and hug you, but that will make me cry. So I'm not going to do that. I'm just going to try to get through the class.' She understood. At the end, she just looked at me and said, 'You did it.'"

On certain days, Nancy made it a point to shop at a supermarket miles from Doylestown, just so there would be less of a chance that she would see a familiar face, that someone would stop her, place a hand on her shoulder, and say, "I'm so sorry . . ." It seemed as if there was always someone saying those words—friends, family, neighbors, people they'd never met before.

"With me at work, I have a customer base," Mark said. "Some I see once a month. Some I see once a week. Some I see once a year. So it's pretty much every day that I run into someone who says, 'I'm very sorry about your son.' And I just say, 'I appreciate that.' That's how I've dealt with it."

Over the five months since Colby's death, they had been invited to a series of ceremonial events, public acknowledgments of their son's sacrifice that stirred in them equal parts pride and grief. A groundbreaking at Doylestown's Veterans Park for a war memorial. The adoption of a Pennsylvania House resolution, honoring Colby's service, introduced by a local legislator. The unveiling at the Bucks County Courthouse courtyard of sixteen commemorative flags, one for each Bucks County soldier killed in Afghanistan and Iraq. The Bucks County All-Star Football Classic, where everyone observed a moment of silence for Colby. A halftime tribute during a Wyoming Seminary football game. They had been to all of them, but there remained that inner emotional conflict.

"Everything that's happy is sad," said Colby's sister, Casey.

Mostly, they went because they wanted people to remember what he had done and why. On the afternoon of May 4, the day after Colby died, when television camera crews and newspaper reporters started lining up outside their house and Nancy didn't think she could summon the strength to speak to them, Mark told her, "Listen, honey. This might be the one time you're going to get his story told. If you say no, they're not coming back." The irony was, Philadelphia-area media were going to be up in Doylestown that day, anyway, because of the First Friday vigil for Marine Lt. Travis Manion. There had been hundreds of people lining the streets of Doylestown that night, observing a moment of silence at 8 P.M., some of them holding candles. The turnout had been even greater for Doylestown's Memorial Day parade: more than twenty-five thousand people. Mark himself marched in the parade.

Through their shared sadness, Mark and Nancy had become friends with Manion's parents, Tom and Janet. Here was another couple who understood. Tom Manion, himself a Marine, interpreted his son's death as a call to service. The following year, he would run as a Republican for Congress, vying for the 8th District seat with incumbent Democrat Patrick Murphy, the only veteran of the Iraq war in Congress (he had served as a paratrooper with the 82nd Airborne) and a sharp critic of the Bush administration's war policies. Murphy (who shared the name of the owner of Doylestown's Bagel Barrel) would beat Manion in November 2008, winning 57 percent of the vote, but Tom Manion had made his point about the importance of his son's service in a very public manner. Mark and Nancy would support Manion's candidacy, would admire him for it, but they themselves were content to spend more time in the background. What's harder for parents whose son has died during a war: The private moments of heartache, when Nancy would break down and Mark would be there to hold her, or the public moments, when they would have to try to smile after strangers called Colby a hero?

"There are days when it would be easier if you just didn't wake up," Nancy said. "We're not suicidal or anything, but it is hard, especially when . . . you miss them. . . . It's the forever thing. It's hard. But I think it could be worse. We talk about that a lot."

The two of them were sitting in their living room. Mark gently rested his hand on the back of her neck.

"There are people who lose kids to car accidents or suicides, or a three-year-old drowns in a swimming pool," he said. "Can you imagine being a parent and having guilt? We have no guilt. Colby died doing what he wanted to do, and that's almost a good thing."

Friday, November 9, 2007
The Central Bucks East auditorium was nearly full for the school's annual Veterans Day ceremony, the audience of a thousand students, teachers, soldiers, and parents still and reverent. Mark and Nancy sat

among them, listening to the school band perform Samuel Hazo's "Each Time You Tell Their Story."

When the final note, the light gong of a bell, faded and the polite applause stopped, two Marines stood up to demonstrate a flag-folding ceremony, the symbolic ritual that transforms an American flag into a tight, blue, triangular field of stars. For the demonstration, the Marines used the flag that flew at half-staff over Delaware Company's base in Musayyib on May 3, the day Colby died. The Umbrells had donated it to East.

This was no small donation. The Musayyib flag was Mark and Nancy's single tangible connection to the events surrounding Colby's death, the one remembrance of his last day alive that they could touch.

"I do believe his soul's gone, and that's what gets us through, that he's in a better place," Nancy said, "but I don't feel like I'm visiting Colby when I go to Arlington. I'm honoring him."

After the ceremony, Mark and Nancy mingled for a short while, talking with Larry Greene, who had just stepped down as East's football coach. Greene had contracted bone marrow cancer in the summer of 2005, and though after taking a year away from coaching he was now in good health, he had decided he no longer had a fire in his belly to coach football anymore. His retirement was only the latest change to the landscape of high school football in the area. But for short stints as an assistant at North Penn High School and CB West, Mike Pettine had remained retired from coaching, and his son, Michael, had left North Penn to take a position with the NFL's Baltimore Ravens. (In 2009, after eight years in Baltimore, Michael was hired as the defensive coordinator of the New York Jets.) Since the opening of Central Bucks High School South in 2004, the rivalry between CB East and CB West hadn't carried the same gravity that it had when Mark and Colby played. Once the premier football program in Pennsylvania, West hadn't had a winning season since 2005, Randy Cuthbert's and

Bryan Buckley's final season there as coaches. CB South, in fact, had emerged as the district's football jewel, going 11–1 in 2007. And now, East—still without a stadium on its campus—had to find Greene's successor.

When Colby was playing, Mark had headed a successful push to build a new weight room at East. *Soon*, Greene told Mark and Nancy, *Colby's picture will hang in that weight room.*

Later, Mark and Nancy sipped coffee from foam cups in a faculty lounge before heading home. In a rotunda down the hall from the lounge, East students and staff members had erected a tribute to graduates who had served in the military. There was a glass case displaying newspaper articles about Colby. The Musayyib base flag would soon rest there, too.

On the wall above the case, there was a photo collage and, bracketing the collage, two mahogany plaques. On the plaques were 129 gold plates, the name and graduation year of an East soldier engraved on each.

Of the thirty-eight classes that had graduated from Central Bucks High School East since 1969, only one alumnus was known to have been killed in action. His was the only gold plate bordered in black. Left plaque, second row from the left, twelve plates down.

COLBY UMBRELL
'99—ARMY

Outside, with a brisk wind picking up in what had been a warm autumn, a mother and a father walked slowly to their car, holding hands. People who had known their son when he was young remembered him. Behind them, teenagers hustled through the hallways to class. The football field was empty and quiet. The mother and father had somewhere to go that weekend. They never looked back.

Sunday, November 11, 2007

The plane carrying Sgt. Bryan Druce touched down at Fort Richardson, Alaska, on Veterans Day. He had finished his first deployment to Iraq—fourteen months. His wife, Holley, greeted him at the airport with a kiss and a long, tight hug. Druce wore an extra dog tag around his neck, and in an e-mail to Mark and Nancy that he had written on May 9, while he was still in Iraq, he had explained why.

My name is SGT Bryan Druce. I am one of the Squad Leaders in 1st LT Umbrell's platoon. I was with him on the day the Lord took him.... 1st LT Umbrell was a great person that always meant well in everything that he did. He was always trying to push himself to the limits just to see how far he could go. I treasure serving with him as one of his Squad Leaders. I think we both learned a lot from one another. Our platoon was thankful to have him as a platoon leader for as long as we did. I kept one of the dog tags that LT Umbrell wore around his neck and I would like to personally give this to you. Until I make it back I will keep it around my neck in tribute to our fallen brother.

Monday, November 12, 2007

Mark and Nancy Umbrell walked from their car to Grave No. 60 8623 in Section 60 of Arlington National Cemetery—Section 60, where the remains of the men and women killed in Iraq and Afghanistan lie.

"The saddest acre in America," Mark said, repeating a phrase often used to describe Section 60. Above the dead, the air was still chilly and dewy, the sky a slate of gray, the ground soft and wet. Grass had been torn up from large patches of the earth so that more graves could be dug.

One of Colby's dog tags dangled from Nancy's neck, and she clutched a camouflage-colored bucket hat in the left pocket of her "ARMY" Windbreaker. Wearing a baseball cap festooned with military pins, Mark kept his left arm snug around his wife's waist as they stood together, staring down at one of the white watermarked marble stones, a pair of black Nike football cleats resting on the plot.

COLBY J
UMBRELL
1 LT
US ARMY
APR 3 1981
MAY 3 2007
BRONZE STAR
PURPLE HEART
OPERATION
IRAQI FREEDOM

Nancy had considered leaving the bucket hat at the gravesite. But the groundskeepers at Arlington often collect such mementos after a few days, and the hat had been in a crate full of Colby's personal effects that the Army had sent to Mark and Nancy's house after his death. How could she risk losing that connection to him? "I don't want to leave this," she said, holding out the hat, then stuffing it back into her pocket.

Then she turned from Colby's grave. Holding a tissue in her right hand, she waved it in a what-can-you-do gesture.

"It never gets easy," she said, little tears below her eyes. "I want to come, but I don't want to come, you know?"

She and Mark began to examine the headstones near Colby's. In their monthly visits to Arlington, they had met family members of several of the other soldiers buried there. To their left was the grave of Capt. Jonathan D. Grassbaugh, killed in action on April 7. He graduated from Johns Hopkins University in 2003, one year before Colby. To Mark and Nancy's right was the grave of Sgt. Ashly Moyer, twenty-one, from Emmaus, Pennsylvania, near Allentown. She died in Baghdad when a roadside bomb incinerated her armored patrol vehicle. Her boyfriend was part of her unit and witnessed her death. He couldn't get close enough to the fireball to rescue her.

"Everyone has a story," Nancy said, the perfect rows of headstones stretching out before her.

Except for some scattered pockets of people keeping similar vigils, everything was quiet around the Umbrells—unusually so, Mark said. There were no fighter jets screaming overhead, no three-volley rifle salute piercing a family's veneer of composure, no loved ones on their knees, sobbing. It was 11 A.M., and there were only the solemn chimes of the clock at the Tomb of the Unknown Soldier, the fading echoes filling the cemetery. There was only a mother and a father.

Everyone has a story.

The stone told only part of their son's.

Epilogue

Tuesday, June 24, 2008

Across the street and half a block south from a bar called The Other Side, war protesters, no more than ten or so, had gathered in a loose group on the northwest corner of Main and State streets in Doylestown, in front of the Fountain House. They had moved their hour-long weekly vigil to that intersection in 2003, after members of various veterans groups had requested that the protesters stage their demonstrations somewhere other than the sacred ground of the Bucks County Vietnam Veterans Memorial. The protesters had acquiesced without quarrel. Larry Miller, the Quaker and local activist who had organized the vigils in the aftermath of the war in Afghanistan, had died in June 2007 at age eighty-seven, but his friends and political soulmates still assembled every Tuesday evening at six to hold their signs and make their quiet statements. No one bothered them much anymore, not the motorists weaving through town, not the teenagers and frappuccino seekers gliding in and out of the Starbucks, not the crowd now gathering and growing inside The Other Side.

On one Tuesday night each month, the bar ran a "celebrity bartend-
ing night" to benefit a charity. Tonight, that charity was the Colby
Umbrell Memorial Fund, started by Mark and Nancy to subsidize
scholarships for local high school football players, and there were two
bartenders. One was Michael Barkann, an anchor and talk-show host
for Comcast SportsNet, the Philadelphia region's all-sports television network. The other was Bryan Scott, Colby's teammate and
classmate at Central Bucks East, now a defensive back for the NFL's
Buffalo Bills.

Nancy wore Colby's blue Central Bucks East jersey, the number 67
on the back bunching up because the jersey was so big on her. Mark
wore a smile and a black *Crayola Rocks!* T-shirt. They were in good
spirits. The turnout had exceeded their expectations. An advertisement,
touting Barkann's and Scott's appearances, had run in the *Intelligencer*,
and word about the party had spread quickly among Colby's friends
and former East teammates. Scott had flown in earlier in the day.
Anthony Greene, working at the Bronx County Historical Society and
studying for his Ph.D. in history and education at Columbia University,
had taken the train down from New York to be there. Brandon
Heath, Mark Reilly, and Steve Gonzalez had arrived early and would
stay late. There were people who had worked with Colby, had known
him through Mark and Nancy, had attended middle school with him.
One of those old middle-school friends was Dana Cumberbatch. She
had invited Bryan Buckley and his parents, and they entered the bar
with her.

Bryan's second seven-month stint in and around Fallujah, this
time as a platoon leader in the Marine's 2nd Reconnaissance Battalion,
had ended in May, this deployment less eventful than his first. The
implementation of the "surge"—the brainchild of David Petraeus,
the commanding general of Multi-National Force–Iraq—in early 2007
had begun to reap benefits for the American forces and to stabilize Iraq.
The additional thirty thousand U.S. troops, the Sunnis' "awakening"

and their turning against al-Qaeda, the troops' more restrained interactions with Iraqis, the implementation of new counterinsurgency tactics—these and other factors had calmed the cauldron that Iraq had once been.

There were still daily threats. A twenty-two-year-old sergeant in Bryan's platoon, Kyle Kaczmarek, a former high school wide receiver from Cleveland, had been riding in a Humvee near the city of Samarra when an IED detonated and destroyed the vehicle. (Kaczmarek survived the blast with only some ringing in his ears.) But on the whole, things were better.

"In reality, as weird as it sounds, our getting hit by an IED was the best thing to happen," Bryan had said, "because we had Iraqis looking down, and they saw the vehicle that did it, and they watched where it went from house to house to house, and they found a lot of info.

"The first time we went out on a mission, we went on a route that was a bad route when I was in the 2–8. I'm like, 'Oh, man, we're in trouble here. Something's going to happen.' And now you'd see all the Iraqi people working, doing security and stuff. It had totally changed. We worked ourselves out of a job, which is good, but it was very low impact. You're trying to make things happen, go the way you were when you were there eight months earlier, but it's a totally different ball game now. You hate to say it, but it was boring."

On June 22, only two days before the party at The Other Side, Bryan and I sat down together in his parents' kitchen for the first of many interviews about his high school football career, his military experience, and his time in Iraq. As this book took shape, we would talk in person and over the telephone, sometimes for several hours, and exchange dozens of e-mails, and as our correspondence continued, Bryan became more comfortable in opening up about what he had done in his life and why he had done it. Initially, though, he had been uncomfortable about my desire to write a book that was, in any way, about him. He did not consider himself a hero and did not want anyone who read the book to think of him as one. He had agreed to participate for one reason, he said: "Colby." If the book would cause more people to remember Colby and his service and fewer to forget him, then Bryan would help however he could. His reasons for participating in the project were no different from Mark and Nancy's.

Now, here were the five of them—Bryan and Bill and Connie, Mark and Nancy—in the center of the bar, shaking hands and exchanging hugs and thank-yous, mentioning what a long time it had been since Colby and Bryan had played together at Lenape Middle School and against each other at East and West. Their conversation was halting, awkward. Connie tried her best to hold herself together, to keep from crying, but the woman in front of her had lived the awful dream that kept Connie up at night. Connie wasn't sure what to say. How do you tell a mother and father who have lost their son that you're sorry, that you understand—when your son is standing next to you?

So Connie, tears welling in her eyes, didn't say anything.

Her son did.

"I don't know quite how to put this," Bryan said, "but his sacrifice won't be in vain."

They talked for only a few moments. It was enough. Mark and Nancy had hellos to hand out, a raffle to run. "They couldn't have been nicer," Nancy said later. "That was good. I felt like I could be their friend, even though we'd never met them before. I think that'll happen. I thought it was really nice that they came. To see Bryan was really nice. It felt good to see him."

The party felt like a high school reunion, as if everyone there had been friends in another era, at another time, and in a sense, that's exactly what it was. Soon, the Bryans—Buckley and Scott—were rehashing those old East-West games. (Buckley: "Our plan was that, as soon as you got the ball, we wanted you to see four yellow helmets hitting you." Scott: "I did.") People recognized each other. They caught up. Afterward, Mark Umbrell would say, "I don't care if we made a dime.

It was just so nice that all those people came together." And they stayed together for hours, laughing and carousing, remembering a young, brave man and thinking of others like him, their voices drifting out of that neighborhood bar long after the rest of Main Street in Doylestown had gone empty in the twilight.

ACKNOWLEDGMENTS

Over the months I spent researching and writing *Fading Echoes*, people often asked me if I had ever written a book before. *Yes*, I would tell them, *I cowrote a book a few years ago.* Usually, the person I was speaking with would then say, "But this one, you're writing alone, right?" As any honest author will admit, no one writes a book alone, and as I think of all those who contributed to this project in ways big and small, I am grateful for and humbled by their help.

Researching and writing the stories of Colby Umbrell and Bryan Buckley carried a grave responsibility to be accurate and thorough. Mark and Nancy Umbrell continue to amaze me with their daily displays of strength, and the Buckleys welcomed this project with open minds and hearts. My first duty was to them, to make sure I got Colby's and Bryan's stories right. Bryan, in particular, had little to gain from having me pepper him with questions about the most challenging and difficult days of his life, yet he was always willing to share his memories and thoughts with me. If, at any time, he or any member of the Umbrell or Buckley families had asked me not to pursue this project, I would have complied with the request. None of them did. I thank them for their trust, and I'm fortunate to count them as friends.

On the day I decided I had to write a book about Colby and Bryan and Doylestown, I e-mailed query letters to a dozen literary agents. Only one called me. From that moment, Scott Miller of Trident Media Group was a tireless, reassuring advocate for the idea behind this book. He and his assistant, Stephanie Sun, handled my repeated questions and concerns with grace and aplomb. Natalee Rosenstein and Michelle Vega, who shepherded *Fading Echoes* through its editing and publication processes at The Berkley Publishing Group, were as enthusiastic about and committed to this book as anyone.

Among Colby's friends and teammates, Brandon Heath, Steve Kreider, Mark Reilly, Dan Tamaroff, Anthony Greene, Steve Gonzalez, Bryan Scott, Bobby Hulmes, Neil Bardham, Ben Stopper, and Tom Deveney helped me understand just who Colby was. Katie Armstrong, Cynthia Magnuson, and Jenna Menard shared their memories of Colby and their years at Central Bucks East. Amal Agalawatta, Eric Lawless, Bryan Druce, John Zaremba, and Doug Smith introduced me to 1st Lt. Colby Umbrell, Army Ranger.

Among Bryan's friends and teammates, Dave Armstrong, Brian Spratt, Ed Hillman, Erich Maerz, and Dana Cumberbatch were more than accommodating. Phil DiGiacomo, Mike Orihel, and Dustin Picciotti provided insight into their years with the Central Bucks West football program and Bryan's role in the Bucks' success. Don Moeller and Jim Mingus were invaluable resources for understanding the mindset of a Marine. Dan Clark was available at a moment's notice to fill in details and answer elementary questions about Fox Company's seven months in Fallujah in 2006–07. I would sit down for a beer with him, Stephen Turpin, Spencer Hurley, Joe Luevano, Ed Skelly, and Kyle Kaczmarek anytime, anywhere. Ken Urquhart was an impeccable host during my visit to his and his family's home, and he grills a mean steak.

Larry Greene, Mike Pettine, Mike Carey, Michael Pettine, Randy

Cuthbert, Joe Hallman, and Jim Benstead seemed to have total recall of their years coaching middle school and high school football. Rod Stone, Mike Dougherty, Sean Kelly, John Reading, Paul Wilson, and Ann Kuntzmann are as devoted now to the well-being of the Central Bucks School District's student-athletes as they have ever been.

Betty Strecker and Ed Ludwig of the Doylestown Historical Society guided me on a tour of the Doylestown that was. Dr. Jim Bumgardner talked with me about his treatment of Colby's knee injury, and Dr. Christopher Aland explained, in layman's terms, the physiology behind a torn anterior cruciate ligament. David Davies, Corey Goff, Randy Granger, Mike Stubljar, Ernie Larossa, Jim Margraff, Don Brown, Keith Dudzinski, and Mark Whipple bridged for me the gaps in Colby's and Bryan's lives between high school and the military.

Jeff Beideman, the sports editor of the *Bucks County Courier Times* and the *Intelligencer*, gave me my first internship and my first full-time job in daily journalism. I owe him much. He and Pat Walker, the papers' executive editor, graciously allowed me to take three months of part-time leave to complete this book. Even with the Philadelphia Phillies on the way to winning their first World Series in twenty-eight years and with the demand for copy about the team insatiable, Pat and Jeff did everything they could to accommodate their often-frazzled sports columnist and his quest to be an often-frazzled author.

I treasure my long-standing friendships with Brian Parks, Tom Schurtz, John McGrath, Mark Prybutok, and Seth Oltman, and my colleagues and friends at Calkins Media and around the sportswriting profession assisted me in ways overt and subtle. Dom Cosentino, Rich Hofmann, and Gordie Jones were kind enough to review excerpts of the manuscript and lend their advice and recommendations. Kevin Cooney and Mike Radano broke up long stretches of writing with welcome bursts of humor, and Jack Scheuer's weekly pickup basketball games at the Palestra kept my muscles from atrophying and allowed me to clear my head and make a few jump shots (depending on who was guarding me). With my deadline fast approaching, Adrian Wojnarowski needed only five minutes over the phone to calm me down enough so I could finish the manuscript. Phil Sheridan, Kevin Roberts, Dana O'Neil, Reuben Frank, Bob Ford, Ed Kracz, Tom Moore, Christina Kristofic, Jayson Stark, Mike Vaccaro, and Michael Rosenberg were always encouraging. I appreciated the help and camaraderie that they provided.

Gabriel Fagan and Bill Lyon are the finest mentors anyone could ask for.

It is a blessing that most members of my immediate and extended family live in or near the Philadelphia area. It is a greater blessing that all of us have remained so close and loyal and loving to each other, particularly during times of unsurpassable joy and unbearable sorrow.

My in-laws—Pam, Bob, and Jeff Zilahy—have embraced me from the moment I met them, and if not for their assistance, this book would feature no photographs.

My sister and her husband, Jessica and Martin Cunningham, were supportive of this project from its beginning, and I'm thankful that each of them has pledged to buy a dozen copies of this book at full price.

Chuck and Ann Sielski impressed upon me at an early age the importance of academics, of hard work, of the value in striving to be an upright, moral person. There is still nothing more satisfying to me, after writing something, than to have my parents read it and hear them say, "That was good." My mother and father are the wisest people I know, and I'm proud to be their son.

Finally, this book belongs to my wife, Kathryn Marie Sielski, as much as it does to me. Kate had to deal with a husband who, for the better part of seven months, kept himself sequestered in a third-floor office, rarely came to bed before 2 A.M., and had the same excuse whenever he neglected to complete a simple task around the house. (Wife: "You were home for eight hours and couldn't empty the garbage?" Husband: "Sorry. Working." Wife: "Did you know you left the coffeepot on all day and burned down the house?" Husband: "Sorry. Working.") She was my editor, photographer, counselor, and chef. She was patient and gentle and giving. Such is her nature. It is why I love her, and why I could not have finished this book without her.

Mike Sielski
April 2009

NOTES AND SOURCES

In writing this book, I relied on two primary sources: my own interviews with the participants in the story, and archived newspaper articles from two of the newspapers for which I work, the *Intelligencer* and the *Bucks County Courier Times*. The book's genesis was a four-part series that I wrote about Colby Umbrell and that the papers published in December 2007. With the permission of Pat Walker, the papers' executive editor, much of that series appears almost verbatim in this book. I was also the *Intelligencer's* beat writer for Central Bucks East and West football from August 1998 to September 2002, and I drew on much of my work from those years in unfurling the book's narrative: stories, columns, interview transcripts that I have kept. Virtually all of the information regarding the 1998 football seasons for Central Bucks East and Central Bucks West and the programs' subsequent history comes from this research. The information that doesn't has been cited.

In addition to allowing me to review some of Bryan's letters to them and others, Bill and Connie Buckley lent me their homemade videotapes of every CB West football game from the 1998 season and several of

Bryan's prep-school games, and those tapes were invaluable for confirming and providing details. T. Patrick Murray and Alex Weinress's excellent documentary on the 1999 CB West football season, *The Last Game*, was also a terrific resource. Members of Fox Company's 4th Platoon provided me with the unit's daily log book and documents verifying the platoon's actions.

I have changed the name of one member of 4th Platoon for the sake of the man's privacy.

Mark and Nancy Umbrell allowed me access to Colby's recruiting tape, some of the coursework that he completed at Johns Hopkins, his letters and e-mails to them, several letters and e-mails that they received from Colby's friends and fellow soldiers, and the official U.S. Army report on Colby's death. The report was invaluable in reconstructing the events of May 3, 2007.

I have supplemented this reporting by relying on research and details from books; speech transcripts; reputable websites; and articles from magazines, newspapers, journals, and news services. I have cited these sources.

Any direct quotations that appear in the text came from published accounts, from interview or speech transcripts, or from the memories of those who either uttered or heard the quote. I have not fabricated dialogue for the sake of drama or detail. Where there were differing recollections of a particular incident or anecdote, I have attempted to present each of those varying perspectives. In those instances in which I use the phrases "he thought" or "she thought," I have done so because an interviewee told me what he or she was thinking in that moment or because my reporting and research revealed a person's thoughts to be obvious and indubitable (e.g., Colby and Bryan's e-mails and letters). Where possible, I have relied on firsthand witnessing or reporting of events to reconstruct scenes.

PREFACE: CONNECTIONS

"At the schools": *Interview*, Andy Kozar.

In 1890: Steven W. Pope, "An Army of Athletes: Playing Fields, Battlefields, and the American Military Sporting Experience, 1890–1920," *The Journal of Military History*, July 1995.

Under the presumption: Ibid.

U.S. military leaders: Ibid.; "Athletics in Army to Be Compulsory," *The New York Times,* March 31, 1918.

By 1921, seventeen states: Pope, "An Army of Athletes."

CHAPTER 1: DEPARTURE

Interviews: Bill Buckley, Bryan Buckley, Connie Buckley, Dan Clark, Mike Pettine, Chris DiSciullo, Kim DiSciullo, James Mingus.

The temperature was climbing to 90 degrees: www.almanac.com.

To that end: David Kilcullen, "Twenty-Eight Articles: Fundamentals of Company-Level Counterinsurgency," *Military Review*, May–June 2006.

In May: Woodward, *State of Denial*.

The number of attacks: Ibid.

Insurgents had ambushed and killed: West, *No True Glory*.

Lance Cpl. James Higgins: Nelson Hernandez, "Marine Fought for Place in History; Frederick County Native Was Due Home This Month," *The Washington Post*, August 2, 2006.

The three other Marines: "Four Marines Die July 27 from Wounds Received While Conducting Combat Operations in Al Anbar Province, Iraq," States News Service, July 31, 2006.

At the time of the classified report's release: Woodward, *State of Denial*.

Kuwait City's mean temperature: www.weather.com.

To that moment: www.icasualties.org.

CHAPTER 2: HISTORY

Interviews: Jim Benstead, Bill Buckley, Bryan Buckley, Connie Buckley, Stephen Buckley, Leo Carey, Mike Carey, Steve Gonzalez, Anthony Greene, Larry Greene, Steve Kreider, Ann Kuntzmann, John Perno, Maureen Perno, Mike Pettine, Bryan Scott, Brian Spratt, Betty Strecker, Casey Umbrell, Mark Umbrell, Nancy Umbrell.

The extra weight: Central Bucks East football official game program, September 25, 1998.

By 1998: Report entitled "Central Bucks School District Twelve-Year Comparison of Enrollment Increases," 2002. Ed Levenson, a former reporter at the *Intelligencer*, provided the report.

There were older high school football rivalries: Gordie Jones, "Supper Club, Courage Bowl and Old Shoes," ESPN.com, September 30, 2008.

There are two Doylestowns: U.S. Census Bureau, Census 2000.

William Penn: Ludwig, McNamara, and Strecker; *Images of America: Doylestown.*

"With the opening of Doyle's Tavern": Baldwin, Klein, Luce, Spare, Strecker; *Doylestown: 150 Years.*

Amid verdant, fertile land: Ibid.

Soon, Michener's hometown: Ludwig, McNamara, and Strecker; *Images of America: Doylestown.*

From 1960 to 2000: Ibid.; U.S. Census Bureau, Census 2000.

By 1962: Baldwin, Klein, Luce, Spare, Strecker; *Doylestown: 150 Years.*

Doylestown mutated: U.S. Census Bureau, Census 2000.

But the people of Doylestown were also supportive: Davis, *History of the Doylestown Guards.*

Not long after: Lebegern, *Episodes in Bucks County History.*

CHAPTER 3: THE OPENING WEEKEND

Interviews: Dave Armstrong, Phil DiGiacomo, Mike Dougherty, Steve Gonzalez, Anthony Greene, Larry Greene, Brandon Heath, Ed Hillman, Bobby Hulmes, Sean Kelly, Steve Kreider, Mike Orihel, Mike Pettine, Dustin Picciotti, Bryan Scott, Rod Stone, Mark Umbrell, Nancy Umbrell.

He coached the Patriots' offensive line: Bill Lyon, "For CB East Coach, Best Is Quite Good," *The Philadelphia Inquirer*, August 29, 2002.

At the beginning of the twentieth century: Baldwin, Klein, Luce, Spare, Strecker; *Doylestown: 150 Years.*

"They were wondering if he'd be able to do the job": Adam Gusdorff, a former sportswriter for the *Intelligencer*, conducted an interview with Bob Schaffer in anticipation of Mike Pettine's three hundredth career victory. This quote from Schaffer, who died in 1999, comes from that interview.

He had designs: Maximillian Potter, "I Don't Lose," *Philadelphia Magazine*, October 2000.

CHAPTER 4: RITUALS AND SACRIFICES

Interviews: Bill Buckley, Bryan Buckley, Connie Buckley, Stephen Buckley, Dana Cumberbatch, Chris DiSciullo, Kim DiSciullo, Steve Gonzalez, Anthony Greene, Larry Greene, Steve Kreider, Bobby Hulmes, Mike Pettine, Dustin Picciotti, Bryan Scott, Mark Umbrell, Nancy Umbrell.

Connie had heard stories about Pettine: Interview, Connie Buckley; Bill Lyon, "CB West's Pettine Rolls Toward 300th Win," *The Philadelphia Inquirer*, September 20, 1998.

Pettine's mother: Mark Schiele, "Conshohocken's Pettine Wins 300th," *The Times Herald*, September 26, 1998.

Before every game: T. Patrick Murray and Alex Weinress, directors; *The Last Game;* Crystal Spring Productions; 2002.

CHAPTER 5: SHELTER FROM THE STORM

Interviews: Bryan Buckley, Mike Carey, Phil DiGiacomo, Anthony Greene, Larry Greene, Steve Kreider, Michael Pettine, Mike Pettine, Dustin Picciotti, John Reading, Bryan Scott, Rod Stone, Casey Umbrell, Mark Umbrell, Nancy Umbrell.

He ended his career: After Mike Pettine's retirement in 1999, the CB West football program compiled a book of West's season-by-season results and individual school records during Pettine's tenure.

At UVA: www.newyorkjets.com/team/coach/1414-mike-pettine.

For the first time in a long time: Liz Sullivan, "The Son Didn't Want to Jump Right In," *The Reporter*, October 2, 1997.

The West football coaches: Mike Kern, "Pettine Family Values Winning," *The Philadelphia Daily News*, October 3, 1997.

Now, here he was: Christine Liberaski, the spokesperson for the North Penn School District, provided the district's enrollment statistics for the 1998–99 scholastic year.

Then, on October 3, 1997: Fran McLaughlin, "NP vs. CB West Will Be First Match of Father, Son in Pa.," *The Montgomeryville Spirit*, October 1, 1997.

CHAPTER 6: CRISES AND COMEBACKS

Interviews: Christopher Aland, Katie Armstrong, Bryan Buckley, Jim Bumgardner, Leo Carey, Mike Carey, Phil DiGiacomo, Steve Kreider, Mike Orihel, Michael Pettine, Mike Pettine, John Reading, Bryan Scott, Mark Umbrell, Nancy Umbrell.

Over the thirty-five years that Curry coached there: Dave Krider, "Pennsylvania's Curry Retiring After 42 Years," MaxPreps.com, December 17, 2008.

CHAPTER 7: TRADITIONS

Interviews: Dave Armstrong, Bryan Buckley, Mike Carey, Mike Dougherty, Anthony Greene, Larry Greene, Bobby Hulmes, Sean Kelly, Jenna Menard, Mike

Orihel, Mike Pettine, Dustin Picciotti, Casey Umbrell, Mark Umbrell, Nancy Umbrell.

CHAPTER 8: BEYOND THE GAME

Interviews: Dave Armstrong, Bill Buckley, Bryan Buckley, Connie Buckley, Mike Carey, Brandon Heath, Sean Kelly, Ann Kuntzmann, Cynthia Magnuson, Michael Pettine, Mike Pettine, Mark Umbrell, Nancy Umbrell, Paul Wilson.

And because Division III colleges: www.collegescholarships.org/scholarships/sports/football.htm.

"Their streak has to end sometime": Keith Groeller, "PIAA Eastern Finalist Parkland Doesn't Mind Underdog Role in 4A," *The Morning Call*, December 4, 1998.

Because the Umbrells' seats were underneath: www.usna.edu/LibExhibits/Archives/Armynavy/An1998.htm.

As grim proof: Alan Goldstein, "For Navy, Excruciating Loss," *The Baltimore Sun*, December 6, 1998; Drew Markol, "Comeback Carries Army past Navy," *The Intelligencer*, December 6, 1998.

In 1996, on the heels of his reelection: Malcolm Moran, "Army Rally Holds Up, but Just Barely," *The New York Times*, December 8, 1996.

CHAPTER 9: DOMINANCE

Interviews: Jim Benstead, Bryan Buckley, Mike Carey, Phil DiGiacomo, Mike Orihel, Mike Pettine, Dustin Picciotti, Mark Umbrell.

The Western Pennsylvania Interscholastic Athletic League: www.wpial.org/history.asp.

"Pennsylvania football": Bob Herman, "Pennsylvania Football Springs from Rich History," www.nfhs.org/web/2007/10/pennsylvania_football_springs_of.aspx.

This was still the town: Michener, *The Fires of Spring.*

Until the day in 1945: Pomerantz, *Wilt, 1962.*

As Clinton was preparing: Clinton, *My Life.*

At 5 P.M. on December 16: Text of a letter from the President to the Speaker of the House of Representatives and the President Pro Tempore of the Senate, December 18, 1998. Transcript provided at www.globalsecurity.org/wmd/library/news/iraq/1998/981218-wh1.htm.

In an address: Clinton, *My Life.*

In all: Gordon and Trainor, *Cobra II*; transcript of a Department of Defense briefing, December 18, 1998. Transcript provided at www.globalsecurity.org/wmd/library/news/iraq/1998/98121905_tlt.html.

CHAPTER 10: CLOSURE
Interviews: Bill Buckley, Bryan Buckley, Larry Greene, Ed Hillman, Steve Kreider, Bryan Scott, Brian Spratt, Mike Stubljar, Mark Umbrell, Nancy Umbrell, Paul Wilson.

CHAPTER 11: AWAY FROM HOME
Interviews: Don Brown, Bill Buckley, Bryan Buckley, Connie Buckley, Mike Carey, David Davies, Phil DiGiacomo, Corey Goff, Randy Granger, Jim Margraff, Mike Orihel, Mike Pettine, Dustin Picciotti, Rod Stone, Mike Stubljar, Mark Umbrell, Nancy Umbrell.

Though Colby was unaware of it: Gerald Eskenazi, "Night Football Celebration: Lights Out on Re-creation of 1892 Game?" *The New York* Times, December 16, 1991; Angus Lind, "Illuminating Experience," *The Times-Picayune*, September 28, 1997.

Had it been: Wilkes University football media guide, 2007.

In truth: www.wyomingseminary.org.

But here, at Worcester: www.worcesteracademy.org.

Bryan's roommate: Ken Powers, "He's Got Name and Game; Rockne's a Star for WA," *The Sunday Telegram*, October 24, 1999.

He had told no one: Murray and Weinress, *The Last Game*.

Unhappy over how Pettine was using him: Ibid.

CHAPTER 12: CHANGE
Interviews: Neil Bardham, Don Brown, Bill Buckley, Bryan Buckley, Connie Buckley, Mike Carey, Randy Cuthbert, Tom Deveney, Ernie Larossa, Jim Margraff, Chris Said, Rod Stone, Ben Stopper, Casey Umbrell, Mark Umbrell, Nancy Umbrell, Mark Whipple.

Following those months: Colby described the scene at the pool and the doctor's phone call in an essay that he wrote for an English course at Johns Hopkins.

There were five colleges: www.fivecolleges.edu.

For a Hopkins team: Ernie Larossa, the sports information director at Johns Hopkins, provided Colby's career statistics.

According to one report: The Associated Press, January 20, 2001.

For many of the protesters: Ibid.; Daryl Lindsey, "Thousands Protest Bush's Inauguration," Salon.com, January 20, 2001.

The protesters: Lindsey, "Thousands Protest."

Someone lobbed an egg: The Associated Press, January 20, 2001.

In October: Wayne Washington, "Once Against Nation-Building, Bush Now Involved," *The Boston Globe*, March 2, 2004.

"We will build": First Inaugural Address, George W. Bush, transcript provided by the Miller Center of Public Affairs, University of Virginia.

CHAPTER 13: DECISIONS

Interviews: Dave Armstrong, Neil Bardham, Don Brown, Bill Buckley, Bryan Buckley, Connie Buckley, Chris DiSciullo, Kim DiSciullo, Keith Dudzinski, Erich Maerz, Jim Margraff, Ben Stopper, Mark Whipple.

In the apartment: www.almanac.com.

Amherst did not share: Longman, *Among the Heroes.*

Off to an 0-2 start: Matthew F. Sacco, "Minutemen Prove True Test for I-A Marshall," *The Massachusetts Daily Collegian*, September 10, 2001.

At 7:59 A.M.: John Kifner, "After the Attacks: American Flight 11; A Plane Left Boston and Skimmed Over River and Mountain in a Deadly Detour," *The New York Times*, September 13, 2001.

Flight 11: Glen Johnson, "Probe Reconstructs Horror, Calculated Attacks on Planes," *The Boston Globe*, November 23, 2001.

Flight 175: Johnson, "Probe Reconstructs"; Kifner, "After the Attacks."

Clark Hall: Lois Perschetz, editor; "Terrorist Acts Send Shock Waves through JHU," *The Johns Hopkins Gazette*, September 17, 2001.

Because McGuirk Alumni Field: Matthew Sacco, "UMass Coach Deals with NCAA Decision-Making," *The Massachusetts Daily Collegian*, September 13, 2001.

The American retaliation: Transcript of a press conference held by Secretary of Defense Donald Rumsfeld and Joint Chiefs of Staff Chairman Richard Myers, October 7, 2001. Transcript provided at www.globalsecurity.org/military/library/news/2001/10/mil-011007-usia04.htm.

Bush had first discussed: Gordon and Trainor, *Cobra II.*

"That's what I think": Ibid.

"Every nation has a choice to make": Statement by the president announcing military strikes in Afghanistan. Statement provided at www.globalsecurity.org/military/library/news/2001/10/mil-011007-usia01.htm.

In his thirteen previous years: http://umassathletics.cstv.com/sports/m-footbl/mtt/whipple_mark00.html.

The following week: Tim Casey, "UMass Hurt by Penalties; Richmond Takes Control Early," *The Boston Globe*, November 24, 2001.

CHAPTER 14: "END OF AN AURA"

Interviews: Bill Buckley, Bryan Buckley, Connie Buckley, Randy Cuthbert, Tom Deveney, Steve Gonzalez, Larry Greene, Brandon Heath, Steve Kreider, Ernie Larossa, Don Moeller, Mike Pettine, Rod Stone, Ben Stopper, Mark Umbrell, Nancy Umbrell.

Their defense had not allowed a touchdown pass: http://hopkinssports.cstv.com/sports/m-footbl/spec-rel/113001aaa.html.

In the seven games: Interview, Larossa.

Since 1990: U.S. Census Bureau, Census 2000.

Over the same period: Central Bucks School District enrollment report.

Their school-record nine victories: http://hopkinssports.cstv.com/sports/m-footbl/spec-rel/121202aaa.html.

It had been more than a month: Transcript of speech by Secretary of State Colin Powell to the United Nations Security Council, February 5, 2003. Transcript provided at www.cnn.com/2003/US/02/05/sprj.irq.powell.transcript.

It had been two days: Gordon and Trainor, *Cobra II*.

Bush ordered the strikes: Ibid.; Ricks, *Fiasco*.

On March 22: Degen, Fontenot, and Tohn; *On Point*.

Constructed in 1949: www.villanova.edu/artsci/nrotc/about/history/inception/jbarryhall.htm.

At the institute: Naval Science Institute student information package.

CHAPTER 15: TRAINING, IN BRYAN'S WORDS

Interviews: Bryan Buckley, Randy Cuthbert, Don Moeller.

(The italicized excerpts are the transcripts of several interviews with Bryan Buckley. His remarks have been edited for continuity's sake.)

From classroom instruction: John Grant, director; *The Marines*; Driftwood Productions; 2006.

SERE was a Cold War creation: Mayer, *The Dark Side*.

The military officials who conduct the school: Press release regarding a report on the treatment of detainees in U.S. custody by the Senate Armed Services Committee, December 11, 2008. Release was provided at http://levin.senate.gov.

Together, TBS and IOC: www.marinecorpstimes.com/class186.

CHAPTER 16: TRAINING, IN COLBY'S WORDS

Interviews: Mark Umbrell, Nancy Umbrell.

(The italicized excerpts come from several of the letters and e-mails that Colby sent to his family during his training. They have been edited for continuity's sake.)

The school had a graduation rate: Bryant, *To Be a U.S. Army Ranger.*

Through those phases: Ibid.

Should Colby endure the ordeal: *U.S. Army Ranger Handbook.*

CHAPTER 17: SAND AND SNOW

Interviews: Amal Agalawatta, Dave Armstrong, Bill Buckley, Bryan Buckley, Connie Buckley, Stephen Buckley, Dan Clark, Chris DiSciullo, Kim DiSciullo, Bryan Druce, Steve Gonzalez, Brandon Heath, Ed Hillman, Spencer Hurley, Eric Lawless, James Mingus, John Perno, Maureen Perno, Mike Pettine, Doug Smith, Brian Spratt, Dan Tamaroff, Stephen Turpin, Mark Umbrell, Nancy Umbrell.

The monthlong exercise: www.pbs.org/wgbh/pages/frontline/haditha/view/extra. html.

Since September 2005: Ibid.; Cragg, *Guide to Military Installations.*

Smith, who had worked in a grain elevator: U.S. Census Bureau, Census 2000.

Early on: Letter from Kevin McDaniel to Mark and Nancy Umbrell.

Come the fall: Andy Mosher and Saad Sarhan, "Death Toll Rises to 100 in Suicide Blast in Iraq," *The Washington Post,* Monday, July 18, 2005; Anthony Shadid, "Iraq's Forbidding 'Triangle of Death'," *The Washington Post,* November 23, 2004.

On July 16, 2005: Mosher and Sarhan, "Death Toll Rises."

Colby, Agalawatta, and the battalion's other platoon leaders: www.wainwright .army.mil/nwtc/cwlc.htm.

On August 4: www.jrtc-polk.army.mil.

Weeks earlier: E-mail message from Colby Umbrell to Mark and Nancy Umbrell, August 2, 2006.

CHAPTER 18: FALLUJAH

Interviews: Dave Armstrong, Jim Benstead, Bill Buckley, Bryan Buckley, Connie Buckley, Stephen Buckley, Mike Carey, Dan Clark, Chris DiSciullo, Kim Di-Sciullo, Ed Hillman, Spencer Hurley, Joe Luevano, Erich Maerz, James Mingus, Don Moeller, John Perno, Maureen Perno, Mike Pettine, Ed Skelly, Brian Spratt, Stephen Turpin.

The situation: www.weather.com; Jennifer Griffin, "Marines Call New Body Armor Heavy, Impractical," FOXNews.com, February 27, 2008.

Though their leader: The Associated Press, June 8, 2006.

After coalition forces: Rick Atkinson, "Left of Boom: The Fight against Roadside Bombs," *The Washington Post,* September 30-October 3, 2007.

Often made: Nance, *The Terrorists of Iraq.*

The number of IED attacks: Atkinson, "Left of Boom"; James Mingus, summary of action in the case of 2nd Lieutenant Bryan Buckley, recommendation for the Navy and Marine Corps Achievement Medal.

In all: 4th Platoon logbook; Mingus, summary of action; Solomon Moore, "Iraq Violence Continues," *The Los Angeles Times,* September 15, 2006.

They moved in: 4th Platoon logbook; Mingus, summary of action.

CHAPTER 19: MUSAYYIB

Interviews: Amal Agalawatta, Bryan Buckley, Dana Cumberbatch, Bryan Druce, Larry Greene, Brandon Heath, Ed Kracz, Steve Kreider, Christina Kristofic, Ann Kuntzmann, Eric Lawless, Dan Tamaroff, Casey Umbrell, Mark Umbrell, Nancy Umbrell, John Zaremba.

The four smokestacks: Monte Morin, "Faltering Power Plant Brings Iraq's Electrical Woes to Light," *Stars and Stripes,* September 29, 2006.

The plant: Ibid.

On December 20: Tom Junod, "The Six-Letter Word That Changes Everything," *Esquire.* July 2008.

The following month: Ibid.

Together, Iraqis: Major Eric Verzola, "Rule of Law Finds Home in Musayyib," U.S. Fed News, March 19, 2007.

In Musayyib: Department of the Army, report on the official investigation of the death of 1st Lieutenant Colby Umbrell; Nance, *The Terrorists of Iraq.*

In turn: Army investigation.

On May 15, 2004: Atkinson, "Left of Boom."

By July 2005: Ibid.; Nance, *The Terrorists of Iraq.*

One measure: Atkinson, "Left of Boom."

From July 2003: www.icasualties.org.

There were 6: Army investigation.

The Army had recently extended: E-mail message from Colby Umbrell to Mark and Nancy Umbrell, April 13, 2007.

He was taking out half: Army investigation.

After Colby: Ibid.

The Humvees: Ibid.

That night: Letter from Frank Aguilar to Mark and Nancy Umbrell, May 3, 2007.

But at 1:07 P.M.: Army investigation.

CHAPTER 20: REMEMBRANCES

Interviews: Larry Greene, Casey Umbrell, Mark Umbrell, Nancy Umbrell.

The turnout had been even greater: Larry King, "A Silent Community in a Nation at War," *The Philadelphia Inquirer*, September 9, 2007.

The plane carrying: Beth Bragg, "Back Home, With a Welcome New Assignment, *The Anchorage Daily News*, November 12, 2007.

Druce wore an extra dog tag: E-mail from Bryan Druce to Mark and Nancy Umbrell, May 9, 2007.

To their left: Sumathi Reddy, "'We Wanted to Love Each Other Forever'," *The Baltimore Sun*, April 13, 2007.

To Mark and Nancy's right: Daniel Patrick Sheehan, "Soldier's Boyfriend Couldn't Save Her," *The Morning Call*, March 8, 2007.

EPILOGUE

Interviews: Bill Buckley, Bryan Buckley, Connie Buckley, Kyle Kaczmarek, Mark Umbrell, Nancy Umbrell.

The additional thirty thousand U.S. troops: John Hendren, "'Sunni Awakening': Insurgents Are Now Allies," www.abcnews.com, December 23, 2007; Bing West, "Decency, Toughness . . . and No Shortcuts," www.theatlantic.com, September 24, 2008; Bob Woodward, "Why Did Violence Plummet? It Wasn't Just the Surge," *The Washington Post*, September 8, 2008.

SELECTED BIBLIOGRAPHY

Ambrose, Stephen E. *Band of Brothers: E Company, 506th Regiment, 101st Airborne from Normandy to Hitler's Nest.* Simon & Schuster, 1992.

Baldwin, Toni; Phil Klein; William Luce; William Spare; and Betty Strecker. *Doylestown: 150 Years.* Bucks County Historical Society, 1988.

Bryant, Russ. *To Be a U.S. Army Ranger.* Zenith Press, 2003.

Buzzell, Colby. *My War: Killing Time in Iraq.* G. P. Putnam's Sons, 2005.

Clinton, Bill. *My Life.* Random House, 2004.

Cragg, Dan. *Guide to Military Installations, 6th Edition.* Stackpole Books, 2000.

Davis, William W. H. *History of the Doylestown Guards.* Press of "Democrat" Job Department, 1887.

Degen, Lt. Colonel E. J.; Ret. Army Col. Gregory Fontenot; and Lt. Colonel David Tohn. *On Point: The United States Army in Operation Iraqi Freedom.* Combat Studies Institute Press, 2004.

Fick, Nathaniel. *One Bullet Away: The Making of a Marine Officer.* Houghton Mifflin, 2005.

Gordon, Michael R.; and General Bernard E. Trainor. *Cobra II: The Inside Story of the Invasion and Occupation of Iraq.* Vintage Books, 2006.

Lebegern, Jr.; George. *Episodes in Bucks County History: A Bicentennial Tribute, 1776–1976.* Bucks County Historical Tourist Commission, 1975.

Lock, J. D. *Rangers in Combat: A Legacy of Valor.* Wheatmark, 2007.

Longman, Jere. *Among the Heroes: United Flight 93 and the Passengers and Crew Who Fought Back.* HarperCollins, 2002.

Ludwig, Ed; Brooks McNamara; and Betty Strecker. *Images of America: Doylestown.* Arcadia Publishing, 2000.

Mayer, Jane. *The Dark Side: The Inside Story of How the War on Terror Turned into a War on American Ideals.* Doubleday, 2008.

Michener, James. *The Fires of Spring.* Fawcett Publications, 1949.

Nance, Malcolm W. *The Terrorists of Iraq: Inside the Strategy and Tactics of the Iraq Insurgency.* Malcolm W. Nance, 2007.

Pomerantz, Gary. *Wilt, 1962: The Night of 100 Points and the Dawn of a New Era.* Crown Publishers, 2005.

Ricks, Thomas E. *Fiasco: The American Military Adventure in Iraq.* The Penguin Press, 2006.

The U.S. Army and Marine Corps Counterinsurgency Field Manual. The University of Chicago Press, 2007.

The U.S. Army Ranger Handbook. Skyhorse Publishing, 2007.

West, Bing. *No True Glory: A Frontline Account of the Battle for Fallujah.* Bantam Books, 2005.

Woodward, Bob. *Bush at War.* Simon & Schuster, 2002.

—. *Plan of Attack: The Definitive Account of the Decision to Invade Iraq.* Simon & Schuster, 2004.

—. *State of Denial: Bush at War, Part III.* Simon & Schuster, 2006.

Wright, Evan. *Generation Kill: Devil Dogs, Iceman, Captain America, and the New Face of American War.* G. P. Putnam's Sons, 2004.

Yon, Michael. *Moment of Truth in Iraq.* Richard Vigilante Books, 2008.